Learning Language Through Literature 1

英語圏版
マンガ『坊っちゃん』

原作　夏目漱石 Natsume Soseki
監修　ジョーン・E・エリクソン Joan E. Ericson
著　　増山和恵 Masuyama Kazue
マンガ　月館蛍人 Tsukidate Keito

ゆまに書房

Learning Language Through Literature 1

マンガ『坊っちゃん』

目次(もくじ)

- この本の特徴(とくちょう)と使(つか)い方(かた) Features and Use of the Text …… 4
- 本の構成(こうせい) The Structure of the Text …… 6
- 日本の地図(ちず) Map of Japan …… 7
- おもな登場(とうじょう)人物(じんぶつ) The Main Characters …… 8
- 物語(ものがたり)文でよく使われるキーワード Keywords Used to Introduce, Explain, and Discuss the Story
- マンガの読み方 How to Read Manga …… 12
- オノマトペ Onomatopoeia …… 13

- 第1章 ✦ 清(きよ)と坊っちゃん Kiyo and Botchan …… 15
  - 原文に挑戦しましょう 28 / 第1章を読む前に 14

- 第2章 ✦ 四国(しこく)へ Going to Shikoku …… 29
  - 原文(げんぶん)に挑戦(ちょうせん)しましょう 27 / 第2章を読む前に 28

- 第3章 ✦ 坊っちゃん先生 Botchan Sensei …… 43
  - 原文に挑戦しましょう 42 / 第3章を読む前に

- 第4章 ✦ 宿直(しゅくちょく) Night Watch …… 57
  - 原文に挑戦しましょう 56 / 第4章を読む前に

- 第5章 ✦ 陰謀(いんぼう) Conspiracy …… 73
  - 原文に挑戦しましょう 72 / 第5章を読む前に

- 第6章 ✦ 山嵐(やまあらし)との決裂(けつれつ) The Falling Out with Yama-Arashi …… 87
  - 原文に挑戦しましょう 100 / 第7章を読む前に

Contents

第7章 うらなりとマドンナ　Uranari and Madonna ……… 101
　原文に挑戦しましょう ……… 118
第8章 増給話(ぞうきゅうばなし)の裏(うら)　The Other Side of the Salary Increase Story ……… 119
　原文に挑戦しましょう ……… 132
第9章 さらばうらなり君　Farewell to Uranari ……… 133
　原文に挑戦しましょう ……… 146
第10章 祝勝会(しゅくしょうかい)のわな　The Victory Celebration Trap ……… 147
　原文に挑戦しましょう ……… 158
第11章 天誅(てんちゅう)　Heaven's Punishment ……… 159
　原文に挑戦しましょう ……… 175

練習問題の構成(こうせい)　The Structure of the Exercises ……… 177
ことば・文化ノート　Language and Culture Notes ……… 178
理解(りかい)しましょう　Let's Understand ……… 181
原文(げんぶん)に挑戦しましょう　Be Challenged by the Original Text ……… 182
表現(ひょうげん)しましょう　Let's Express Ourselves ……… 184
【著者(ちょしゃ) 夏目漱石(なつめそうせき)について】　About Natsume Soseki ……… 186

エッセイ　ジョーン・E・エリクソン　Essay by Joan E. Ericson ……… 187
語彙索引(ごいさくいん)　Vocabulary Index ……… (22)

(5)

◆この本の特徴と使い方

マンガ『坊っちゃん』は日本語を300時間勉強した中級レベルの学習者向けに作られたものですが、初級の学習者でも、上級の学習者の方々でも楽しく読んでいけます。

● マンガ形式なので、物語のあらすじ、場面の様子、人物の気持ちなどが理解しやすく、日本文学を身近なものに感じます。

● 語学テキストという枠を超えて、マンガ化された小説を通して、日本の文化、社会、生活習慣に触れ、その文化的背景や価値観を考える機会となります。

● 日本語を用いて他の分野（地理、歴史、経済、社会、美術など）の知識を学びます。

● 会話を通して、自然な日本語表現（語彙、漢字、言い回し、慣用句、オノマトペなど）が学べます。

● 自主学習 教材として使えるように、Webサイトには各章の質問や練習問題があり、答えながら自分の理解度をチェックできる構成になっています。

● 『坊っちゃん』を文学作品として深く理解するために英語での解説やコラムも入っています。このマンガ『坊っちゃん』を読むことで、ほかの日本文学作品への興味をもつきっかけになるでしょう。

◆ Features and Use of the Text

The manga Botchan was designed for intermediate Japanese language learners who have completed approximately 300 hours of college-level classroom instruction. However, beginning and advanced Japanese language learners will also enjoy this text.

• The manga format makes it easy to understand the storyline, the setting, and the feelings of the main characters. It also provides a means for language learners to become familiar with an important piece of Japanese literature.
• In addition to learning the Japanese language, this text presents an opportunity to explore Japanese daily customs, manners, cultural values, and perspectives.
• Students will learn about other subjects (e.g., geography, history, economics, society, and arts) in Japanese.
• Dialogues in the manga provide a natural setting for authentic Japanese language (e.g., vocabulary, kanji, sayings, idioms, and onomatopoeia).
• This text can be used for independent study. The website includes exercises based on each chapter. Language learners can use the exercises to self-check their understanding of the material.
• A literary essay in English, together with supplementary information about Japanese literature, helps the readers to understand Natsume Soseki's novel more fully. We hope that this manga text will serve as a gateway to the further exploration of Japanese literature.

◆ 本の構成

◎ 各章の初めでは登場人物の一人がみなさんをこれから読む章に案内します。

◎ マンガは各章10ページから16ページで構成してあり、各ページの下に語彙の説明があります。

◎ 各章の終わりには原文からの引用文と質問があります。

◎ マンガの後に、練習問題のサンプル（第1章）と英語と日本訳の解説があります。

◆ The Structure of the Text

• At the beginning of each chapter, one of the main characters guides you through the chapter.

• The manga text is composed of 10 to 16 pages per chapter. There is a list of vocabulary on the bottom of each page.

• At the end of each chapter, there is an extract from the original novel, followed by questions.

• After the manga text, there is a sample chapter exercise (Chapter 1) and a literary essay on Botchan in English, followed by a translation in Japanese.

日本の地図
Map of Japan

Ⓐ 福島県会津若松市……山嵐の出身地。武士的気質を持つ地。

Ⓑ 東京……坊っちゃんが生まれた所。

Ⓒ 箱根……清が知っている一番遠い所。

Ⓓ 愛媛県松山市……夏目漱石が教えていた中学校があり、坊っちゃんの舞台になった所。

Ⓔ 宮崎県延岡市……うらなりの転勤先。

【 おもな登場人物 とうじょうじんぶつ The Main Characters 】

東京の人々 The People of Tokyo

「清」
きよ
坊っちゃんの家に仕える奉公人
ほうこうにん
明治維新で落ちぶれた
めいじ いしん
身分のある家の出
みぶん
坊っちゃんをかわいがる

Kiyo
A servant who works in Botchan's home.
Kiyo is from an aristocratic family that lost everything after the Meiji Restoration. She loves Botchan unconditionally.

「坊っちゃん」
主人公
しゅじんこう
無鉄砲な江戸っ子
むてっぽう えど
義理人情に厚い
ぎりにんじょう あつ
中学校の数学 教師になる
きょうし

Botchan
The protagonist of the story.
Botchan is a reckless, true Tokyoite with a sense of strong moral obligation. He becomes a mathematics teacher at a middle school.

「坊っちゃんの家族」
坊っちゃんに厳しい父親と愛想をつかした母親
きび　　　　　　　　　　　　あいそ
坊っちゃんの兄

Botchan's family
Botchan's father is strict; his mother becomes fed up with his antics.
His older brother.

8

四国の人々 The People of Shikoku

「赤シャツ」
教頭
ずるくて腹黒い
年中赤いシャツを着ている
"Red-Shirt"
The vice principal of the middle school. He is a sneaky, scheming man who always wears a red shirt.

「山嵐」
本名：堀田　数学教師
正義感が強く、生徒に人気がある
"Porcupine"
His real family name is Hotta.
He is a popular mathematics teacher who has a strong sense of justice.

「野だいこ」
本名：吉川　画学教師
赤シャツの太鼓持ち
"Nodaiko-The Clown"
His real family name is Yoshikawa.
He is an art teacher and an ally of Red-Shirt.

「うらなり」
本名：古賀　英語教師
おとなしくて消極的
マドンナの元婚約者
"A pale-faced, sickly person"
His real family name is Koga.
He is an English teacher who is docile and passive.
Madonna is his former fiancée.

「マドンナ」
本名：遠山
町一番の美人
うらなりの元婚約者
"Madonna"
Her real family name is Toyama.
She is the town's most beautiful woman and Uranari's former fiancée.

「狸」
校長
事なかれ主義
"Tanuki"
The principal of the middle school. He is a passive person who plays it safe all the time and abides by "don't-rock-the-boat" principles.

「江戸っ子」とは　What is *Edokko*?

江戸っ子 (*Edokko*, a true Tokyoite, literally 'child of Edo') refers to a person born and raised in 江戸 (*Edo*, renamed Tokyo in 1869). A true 江戸っ子 was born and raised in 江戸 to parents who were also born and raised there. Certain personality traits associated with the status of 江戸っ子 include being assertive, straightforward, cheerful, and having a sense of moral ground such as 義理 (*giri*, duty, obligation) and 人情 (*ninjō*, feeling).

「無鉄砲」とは　What is *muteppō*?

無鉄砲 (*muteppō*, reckless), written as 無 (*mu*, nothing) + 鉄砲 (*teppō*, gun), describes a reckless action such as going hunting or going off to war without a gun. It may also be derived from the phrase *mutenhō*: 無 (*mu*, nothing) + 点法 (*tenpō*, punctuation rule). In much the same way that a text is very difficult to read without proper punctuation, a *muteppō* person acts in an absurd or a rash manner without much forethought. However, a *muteppō* action is often not intentional or done out of stupidity; rather, one might be *muteppō* simply out of a kind of innocence and naïve optimism as in the case of Botchan.

「太鼓持ち」とは　What is *taikomochi*?

太鼓持ち (*Taikomochi*, drum holders) were the original male geisha of Japan. From the early Edo period on, they entertained patrons with comic performances and lewd stories at intimate gatherings in the traditional adult entertainment quarters of Tokyo and Kyoto. While talented musicians and dancers kept the name of geisha, clowns and professional fools were called *Taikomochi* and talentless *Taikomochi* were called *Nodaiko*. Botchan nicknamed Yoshikawa, who teaches drawing as Nodaiko, since he has the appearance of a frivolous performer. Nodaiko calls himself a Tokyoite and prides himself on his good taste. Nodaiko fawns upon men of influence, and follows others without much thought.

「事なかれ主義」とは　What is *kotonakare shugi*?

事なかれ主義 （*Kotonakare shugi*） means someone who abides by "don't-rock-the-boat" principles. *Kotonakare shugi* breaks down into three parts 事 (*koto*, matter, thing), なかれ (*nakare*, must not, do not), and 主義 (*shugi*, belief system, ideology). A person who practices this passive approach to life, in which one desires a peaceful and uneventful life, may be viewed as a negative thinker, a selfish individual who thinks of matters only from the perspective of his or her own loss or gain, and/or a conservative who plays it safe all the time without taking any risks. Ignoring other people's wrongdoings, *kotonakare shugi* people settle matters quietly, frequently using vague expressions to avoid any direct conflict. In addition to describing his school principal as a typical *kotonakare shugi* person, *Botchan* nicknames him *Tanuki* (Badger), an animal traditionally viewed as a symbol of slyness. The term *Tanuki* is used to describe someone who makes evil plans without ever showing emotion. The Tanuki's folkloric shape-shifting ability makes him a symbol of duplicity and indicates he is not to be trusted at face value.

◇ 物語文でよく使われるキーワード
Keywords Used to Introduce, Explain, and Discuss the Story

❶ 物語を説明したり話し合ったりする時に、よく使われる20のキーワードです。言葉の意味を調べてみましょう。

登場人物　主人公　場面　出来事　状況　様子　性格　気持ち　考え　表情　行動　態度
原因　理由　あらすじ　重要（な）　要点　段落　まとめ　結末

読み方ヒント：だんらく　できごと　ようてん　けつまつ　しゅじんこう　ばめん　とうじょうじんぶつ　せいかく　きもち
じゅうよう　こうどう　ようす　げんいん　りゆう　じょうきょう　ひょうじょう　かんがえ　たいど

意味ヒント：summary, attitude, plot, feeling, facial expression, paragraph, important, ending, event, character(s), thinking, action, protagonist, appearance, personality, setting, essential point, cause, reason, situations

❷ 登場人物の仕事、本名、性格、特徴 (distinguishing characteristic) を
　□の中から言葉を選んで、空欄 (blank column) に書き入れましょう。

あだな								
仕事								
本名								
性格・特徴								

＊あだな、仕事、本名がわからない人もいる

①山嵐　②赤シャツ　③狸　④坊っちゃん　⑤野だいこ　⑥うらなり　⑦吉川　⑧古賀
⑨遠山　⑩堀田　⑪マドンナ　⑫清　⑬英語の先生　⑭画学（美術）の先生　⑮校長
⑯数学の先生　⑰教頭　⑱奉公人　⑲ずるい　⑳おとなしい　㉑坊っちゃんをかわいがる
㉒太鼓持ち　㉓事なかれ主義　㉔無鉄砲　㉕正義感が強い　㉖たくましい　㉗美人

❸ 下の質問に答えましょう。

1. この物語の主人公は誰ですか。仕事は何ですか。どんな人でしょうか。
2. 東京の登場人物を箇条書きに (list) してください。
3. 四国の登場人物を箇条書きにしてください。
4. 清は坊っちゃんの母親ですか。
5. 「事なかれ主義」とは何ですか。日本語で説明してみましょう。
6. 一番おもしろそうな登場人物は誰ですか。どうしてですか。
7. 「坊っちゃん」は英語で、son (of someone else); young master; inexperienced or "green" young man from a well-to-do family という意味です。『坊っちゃん』というタイトルから、この物語のストーリーを想像してみましょう。

❖ マンガの読み方　How to Read Manga ❖

読む方向 (direction) は右上のコマ①をはじめに読みましょう。そして、左のコマ②を読みます。つまり右上→左上です。コマ①の中を読む時も、「右」から「左」(❶→❷→❸→❹)へ読みます。次に、2段目 (the second line) にさがって右中のコマ③を読みます。下図 (the lower illustration) のように、左にコマがなければ、右下のコマ④に行きます。そして、左下のコマ⑤に行きます。

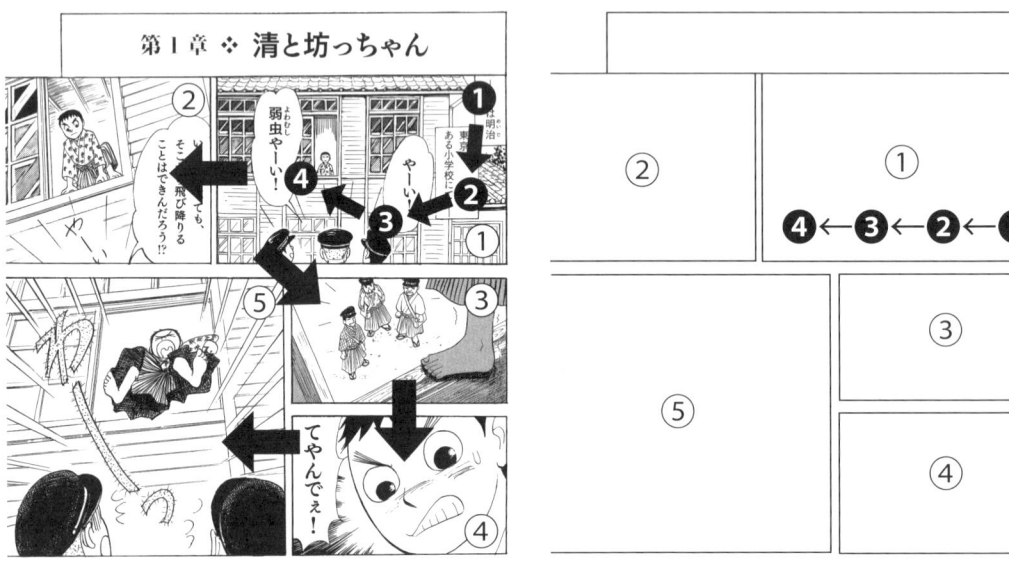

マンガの吹き出し (balloon) には、いろいろな形があります。

という形はマンガの中の登場人物が「言っている」言葉です。

でも、登場人物が怒ったり、大きな声を出して言うと 　　　　という形になります。

心の中で思ったことを表現する時は 　　　　という形になります。

そして、心の中で怒ったりすると 　　　　のようになります。

ナレーションは 　　　　の中に書かれています。

マンガのバックグラウンドの音 (sounds) や声はそのまま (as it is; without any marks) 書いてあります。

オノマトペ　Onomatopoeia

オノマトペ (onomatopée in French; onomatopoeia in English) are sound symbolic words. While English has words such as *bow-wow*, *creak*, *ding*, and *pitapat*, Japanese is abundant with such expressions, even extending to mimetic words that "imitate" soundless states or events. Generally, the Japanese sound symbolic vocabulary is classified into the following three types:

オノマトペ
(French:onomatopée
English:onomatopoeia)

- **擬声語・擬音語** (*giseigo・giongo*)
  Words that mimic actual sounds. *Giseigo* refers to sounds made by animate things (e.g., わんわん a baby bawling or a dog barking), and *giongo* refers to sounds made by inanimate objects (e.g., くしゃ crumpling, さわさわ rustling).

- **擬態語** (*gitaigo*)
  Mimetic words to represent non-auditory external phenomena (e.g., しーん silence, ばらばら scattered in pieces).

- **擬情語** (*gijōgo*)
  Mimetic words that represent psychological states (e.g., ギク being startled, いらいら irritation).

Note: The division between the above types is not always clear. For example, a mimetic word may refer to one's inner emotion as well as to an external expression.

In 坊っちゃん, sound symbolic words that mimic actual sounds are typically used independently to describe scenes, such as シャー (the sound of water flowing while wringing a towel) and ガラガラ (rattling of things falling down). If these words are used in sentences, they function as adverbs, often taking the particle と (typically for action) or sometimes に (typically for results). For example, わんわん（と）泣く to bawl, きらきら（と）光る to sparkle, ひらひら（と）舞う to flutter (in the air), かちかちに凍る to be frozen hard.

There are some patterns in sound-meaning relationships. The vowel う often represents psychological states (e.g., うきうき buoyant and cheerful), and い represents tenseness (e.g., きりきり sharp pain). A long vowel denotes prolongation or continuity and the ん ending denotes prolonged resonance (e.g., ずどーん prolonged bang). Voiced consonants tend to represent stronger, bigger, rougher actions and states. For example, the smooth rustling of tree leaves would be かさかさ, but a heavy or rough rustling would be がさがさ. Pleasant dampness of the skin would be しっとり, but uncomfortable dampness from sweating would be じっとり. Repetition represents repetitive sounds or movements (e.g., ごろごろ rumbling, tumbling).

参考文献　References
Hamano, Shoko (1998). *The sound-symbolic system of Japanese*. Stanford, CA: CSLI.
Makino, Seiichi, and Michio Tsutsui (1989). *Dictionary of Basic Japanese Grammar,* Tokyo:The Japan Times. pp.50-56.
Shibatani, Masayoshi (1990). *The Languages of Japan*. Cambridge: Cambridge University Press. pp.153-157.
Yamaguchi, Toshiko (2007). *Japanese Linguistics: An Introduction*. London & New York: Continuum. pp.63-71.

第1章を読む前に

坊っちゃん

俺は江戸っ子だ。
この物語は俺が子供の時の話から始まる。
俺は小さい時から無鉄砲で、親を困らせてばかりいた。
しかし、奉公人の清は生みの親よりもなぜか俺のことをかわいがってくれた。
清はいつも俺のことを「まっすぐで、いい気性だ」と言ってくれたんだ。
大学卒業後、そんな清と別れる日が来る。

困らせる　to trouble someone　　[V(て form) ばかり]　nothing but 〜　　生みの親　one's true parents
気性　disposition

第1章 ❖ 清と坊っちゃん
Kiyo and Botchan

① 時【とき】 (n) the time ＊時は～ It was (the time/era of) ～　明治【めいじ】 (n) Meiji Period (1868-1912)
　東京【とうきょう】 (n) Tokyo　　ある [Noun] (adj-pn) a certain (place or person)
　小学校【しょうがっこう】 (n) elementary school
　やーい (int) hey ＊Used when one ridicules or humiliates others.
　弱虫【よわむし】 (n) coward
② いくら [V (て form)] も (exp) No matter how much one does ～
　いばる (v5r, vi) to brag; to boast about
　飛び降りる【とびおりる】 (v1, vi) to jump off of ＊飛び降りる is a compound word of　飛ぶ (to fly; to jump) and
　降りる (to go down; to get out/off). 飛びます [V (ます stem form)] + 降りる => 飛び降りる
　～ん (aux) negative verb ending used in informal speech (abbr. of negative verb ending "ぬ・ない"). ＊できんだろう = できないだろう
④ てやんでぇ (exp) (vulg) What're you talking about?! ＊This is an old Edo working-class dialect : 何、言ってやがる！
　=> 何、言ってやんでい => てやんでぇ． [V (form or ます stem form)] やがる indicates contempt, or disdain for
　another's action.
⑤ わー (int) Aahh; a crowd's excited roar ＊The small っ at the end of the sentence convey an interruption, or emotions such
　as surprise, anger, and excitement, and is often followed by an exclamation mark（！）．

⑥ 〜ぞ (prt) (sentence end, mainly masc.) emphasizes what the speaker is saying.
⑧ 校舎【こうしゃ】 (n) school building　　[Number]階【かい】 (ctr) counter for floors of a building
　それで (conj) because of that　　小使いさん【こづかいさん】 (n) janitor *Today, 用務員【ようむいん】 is used instead.
　おぶう (v5u, vt) to carry (child) on one's back * おぶわれる (passive form)
⑨ [Noun] ぐらい (prt) just; only * 二階ぐらいから from about the second floor level
　腰を抜かす【こしをぬかす】 (exp, v5s) to dislocate one's lower back. This expression also means "to be paralyzed with fright."
　奴【やつ】 (n) (col) fellow
　〜か (prt) indicates a question, choice, or doubt. However, here it is more of a rhetorical question (a forceful statement with no expected response).
　*The comment of Botchan's father, "what kind of man dislocates his back just from jumping off the second floor...!" indicates some similarities between Botchan's personality and his father's.
⑩ [V (ず neg. form)] に (exp) without 〜 ing * ぬかさずに is the same as ぬかさないで [V (ない neg. form) で], but it is a more formal expression.
　[V (て form)] みせる (v1, vt) to show the action of　　小ッ (onoma) a suppressed sigh

16

⑫ ある日【あるひ】 (n) one day
　相撲【すもう】 (n) sumo wrestling; a Japanese style of wrestling ＊相撲をとる to wrestle
　はっけよい (int) a phrase shouted by a sumo referee when both wrestlers have stopped moving; "put some spirit in it!"
⑬ のこった、のこった (int) notifies the wrestlers they are still in the ring so the fight is not over yet
⑮ こらー！ (int) hey! ＊Used to scold or reprove someone.
⑯ 人参畑【にんじんばたけ】 (n) carrot garden
⑰ 逃げる【にげる】 (v1, vi) to run away（〜に、〜から）＊逃げろ (command form)

17

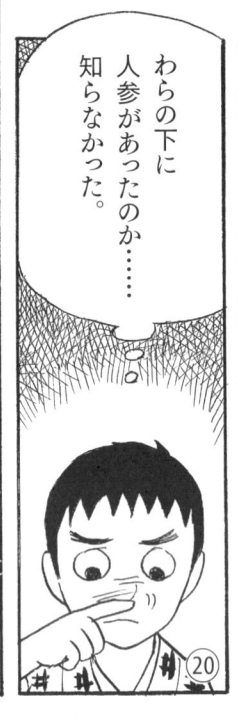

⑲ まだ芽が出たばかりだったんだ。そこで、相撲をとられたら、人参が台無しだよ！

⑳ わらの下に人参があったのか……知らなかった。

㉑ ……まったく

㉒ 農家には罰金を出して許してもらったが……こいつはきっとろくなものにはならん！

㉓ はぐ / ずっ

㉔ この前は年上の近所の男の子とけんかしたり、本当に乱暴で乱暴で行く先が心配です。 / 清、おかわり！

---

⑲ 芽【め】(n) sprouts　　[V (た form)] ばかり (prt) just (finished, etc.)　　人参【にんじん】(n) carrots
　（person に）相撲をとられたら　This passive pattern describes a difficult situation. The farmer indicates his unpleasant feelings and actual inconvenience and suffering caused by Botchan's action.
　台無し（な）【だいなし】(adj-na, n) ruined; spoiled; spoilt
⑳ わら (n) straw
㉑ まったく (exp, int) Good grief
㉒ 農家【のうか】(n) farmer　　罰金【ばっきん】(n) fine
　[V (て form)] もらう (v5u, vt) to get someone to do something (to/for me or someone else)　　許す【ゆるす】(v5s, vt) to forgive
　ずっ (onoma) slurp
㉓ こいつ (pn) (col) this guy　　きっと (adv) most likely (e.g., 90 percent)
　ろくな (adj-pn) decent *Used with a negative predicate. ろくなものにはならん He will not become a decent person.
　はぐ (onoma) chomp; eating, munching sounds
㉔ 年上【としうえ】(n) older; senior　　近所【きんじょ】(n) neighborhood　　けんかする (vs) to fight
　乱暴（な）【らんぼう】(adj-na, n) violent; rough *Repetition twice emphasizes the mother's worries, frustration, and condemnation towards Botchan.
　行く先【ゆくさき】(n) the future　　心配（な）【しんぱい】(adj-na, n, vs) worried; nervous
　清【きよ】(n) Kiyo, a woman's given name * 清 means clear, pure, or noble.　　おかわり (n, vs) another helping

㉕ 俺【おれ】 (n) (male) I; me (tough, rough, or arrogant-sounding first-person pronoun) * 俺 is commonly used to indicate a more macho, rough character while 僕（ぼく）indicates a masculine but less aggressive character.
　無鉄砲（な）【むてっぽう】 (adj-na, n) reckless; rash (see "無鉄砲" p. 10)
　なやむ (v5m, vi) to be worried; to be troubled *(person を) なやませる is a causative form, which means "to cause (someone) to worry."
　タンタン (onoma) tan-tan; tap tap * タンタン is the sound of Botchan hitting the wood floor as he walks on his hands.
㉖ ジャーッ (onoma) sound of flowing water
㉘ はっ (onoma) hah; gasping sound; catching one's breath
　トン (onoma) tap; jump * トン indicates a fairly quiet impact as he does flips.
　よっ (onoma) yah *This is a grunt that one makes when performing a heavy or difficult task.
　ダン (onoma) bang; bam *This indicates a sudden impact.
㉙ あらよっと (int) up we go; off we go; here I go. *This is a set expression when starting some heavy lifting or some physical task.
㉚ ドン (onoma) boom!　　ガラン (onoma) loud (metalic) sound　　ガラガラ (onoma) rattling

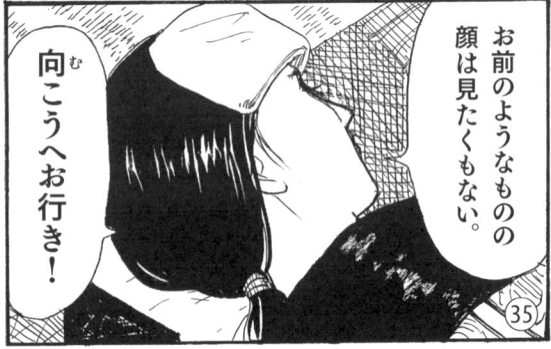

㉛ **大丈夫**【だいじょうぶ】 (adv, n) all right   **いてっ、いてててて** (adj-i) painful *This is a contracted form of いたい.
㉜ **お母様**【おかあさま】 (n) (your) mother *Kiyo refers to Botchan's mother from Botchan's perspective. 〜様 is a more respectful and polite version of 〜さん.   **目を覚ます**【めをさます】 (v5s, vt) to awaken *お母様が目を覚まされましたよ Literally, your mother has awakened, but here it actually means "you woke her up." 覚まされました is an honorific expression using a passive form.
ご [Noun] (pref) honorable *The general rule is ご＋漢語 (Chinese-origin word, e.g., 病気) and お＋和語 (Japanese-origin word).
〜(な)のに (conj) even though; despite the fact that *When 〜のに appears at the end of a sentence, it carries a note of disappointment, regret, or discontent.
宙返りする【ちゅうがえりする】 (vs) to do a somersault   **かまど** (n) kitchen range; cooking stove; hearth
角【かど】 (n) corner   **あばら** (n) ribs   **打つ**【うつ】 (v5t, vt) to hit
㉝ **でへへ** (int) ow ow
㉟ **お前**【おまえ】 (pn) (fam) (male) you * Formerly honorific, now this second person pronoun indicates condescension towards or intimacy with an equal or inferior.   **〜のような [Noun]** (adj-pn) like 〜 ; similar to 〜 *おまえのようなもの someone like you
向こう【むこう】 (n) over there   **お行き**【おゆき・おいき】 (exp) go *お行き is an abbreviation of お行きなさい. お [V (ます stem form)] なさい is a command expression.

20

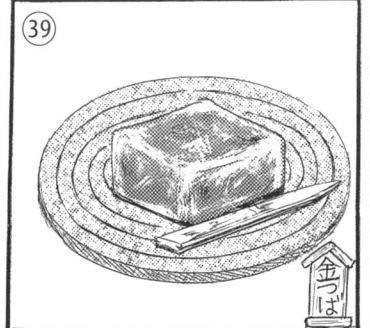

㊲ 坊っちゃん

㊳ 台所に来て金つばをお召し上がりなさいませ。

㊴

㊵ それから

㊶ この帳面—どうぞお使いください。

㊷ なぜ清は自分の小遣いで俺に色々な物を買ってくれるのだ?

㊸ 坊っちゃんがまっすぐで、いいご気性だからです。俺は世辞は嫌いだ!

㊹ そういうところが、いいご気性だというんです!

㊳ 台所【だいどころ】 (n) kitchen　　金つば【きんつば】 (n) a type of traditional Japanese confection, or wagashi
召し上がる【めしあがる】 (v5r, vt) (hon) to eat　　～ませ (aux) (pol) (used to make a polite request or demand) please
㊶ 帳面【ちょうめん】 (n) notebook
㊷ なぜ (adv) why　　自分【じぶん】 (pn) oneself
小遣い【こづかい】 (n) allowance *Kiyo is spending her own money to buy things for Botchan.
[V (て form)] くれる (v1, vt) to do something for me　* 買ってくれる buy for me
～のだ・～んだ (exp) the expectation is that ...; the reason is that ... Botchan is asking for some explanation from Kiyo.
㊸ まっすぐ(な) (adj-na, n) straightforward; honest; frank (in this particular context)
気性【きしょう】 (n) disposition; temperament　* ご気性 your honorable nature. Kiyo uses honorific speech with Botchan.
世辞【せじ】 (n) flattery
㊹ そういうところ (exp) such; that sort of; aforementioned quality or trait *This refers to Botchan's comment ('I dislike flattery'), but Kiyo always finds something good in Botchan's acts whether they are good or bad, simply because she dotes on him.

㊺ **奉公人【ほうこうにん】** (n) maidservant
よい家の出【よいいえので】 (exp) from a well-to-do family *Kiyo's aristocratic family lost everything after the Meiji Restoration.
明治維新【めいじいしん】 (n) Meiji Restoration (1868) *This refers to a series of events that ended the Tokugawa regime and restored imperial rule through the Meiji Emperor. Enormous political and social changes ensued.
落ちぶれる【おちぶれる】 (v1) to be ruined; to fall low
[V (plain form)] そう（だ） (aux) people say that; I hear that
㊻ **不思議と【ふしぎと】** (adv) strangely; curiously **かわいがる** (v5r, vt) to love; to dote on someone
㊼ **〜と** (conj) when **ますます** (adv) increasingly; more and more
㊽ **口癖【くちぐせ】** (n) favorite saying
出世する【しゅっせする】 (vs) to achieve success in the world after leaving home **えらい** (adj-i) great; distinguished
なる (v5r, vi) to become（〜に）* おなりです => お (pref. honorable) + [V(ます stem form)] です
㊾ **ろうか** (n) hallway **立っとれ【たっとれ】** (aux) (arch) Keep standing (in the hall) ! * たっとれ is a contracted form of たっておれ and both are imperative forms. 〜ておる indicates a continuing action or state (i.e., to be ..ing); in this context, it is archaic and sounds haughty.
こんな [Noun] (adj-pn) such (refering to something/someone; or to ideas expressed by the speaker); like this * こんな俺 someone like me... (humble)

母が死んで、六年後に親父も死んだ。

俺には兄がいたが、仕事で九州に行くことになった。それで、兄は家を売った。

本当に残念です。

俺はとりあえず学校に行くつもりだ。

坊っちゃんがお家を持たれるまで、甥のところにやっかいになります。

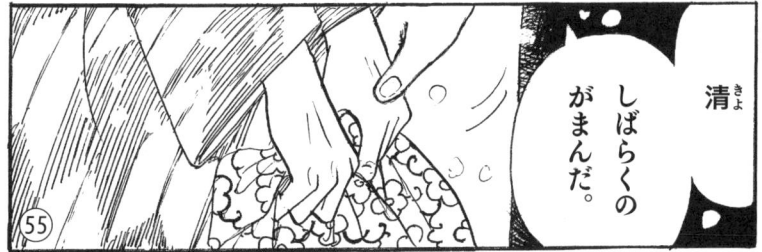

清がまんだ。しばらくの

学校を卒業したら家を持つから！

な？

㊶ 死ぬ【しぬ】 (v5n, vi) to die
　親父【おやじ】 (n) one's father *Father and mother are commonly referred to as お父さん and お母さん. Some men use 親父 and おふくろ to refer to their father and mother.
㊷ 九州【きゅうしゅう】 (n) Kyushu (southernmost of the four main islands of Japan)
　[V (plain form)] ことになる (exp, v5r) it has been decided (so) that 〜; it has been arranged (so) that 〜
㊸ 残念(な)【ざんねん】 (adj-na, n) deplorable; it is a shame
㊹ とりあえず (adv) for the time being
　甥【おい】 (n) nephew
　やっかいになる (exp, v5r) to be under [in] the care of somebody; to throw oneself on somebody's mercy *Kiyo will stay with her nephew.
㊺ しばらく (adv) little while
　がまん (n, vs) patience; endurance
㊻ 卒業する【そつぎょうする】 (vs) to graduate
　な (prt) reassures and confirms. *Here, it is translated as "I promise you. Okay?"

23

三年後—

大学を卒業し、教師として四国に行くことになった。俺は清に会いに行った。

清は風邪を引いて寝込んでいた。

四国に？

そうだ。

ゴホッ

それは箱根の先ですか。手前ですか？

ずっと先の西の方だ。

卒業したら家を持たれると思っておりました。

行くには行くが、すぐに帰ってくる。そうしたら家を持つから、一緒に暮らそう。

㊼ 大学【だいがく】 (n) university; college *Botchan graduated from 物理学校（【ぶつりがっこう】The School of Physics). The school was later renamed 東京理科大学（【とうきょうりかだいがく】Tokyo University of Science).
　教師【きょうし】 (n) teacher　　　四国【しこく】 (n) Shikoku; the smallest of the four main islands of Japan
㊽ 風邪を引く【かぜをひく】 (exp, v5k) to catch a cold　　寝込む【ねこむ】 (v5m, vi) to be sick in bed
　ゴホッ (int) cough; coughing
㊾ 箱根【はこね】 (n) Hakone, a city near Mt. Fuji　　先【さき】 (n) way past that point; the other side　　手前【てまえ】 (n) before; towards this side
㊿ ずっと (adv) far and away　　方【ほう】 (n) side; direction * 西の方 on the western side; to the west
㉑ 持つ【もつ】 (v5t, vt) to possess; to have * 持たれる is honorific using a passive form.
　[V (て form)] おる (aux) (pol) indicates continuing action or state (i.e., to be ..ing). * ～と思っておりました I have been thinking that ～
㉒ [V (plain form)] には [V (plain form)] が Repetition of the same verb creates the atmosphere of an uncertain outcome. * 行くには行くが I will go there (but I don't know how long I will stay there).　　すぐに (adv) soon
　一緒に【いっしょに】 (adv) together (with)　　暮らす【くらす】 (v5s, vi) to live

24

な？
(65)
(64)
出発の日
駅にて——
(66)
歯みがき、楊子に、手ぬぐい……
こんな物、買ってこなくていいのに——
いいから お持ちなさいませ。
(67)
もうお別れになるかもしれません。
(68)
ごきげんよう……
(69)

(66) **出発【しゅっぱつ】** (n, vs) departure　**駅【えき】** (n) train station
(67) **歯みがき【はみがき】** (n) toothpaste　**楊子【ようじ】** (n) toothpick
手ぬぐい【てぬぐい】 (n) hand towel
[V (て form)] くる (aux) to do ～ and come back * 買ってこなくていいのに you didn't have to buy these things (for me)...
[V (ます stem form)] なさい (aux) do (command form) * お as in お持ちなさい makes this statement polite, but Kiyo basically orders Botchan to take it.
～ませ (aux) (pol) indicates a polite request or demand * お持ちなさいませ Please take it.
(68) **もう** (adv) already; now
別れ【わかれ】 (n) farewell
～かもしれない (exp) perhaps; maybe
(69) **ごきげんよう** (exp) please take care of yourself *This colloquial, formal greeting is used for both to say both "hello" and "goodbye." It conveys a wish for a good health.

――振り向いたら

清はやっぱり立っていた。

何(なん)だか大変(たいへん)小さく見えた。

- ⑦② ガッシュ (onoma) hiss *It is the sound of a steam-powered train starting up.
- ⑦④ 振り向く【ふりむく】 (v5k, vi) to turn one's face; to turn around
  [V(た form)]ら (conj) indicates supposition; when; if; after
- ⑦⑤ やっぱり（＝やはり） (exp) as I thought; as expected
  何だか【なんだか】 (adv) somewhat
  大変【たいへん】 (adv) very; greatly

原文に挑戦しましょう

ウェブの練習問題（186ページ参照）をしてから、チャレンジしてみましょう。次の場面は、第1章のマンガのどのコマかわかりますか。引用文（quotation）の後の質問に答えましょう。

原文❶

親譲りの無鉄砲で子供の時から損ばかりしている。小学校にいる時分学校の二階から飛び降りて一週間ほど腰を抜かした事がある。なぜそんな無闇をしたと聞く人があるかも知れぬ。別段深い理由でもない。新築の二階から首を出していたら、同級生の一人が冗談に、いくら威張っても、そこから飛び降りる事は出来まい。弱虫やーい。と囃したからである。小使に負ぶさって帰って来た時、おやじが大きな眼をして二階ぐらいから飛び降りて腰を抜かす奴があるかと言ったから、この次は抜かさずに飛んで見せますと答えた。

【原文❶の質問】どうして無鉄砲は「親譲り」だと言っていますか。お父さんのどんなところが無鉄砲なのですか。

原文❷

出立の日には朝から来て、いろいろ世話をやいた。来る途中小間物屋で買って来た歯磨と楊子と手拭をズックの革鞄に入れてくれた。そんな物は入らないと言ってもなかなか承知しない。車を並べて停車場へ着いて、プラットフォームの上へ出た時、車へ乗り込んだおれの顔をじっと見て「もうお別れになるかも知れません。ずいぶんご機嫌よう」と小さな声で云った。目に涙がいっぱいたまっている。おれは泣かなかった。しかしもう少しで泣くところであった。汽車がよっぽど動き出してから、もう大丈夫だろうと思って、窓から首を出して、振り向いたら、やっぱり立っていた。何だか大変小さく見えた。

【原文❷の質問】坊っちゃんは駅で清と別れる時に泣きましたか。坊っちゃんと清はどんな気持ちだったでしょうか。

第2章を読む前に

清

坊っちゃんが大学を卒業されて、中学校で数学の先生をすることになりました。その仕事で四国という、箱根のずっと先の田舎に行ってしまい、悲しいです。汽車や船に乗って、四国まで行くのは本当に大変だったと思います。坊っちゃんは正直ですが、向こう見ずのところがおありです。もう、いろいろな先生方にあだ名をおつけになって……これからが心配です。

箱根 a place name　**田舎** countryside　**悲しい** sad　**向こう見ず** rash　**おありです**（honorific form of あります）
あだ名をつける to give somebody a nickname　**おつけになる**（honorific form of つける）

第2章 ❖ 四国へ
Going to Shikoku

② やっと (adv) at last
　着く【つく】 (v5k, vi) to arrive at（〜に）
③ 船【ふね】 (n) ship; steamship
　岸【きし】 (n) shore
　はしけ (n) dinghy; launch; a small boat to transport people or goods from a large ship to the shore.
⑤ 中学校【ちゅうがっこう】 (n) middle school
　[Number]里【り】 (n) (ctr) an old Japanese unit of distance ＊一里 is approx. 3.927km or 2.44 miles; thus, 二里 is approx. 5 miles. Japan began to use the metric system after adopting the Treaty of the Metre in 1886.
　[Quantity]ばかり (prt) approximately; just/only (about)
　[(V/adj-i) plain; (adj-na) stem]らしい (aux) seeming ... ＊らしい expresses judgment based on evidence, reason or trustworthy hearsay.

⑥ マッチ箱のような汽車に五分ばかり乗り

⑦

⑧ それから車で中学校に行った。

⑨ 小使がもう放課後だと言ったから、挨拶は明日にすることにした。

⑩ 宿屋に行ってくれ。

⑪

⑫ こちらのお部屋です。

⑥ マッチ箱【マッチばこ】 (n) matchbox　汽車【きしゃ】 (n) steam engine train
　〜のような [Noun] (exp) [Noun] like 〜 ; [Noun] similar to 〜 *マッチ箱のような汽車 (a steam-powered train that looks like a match box) indicates that this train is small. This train, imported from Germany, was in use from 1888 to 1954. In 2001, a replica of the train, *Botchan Ressha* was introduced in the city of Matsuyama, Ehime prefecture. The modern version, now a tourist attraction, runs on diesel.
⑧ 車【くるま】 (n) *jinrikisha*; rickshaw. In the Meiji Period, 車 meant 人力車 (じんりきしゃ, 人 = human, 力 riki = power or force, 車 = vehicle), which literally means "human-powered vehicle." It is a small two-wheeled cart for one or two passengers, pulled usually by one person. The word rickshaw, a commonly used term, is derived from 人力車.
⑨ 放課後【ほうかご】 (n) after school　挨拶【あいさつ】 (n) greeting
　[V (plain form)] ことにする (exp, vs) to decide to do 〜
⑩ 宿屋【やどや】 (n) (Japanese) inn
⑪ 山城屋【やましろや】 (n) Yamashiroya-name of an inn (lit. mountain castle shop) *Yamashiroya was the name of a pawnshop located near the house where Soseki lived during his childhood.

⑬ 狭い【せまい】 (adj-i) narrow; confined ～し (conj) (at the end of a phrase) identifies one of several reasons.
 [V (plain form)] しかない (exp) to have no choice, but (to do something)
 [plain form] のか (exp) (fam) question with the request for further explanation *Same as [Sentence] んですか.
⑭ あいにく (adv) unfortunately; sorry, but ... ふさがる (v5r, vi) to be occupied (e.g., accommodation) ドサッ (onoma) collapse; fall
⑮ ピシャン (onoma) rattle; sound of quickly closing a door.
⑰ さっき (adv) some time ago いっぱい (adv, n) a lot; much 空く【あく】 (v5k, vi) to be empty; to be vacant
 ～な (prt) (sentence end, mainly masc.) indicates emotion, emphasis, or reflection (e.g., How ～!; What ～!). May indicate a command.
 もぐ (onoma) eating; munching sound 押し込める【おしこめる】 (v1, vt) to confine (～に)
⑱ ハッ (onoma) realize *Used when one suddenly realizes something.
⑲ 茶代【ちゃだい】 (n) a (small) tip *There is the custom of handing over 心付け (こころづけ, Japanese style of tipping, consideration of the heart) when staying at a Japanese inn. This custom was common during Soseki's time. Today 心付け is given as a token of appreciation at the end of the stay when a special service has been offered, rather than in anticipation of good service.
⑳ 持っていく (exp, v5k) to take *持っていけ (command form)
㉑ ～も (prt) as much as ～ *五円も！ Five whole yen! This is a big tip since Botchan's salary is 40 yen.

次の日

中学校

校長室で――

辞令です。

色の黒い目の大きな狸のような男だな。

最初に、教育精神について理解してもらいましょう。

まず「教師たるもの生徒の模範であれ」――

教師は生徒によい影響を及ぼさなくてはならないということです。

つまり教育者とは――うんぬんかんぬん

㉒ 次【つぎ】(n) next   校長室【こうちょうしつ】(n) principal's office
㉓ 辞令【じれい】(n) notice of appointment (for his new job)
㉔ 色の黒い【いろのくろい】(adj-i) dark-skinned * の is used to mark the subject in relative clauses; an alternate to が (i.e., 色が黒い).
　 狸【たぬき】(n) Tanuki; badger
㉕ 最初に【さいしょに】(adv) foremost; at first   教育【きょういく】(n) education   精神【せいしん】(n) spirit
　 [Noun] について (exp) about ～; concerning ～; as to ～
㉖ まず (adv) first (of all)   生徒【せいと】(n) pupil * 学生 refers to a college student.   模範【もはん】(n) role model; exemplar
　 [Noun] たる (aux) (usu. as ～たるもの, etc.) (those) who are; (that) which is *Used often in relation to qualifications and requirements for a position (e.g., in the capacity of ～).
　 ～であれ (conj) (command form of である) should * 教師たるもの生徒の模範であれ Teachers should be role models for the students.
㉗ 影響を及ぼす【えいきょうをおよぼす】(exp, v5s) to have an effect on   ～なくてはならない (exp) must do ～
　 ～ということ (だ) (exp) to summarize a point; that means ～
㉘ つまり (adv) in short; in brief; in other words   教育者【きょういくしゃ】(n) educator
　 うんぬん、かんぬん (exp) and so on; and so forth; blah, blah, blah

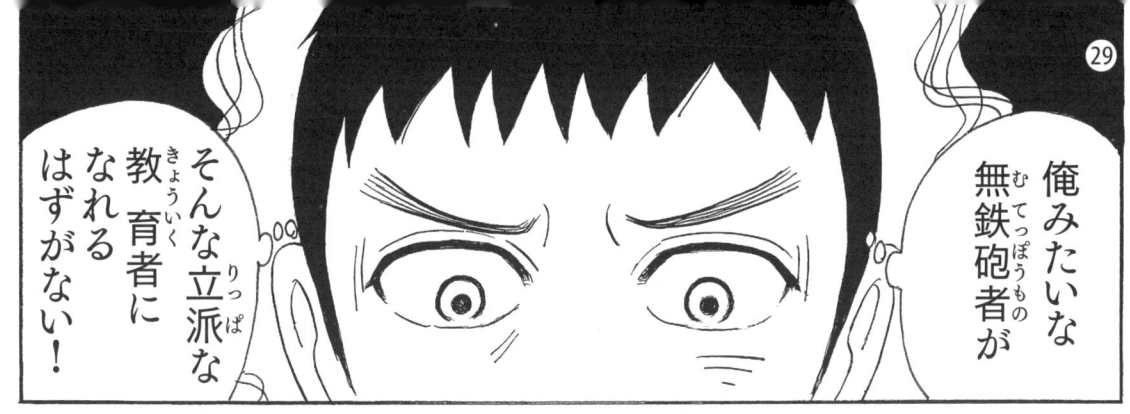

㉙ [Noun] みたい (な) (aux) -like; sort of 〜　　無鉄砲者【むてっぽうもの】 (n) reckless person
　そんな [Noun] (adj-pn) such (about the actions of the listener, or about ideas expressed or understood by the listener); that sort of 〜
　立派 (な)【りっぱ】 (adj-na) fine; exemplary　　[V (plain form)] はずがない (exp) cannot (do); it is impossible that 〜
㉚ 絶対に【ぜったいに】 (adv) absolutely　　無理 (な)【むり (な)】 (adj-na, n) unreasonable; impossible
　ですから (conj) therefore, ... * ですから is more polite than だから
㉛ バン (onoma) bang
㉜ 返す【かえす】 (v5s, vt) to return (something) * お返しします お + [V (ます stem form)] + する (humble expression)
㉝ おっしゃる通り【おっしゃるとおり】 (exp)(hon) as (someone) says * おっしゃる通りにゃ (には) できません I can't possibly do as you say.
㉞ ただの [Noun] (adj-pn) only; mere　　希望【きぼう】 (n) hope; wish
㉟ 〜なら (aux) if it is the case that 〜; if it is true that 〜　　初め【はじめ】 (n) beginning　　おどかす (v5s, vt) to startle; to surprise
　[V (plain form)] な (prt) indicates a negative imperative. * おどかすな do not startle me.
　〜って (prt) indicates annoyance with someone's word or action.
　トテチテタ (onoma) bugle sounds *During the Meiji Period, bugles were sounded to indicate the beginning and end of class time.

33

では、一人ひとりに自己紹介をお願いします。

清へ
昨日四国に着いた。
ここはまったくつまらん所だ。

東京から来ました。
担当は数学です。

㊱ 教員控所【きょういんひかえじょ】 (n) teacher's room; teacher's lounge *The term 教員控所 is no longer used; 職員室【しょくいんしつ】 is a commonly used term.
㊲ ズラリ (adv, onoma) parallel, aligned（〜と）
㊳ 一人ひとり【ひとりひとり】 (n) one by one; one at a time *Botchan introduces himself to each teacher, one at a time, showing his letter of appointment. Today, such an introduction is rare.
　自己紹介【じこしょうかい】 (n) self-introduction
㊵ まったく (adv) really; completely
　つまらん（＝つまらない） (adj-i) uninteresting; boring ん＝ぬ、ない *Botchan refers to Shikoku as the 'absolute boondocks' from the perspective of an *Edokko* who considers Tokyo to be the center of the world.
　担当【たんとう】 (n) (in) charge (of a subject, but not necessarily supervision of the staff)　　数学【すうがく】 (n) mathematics

㊶ 今日はみんなにあだ名をつけてやった。

㊷ 教頭は女のような優しげな声を出す文学士だ。シャツが赤いので、"赤シャツ"。赤は体に良いからと言って、一年中着ているらしい。

㊸ 古賀といいます。よろしくお願いします。

㊹ 英語教師は顔色が悪くふくれているので、"うらなり"。

㊺ 面倒だな、一人ひとりに。

㊻ やあ、君が新しい先生か！ちと遊びに来たまえ。アハハ

㊶ **あだ名をつける**【あだなをつける】 (exp, v1) to give someone a nickname　　**[V (て form)] やる** (aux) (col) to do something for (the sake of someone else) *The use of 〜てやる indicates Botchan's lack of respect towards his colleagues.

㊷ **優しげ(な)**【やさしげ】 (adj-na) gentle; kind; sweet-looking　やさしい＋げ＝やさしげ　*げ（気）is a suffix that when attached to the stems of i-adjectives indicates the meaning of "seeming; giving the appearance of; giving one the feeling of."　　**声**【こえ】 (n) voice
　　文学士【ぶんがくし】 (n) a man of letters; a literary man　*The direct translation is a person with a Bachelor of Arts degree. This degree was given only to graduates of 東京帝国大学 (【とうきょうていこくだいがく】, Tokyo Imperial University) before 1920. The school was renamed 東京大学 (【とうきょうだいがく】, Tokyo University) in 1947.　　**教頭**【きょうとう】 (n) vice principal
　　赤シャツ (n) Red Shirt, the vice princial's nickname　*He wears a red wool flannel shirt.　　**体**【からだ】 (n) body; health
　　一年中【いちねんじゅう】 (adv) all year around　　**[V (plain form)] らしい** (see 第2章 コマ⑤)

㊸ **古賀**【こが】 (n) Koga, family name　　**顔色が悪い**【かおいろがわるい】 (exp, adj-i) looking pale; looking unwell
　　ふくれる (v1, vi) to swell (out)

㊹ **うらなり** (n) Koga's nickname; weak-looking fellow; pale-faced man　*Uranari is a vegetable (Japanese squash) that grows near the top end of the vine.

㊺ **面倒(な)**【めんどう】 (adj-na, n) bother (some) to do; tiresome

㊻ **君**【きみ】 (pn) you; buddy; pal　*An informal way of referring to subordinates; can also be affectionate and friendly.
　　ちと (＝ちょっと) (adv) (fam) (arch) a little bit　　**遊ぶ**【あそぶ】 (v5b, vi) to play; to enjoy oneself
　　[V (ます stem form)] たまえ (aux) (male) please do 〜 (mild command) *imperative form of たまう

数学の主任教師は、たくましい〝山嵐〟。
悪僧って顔つきだ。
画学の吉川でげす。
私も江戸っ子！
お仲間ができてうれしいでげす。
芸人風の〝野だいこ〟。
こんなのが江戸っ子なら、江戸には生まれたくないもんだ。
校長は見ての通りの〝狸〟だ。
今日はもう帰っていいですよ。
授業はあさってから始めて下さい。

㊼ **主任【しゅにん】** (n) person in charge; senior staff **たくましい** (adj-i) burly; strong
山嵐【やまあらし】 (n) nickname of the mathematics teacher * ヤマアラシ is a porcupine (a rodent with a coat of sharp spines). The teacher's hair style looks like a porcupine. The kanji characters also mean "mountain storm." His family name is 堀田【ほった】.
悪僧【あくそう】 (n) dissolute priest **顔つき【かおつき】** (n) look; face

㊽ **画学【ががく】** (n) the study of drawing **吉川【よしかわ】** (n) Yoshikawa, family name
でげす (aux) (arch) **です** *Used by males from the end of the Edo to the beginning of the Meiji Period. Variations include でげしょ and でげし.
江戸っ子【えどっこ】 (n) true Tokyoite **仲間【なかま】** (n) company; fellow; colleague; associate **うれしい** (adj-i) happy; glad

㊾ **芸人【げいにん】** (n) player; performer; actor **〜風（な）【ふう】** (adj-na, n, suf) a style of 〜 ; an appearance of 〜
野だいこ【のだいこ】 (n) the clown, Yoshikawa's nickname. 野だいこ is derived from Taikomochi (see, p.10).
〜もんだ・ものだ (exp) indicates one's wish when used with 〜たい and expresses some degree of shock and surprise when an unlikely event has taken place.

㊿ **見ての通り【みてのとおり】** (exp) as you see; as you already know *Same as 見た通り. 狸（たぬき）is an animal traditionally viewed as a symbol of slyness. It often refers to a scheming person who maintains a poker face. This implies that Botchan views the principal as not only someone who resembles a 狸, but also someone who makes evil plans without ever showing emotion.

(51) **[V（て form)]（も）いいです** (exp) indicates permission; you may (also) do 〜

Panel 52
山城屋

Panel 53
また、色々なことを書いてやる。

Panel 54
これくらい書いておけば十分だろう。
さようなら。

Panel 55
手紙を書くのは大きらいだが、清が心配するからな。
それにしても、こんな立派な十五畳の座敷に寝るのは気持ちいい。

Panel 56
昨日茶代をはずんだからな。

Panel 57
この部屋かい？

㊼ 色々（な）【いろいろ】 (adj-na) various
㊾ [Noun] くらい・[Noun] ぐらい (prt) approximately   [V（て form)] おく (aux) to do something in advance
　　十分（な）【じゅうぶん】 (adj-na, n) enough
㊿ 心配する【しんぱいする】 (vs) to worry   それにしても (exp) nevertheless; at any rate; even so
　　[Number] 畳【じょう】 (ctr) counter for tatami mats; measure of room size (in mat units) *In the region around Tokyo, one tatami generally measures 0.88 m by 1.76 m. 十五畳 approximately 23 square meters; 247 square feet. Botchan moved to this large tatami room from his first small, dark room.
　　座敷【ざしき】 (n) tatami room
㊾ 茶代をはずむ【ちゃだいをはずむ】 (v5m, exp) to tip handsomely
㊿ 〜かい (prt) (fam) marks a yes-no question.

㉘ 先ほどは、失敬！

山嵐（やまあらし）

㉙ 君（きみ）の受け持ちを決めてきた。

㉚ 気の早い男だ。

㉛

㉜ ところでいつまでこんな宿料（やどりょう）の高い部屋に泊（と）まるつもりだい？

㉝ 俺がいい下宿を紹介（しょうかい）してやるから、移（うつ）った方がいい。

はあ……

㉘ **先ほど**【さきほど】 (adv, n) some time ago　　**失敬（な）**【しっけい】(adj-na, n) rudeness; acting impolitely ＊先ほどは失敬 literally means "I'm sorry about earlier" and implies "If I did anything rude before, I'm sorry, but it was nice meeting you." Yama-Arashi refers to the meeting that they had at the school. Equivalent to "Good to see you again!"

㉙ **受け持ち**【うけもち】(n) the class assigned to (Botchan)　　**決める**【きめる】(v1, vt) to decide

㉚ **気の早い**【きのはやい】(exp, adj-i) quick-tempered; hasty ＊気が早い is another option (see コマ㉔).

㉜ **ところで** (conj) by the way　　**いつまで** (exp) how long 〜 ; till when 〜　　**宿料**【やどりょう・しゅくりょう】(n) hotel charges
泊まる【とまる】(v5r, vi) to stay at（〜に）　　**[V (plain form)] つもり** (n) intention to do 〜
〜だい (prt) (fam) marks a WH question (what, where, who, how long). ＊This particle expresses friendliness and affection towards the listener (Botchan in this context).

㉝ **下宿**【げしゅく】(n) boarding; boarding house　　**移る**【うつる】(v5r, vi) to move (to another place)（〜に）
はあ (int) yes; indeed; well; huh 〜 (with some hesitation)

64 あさってから学校だから、今日決めて、明日移れば丁度いいだろう。

65 よろしくお願いします。

66 よし！では、今から見に行こう。

67 い、今？ついて来たまえ。

68 骨董屋か。

69 ここだよ。いか銀いるか？

70 下宿人を連れて来た！

- 64 丁度いい【ちょうどいい】 (exp, adj-i) just right (time, size, length, etc.)
- 65 よろしくお願い【ねが】いします (exp) (hon) please help me; please treat me well
- 66 よし (int) good; all right!; OK!
- 67 ついて来る【ついてくる】 (exp, vk) to come along with one; to accompany
- 69 いか銀【いかぎん】 (n) Ikagin, name of both the antique shop and the proprietor
- 70 骨董屋【こっとうや】 (n) antique store
  - 下宿人【げしゅくにん】 (n) lodger
  - 連れて来る【つれてくる】 (exp, vk) to bring someone along (person を place に)

⑦¹ では明日、女房と一緒にお待ちしております。

⑦² いか銀といか銀の女房か。中学校の時、ウィッチという言葉をならったが、まさにウィッチに似ている。

⑦³ 静かだし、よい下宿だろ？

世話になりました。月給をみんな宿料に払うところでした。

⑦⁴ どうだ？氷水でも？俺のおごりだ。

⑦⁵ 山嵐か……悪い男じゃなさそうだ。

⑦⁶ ハハハ シャカシャカ

⑦¹ **女房**【にょうぼう】 (n) (my) wife *Originally this refered to women who served at the Imperial Palace. These days, 女房 is used less and less while 家内【かない】 and 妻【つま】 are much more common terms. 家内 is literally translated as inside the home. 妻 is formally used by romantically linked men and women to refer to one another and conveys the sense of an equal relationship.

⑦² **ウィッチ** (n) witch *A Japanese word for witch is 魔女【まじょ】.
[Noun] という (exp) said; called thus   **言葉**【ことば】 (n) language; word   **まさに** (adv) exactly; surely
似る【にる】 (v1, vi) to resemble; to be similar (～に)

⑦³ **世話になる**【せわになる】 (exp, v5r) to receive a favor; to be much obliged to someone; to be indebted to someone
月給【げっきゅう】 (n) monthly salary   **払う**【はらう】 (v5u, vt) to pay
[V (plain form)] ところ (n) about to do an action; on the verge of ～

⑦⁴ **氷水**【こおりみず】 (n) (arch) shaved ice (usually served with sweet flavored syrup) * かき氷【かきごおり】 is commonly used now. We can trace the history of shaved ice back to the Heian Period.
[Noun] でも (prt) or something   **おごり** (n) a treat

⑦⁶ **[Noun] じゃなさそう（だ）** (exp) does not seem; unlikely; improbable

原文に挑戦しましょう

ウェブの練習問題（186ページ参照）をしてから、チャレンジしてみましょう。次の場面は、第2章のマンガのどのコマかわかりますか。引用文の後の質問に答えましょう。

【原文❶】

ぶうと言って汽船がとまると、艀が岸を離れて、漕ぎ寄せて来た。船頭は真っ裸に赤ふんどしをしめている。野蛮な所だ。もっともこの熱さでは着物はきられまい。日が強いので水がやに光る。見つめていても眼がくらむ。事務員に聞いてみるとおれはここへ降りるのだそうだ。見るところでは大森ぐらいな漁村だ。人を馬鹿にしていらあ、こんな所に我慢が出来るものかと思ったが仕方がない。威勢よく一番に飛び込んだ。続いて五、六人は乗ったろう。ほかに大きな箱を四つばかり積み込んで赤ふんは岸へ漕ぎ戻して来た。陸へ着いた時も、いの一番に飛び上がって、いきなり、磯に立っていた鼻たれ小僧をつらまえて中学校はどこだと聞いた。

【原文❶の質問】季節はいつですか。

【原文❷】

挨拶をしたうちに教頭のなにがしというのがいた。これは文学士だそうだ。文学士と云えば大学の卒業生だからえらい人なんだろう。妙に女のような優しい声を出す人だった。もっとも驚いたのはこの暑いのにフランネルの襯衣を着ている。いくらか薄い地にはなくっても暑いにはきまってる。文学士だけにご苦労千万な服装をしたもんだ。しかもそれが赤シャツだから人を馬鹿にしている。あとから聞いたらこの男は年がら年中赤シャツを着るんだそうだ。妙な病気があったものだ。当人の説明では赤は身体に薬になるから、衛生のためにわざわざ誂らえるんだそうだが、いらざる心配だ。そんならついでに着物も袴も赤にすればいい。

【原文❷の質問】文学士とは何ですか。どうして教頭先生は赤いシャツを着ていますか。

第３章を読む前に

校長（狸）

私は校長です。
東京から新しい先生が来ましたが、大学を出たばかりで、世間知らずのところがあるようですね。
「生徒の模範になれ」と言ったら、本当に信じていました。
これから、うちの生徒や他の先生方とうまくやっていけるかどうか心配です。
とにかく、問題を起こさないでほしいですね。
さて、坊っちゃん先生の初日はどうだったでしょうか。

世間知らず	to be ignorant in the ways of the world	模範	role model	信じる	to trust
～方	honorific pluralizing suffix	うまくいく	to get along with (others)	問題を起こす	to cause problems

第３章 ❖ 坊っちゃん先生
Botchan Sensei

① 初めての授業は何だか変な感じだった。

② 自分より大きな生徒に「先生」と言われると足の裏がむずむずした。

③ だから、この三角形が——

⑥ つまりこうなるわけだ。

⑦ 早すぎて聞きとれん。

---

① **初めて【はじめて】** (adv,n) for the first time * 初めての授業 the first day of teaching
  変（な）【へんな】 (adj-na) strange; odd; weird   **感じ【かんじ】** (n) feeling
② **大きな【おおきな】** (adj-pn) big *Some other i-adjectives can be modified with な (e.g., 小さな、おかしな、あたたかな).
  足の裏【あしのうら】 (n) sole of the foot
  むずむずする (onoma, vs) to itch; to feel strange * 足の裏がむずむずした I couldn't quite put my finger on it, like having an itch on the bottom of my foot that I couldn't reach.
③ **三角形【さんかくけい・さんかっけい】** (n) triangle   **ハハハハ・アハハ** (int) laughing sounds
  ザワ (onoma) unsettled atmosphere of chatter; people murmuring and fidgeting
  ガヤ (onoma) clamorous racket; chatter; crowd of people talking
⑥ **〜わけ（だ）** (n) conclusion from reasoning, judgment or calculation based on something read or heard *This often gives a summary or restatement of a previous statement. つまり、こうなるわけだ．In short, this is how it turns out.
⑦ **早い【はやい】** (adj-i) quick; fast * 早い＋すぎ => 早すぎる too fast
  聞きとる【ききとる】 (v5r, vt) to catch (a person's words) * 早すぎて聞きとれん（＝聞きとれない）too fast to catch (what Botchan is talking about)

⑧ 俺は弱みを見せないように、どの教室でもできるだけ大声で早口で話した。

⑨ 先生！
ペラペラペラ

⑩ あまり早くてわからんけれ、もうちょっとゆっくり話しておくれんかな、もし。
でかっ

⑪ 俺は江戸っ子で、君らの言葉は使えない。わからなければわかるまで、待っていればいい。

⑫ ……
イーチニーサーン

⑬ 先生！

⑭ ちょっとこの問題を解いておくれんかな、もし。

⑧ 弱み【よわみ】　(n) weakness　　　[V (ない form)] ように　(exp) in order not to (show my weakness)
　どの [Noun] でも　(exp) no matter which 〜 * どの教室でも　no matter which classroom is
　できるだけ　(exp) as much as possible　　大声【おおごえ】　(n) loud voice　　早口【はやくち】　(n) fast-talking * 早口で in a brusque tone
⑨ ペラペラペラ　(onoma) fluent, non-stop talk
⑩ 〜けれ　(prt) (dialect) indicates a reason.　*This may be a variation of a dialect 〜けん, which takes the place of から (because) in standard
　Japanese.　　[V (て form)] おくれんか　(dialect) 〜てくれないか・〜てくれませんか　　　〜かな、もし・〜なもし　(prt) (dialect) (pol)
　makes a request polite. * もうちょっと、ゆっくり話しておくれんかな、もし Can't ya slow down, please?
　でかっ（＝でかい）　(adj-i) (col) huge　*Having a small っ at the end of a word indicates a sudden stopping of sound or the flow of air, and
　adds emphasis or emotional tone.
⑪ 君らの言葉【きみらのことば】　(n) your language. *This refers to a local dialect, Iyo dialect, that the students use. [Noun] ら is a pluralizing suffix.
　〜まで　(prt) until　　　[V (ば form)] いい　(exp) you had better 〜 ; you have only to 〜
⑭ 問題【もんだい】　(n) problem; question　　解く【とく】　(v5k, vt) to solve

⑮ な、なんだこりゃ。

⑯ 何だかわからん。この次に教えてやる。

⑰ わーい♪ 先生なのにわからん！ わからん！ べらぼうめ 先生にだって、解けない問題もある。

⑱ あれが解けたら、四十円でこんな田舎まで来るもんか。

⑲ どうだった？一日目。

⑳ ここの生徒はやっかいだ。それに、授業が終わっても、三時まで帰れないなんておかしいぜ。

⑮ なんだこりゃ（＝こりゃ／これはなんだ）　*Word inversion is common in conversation.
⑯ この次【このつぎ】　(n) next time; another time
⑰ わーい　(int) wow; whee-ee; a crowd's excited roar
　べらぼうめ　(exp) refers to people "You fool" or an incident "It's absurd; it's rubbish"　*This is a combination of べらぼう (absurd) + め (derogatory suffix to refer to others). Here べらぼうめ can be translated as "What's the big deal?"
　[Noun] にだって（＝にでも）　(prt) even 〜 ; even if 〜
⑱ 田舎【いなか】　(n) rural area; countryside
　〜もんか・ものか　(exp) never do; how could 〜　*Used to create a rhetorical question indicating that the speaker actually believe the opposite is true. 四十円でこんな田舎まで来るもんか Would I have had to come to this kind of boondocks for a measly 40 yen salary?
　カチャ　(onoma) the sound of a knob turning
⑲ 一日目【いちにちめ】　(n) the first day
⑳ やっかい（な）　(adj-na, n) trouble; burden　それに　(conj) besides; moreover　終わる【おわる】　(v5r, vi) to finish; to end
　[V(て form)] も　(prt) even if 〜 ; even though 〜　〜なんて　(prt) such as 〜 ; (things) like 〜
　おかしい　(adj-i) ridiculous; strange; funny　〜ぜ　(prt) (male) (sentence end) indicates assertion.

㉑ その通りだが、アハハ

㉒ あまり学校の不平を人前で言わない方がいい。ずいぶん妙な奴もいるからな。

㉓ 赤シャツと野だいこ——

㉔ ——下宿 いか銀

㉕ いかがです？この掛軸。"崋山"ですよ。

㉖ あなたもかなり風流でいらっしゃいますね。道楽に始められてはいかがですか？

㉗ 風流!? この俺が風流だって!?

㉑ その通り【そのとおり】　(exp) just like that; quite so
㉒ 不平【ふへい】　(n) complaint
　　人前【ひとまえ】　(n) the public　＊人前で in public　　ずいぶん　(adv) very; considerably
　　妙（な）【みょう】　(adj-na) strange; unusual　＊妙な奴 a strange guy / a suspicious-looking guy
㉕ いかが（ですか）　(adv) how; how about　＊This is more polite than どうですか．　　掛軸【かけじく】　(n) hanging scroll
　　崋山【かざん】　(n) Kazan, the name of a famous Japanese artist　＊It could be Watanabe Kazan (1793‑1841) or Yokoyama Kazan (1784‑1837). Both artists produced a number of portraits, landscapes, and bird-and-flower genre paintings.
㉖ かなり　(adv) considerably　　風流（な）【ふうりゅう】　(adj-na, n) elegant; refined　＊風流な人 a person of refined tastes
　　道楽【どうらく】　(n) hobby; pastime　＊This term derives from Buddhist teachings about seeking out the path of pleasure but, over time, came to mean pursuit of a decadent and dissipated lifestyle.
㉗ 〜だって（＝〜だと）　(prt) a quotation　＊風流だって？ (You say) I am a connoisseur of art?

㉘ [Noun] にする (exp, vs) to decide on 〜   [V (て form)] おく (aux) to do something with the future in mind *十五円にしておきます
 I will go ahead and make it 15 yen (for your future purchase). 15 yen is too much for Botchan's 40-yen salary.
㉙ [V (ます stem form)] なさい (see 第 1 章 コマ ㊲)
㉚ いらんものはいらんっ (exp) When I say I don't want it, I mean I don't want it!   いつでも (adv) any time; whenever
　結構（な）【けっこう】 (adj-na) sufficient; fine　　〜でございます（＝です） (exp) (pol) to be
㉛ [Noun] 責め【せめ・ぜめ】 (n) persecution; hounding; pestering *骨董責め【こっとうぜめ】means pestering someone to buy antiques.
　たまらん（＝たまらない） (exp, adj-i) intolerable; one can't stand it
㉝ スー (onoma) door sliding smoothly and quietly
㉞ すずり (n) inkstone
　端渓【たんけい】 (n) Tankei inkstone *Chinese inkstones produced in 端渓 (Duanqi in Chinese) are regarded as the finest quality.

そば東京
ある日、散歩の途中「そば・東京」と書いた看板を見つけた。
そば東京
俺はそばが大好きなのだ。
天ぷらそば、もう一杯！
つる
ペコ
なんだ、うちの学校の生徒たちか——
もう一杯！
ひさしぶりに食ったそばはうまかった。

㉟ **散歩【さんぽ】** (n) walk; stroll **[Noun] の途中【とちゅう】** (n) on the way to ～; en route to ～
看板【かんばん】 (n) sign; signboard **見つける** (v1, vt) to discover; to find

㊱ **もう一杯【いっぱい】** (exp) another bowl

㊲ **つる** (onoma) slurping noodle soup ＊ずる（ずる） is another common word to describe a style of eating noodle soups that is more noisier and done without much regard for one's surroundings.

㊳ **ペコ** (onoma) action of quickly bowing or lowering one's head

㊴ **うち** (n) my; our (referring to one's family, school, company, etc.) ＊うちの学校の生徒たち students of the school where I teach
[Noun] たち (suf) plural suffix (esp. for people & animals; formerly honorific)

㊵ **ひさしぶりに** (adv) after a long time **食う【くう】** (v5u, vt) (male) (vulg) to eat
うまい (adj-i) (fam) delicious ＊おいしい is a more neutral expression, used by both male and female speakers.

㊶ 翌日（よくじつ）中学校—

㊷ 天ぷら先生 わあぁっ

㊸ サッ

㊹ 天ぷら食っちゃおかしいか？

㊺ しかし、四杯は食いすぎぞなもし。どっ

㊻ ム〜

㊼ 俺の金で何杯食おうと勝手だろう。さあ、授業を始める。

㊶ 翌日【よくじつ】 (n) next day
㊷ わあぁっ (int) wahaha; a crowd's excited roar
㊸ サッ (onoma) swoosh; a quick motion of erasing the blackboard
㊹ 食っちゃ（＝食べては） * 食っちゃおかしいか Botchan is asking students if eating tempura is something funny. This is a rhetorical question; thus, Botchan is really saying that nothing is wrong with eating tempura. This pattern is similar to 〜ては（ちゃ）だめか、〜ては（ちゃ）いけないか (Is there something wrong with doing 〜 ?)
㊺ しかし (conj) however; but   [V (ます stem form)] すぎ (n) too (much) * 食いすぎ eat too much
〜ぞなもし (prt) (dialect) (pol) indicates polite certainty, emphasis, or contempt (similar to よ, but it is a polite expression); states one's opinion politely （〜と申し上げます）; and makes a request polite (similar to 〜なもし see コマ⑩).
どっ (onoma) rushing, sudden, louder laughter
㊻ ム〜 (onoma) grrr *It is used when someone gets angry or annoyed.
㊼ 勝手（な）【かって】 (adj-na, n) one's own convenience; one's way

㊽ 見物する所もない狭い町だから、天ぷらぐらいで大騒ぎするんだ。

あわれな奴らだ。

㊾ ガチャッ

二年四組

㊿ 一つ、天ぷら四杯なり ただし、笑うべからず

(51) 卑怯な冗談はやめろ！

(52) 自分のしたことを笑われて怒るのが、卑怯じゃろうがなもし。

そうじゃ、そうじゃ

(53) へらず口利かずに勉強しろ！

㊽ 見物する【けんぶつする】 (vs) to sightsee　　[Noun]ぐらい (prt) to (about) the extent that; like ～ *天ぷらぐらいで with something like tempura　　大騒ぎする【おおさわぎする】 (vs) to clamor; to make a big fuss
　　あわれ（な） (adj-na) pitiable; pitiful; pathetic; miserable *あわれな奴ら pitiful folks

㊾ 組【くみ】 (n) class; homeroom; there are several kumi for each grade. *In the Meiji period, the compulsory education (elementary school) was set at four years in 1872 and later extended to six years in 1908. Middle school was five years. This system lasted until 1945 (the end of WWII).
　　ガチャッ・カチャッ (onoma) the sound of a knob turning *Both ガチャッ and カチャッ are the sounds of a door latch, except that the latter makes more of a clicking sound.

㊿ 一つ【ひとつ】 (n) for one thing (often used in itemized lists)　　～なり (aux) (arch) (meaning ～だ、～である) be (an affirmation)
　　ただし (conj) but; however　　笑う【わらう】 (v5u, vi) to laugh
　　[V (plain form)]べからず (exp) (arch) must not; should not; do not * 笑うべからず Laughing is not allowed.

(51) 卑怯（な）【ひきょう】 (adj-na) cowardly; unfair　　冗談【じょうだん】 (n) jest; joke
　　やめる (v1, vt) to end; to stop; to cease * やめろ (command form).

(52) 怒る【おこる】 (v5r, vi) to get angry　　～じゃろうが (dialect) to question or state something *～じゃろうがなもし means ～ではないでしょうか. In this scene, students are just talking back politely in their dialect by saying "You getting mad at us for laughing at things you did...isn't that cowardly, sir?"

(53) へらず口を利く【へらずぐちをきく】 (exp, v5k) to talk back *Literally, へらず口 means impudent talk/needless retort, and 利く to do its work.

(55) **もの** (n) thing; a natural reaction *(On chalkboard) 天ぷらを食うとへらず口が利きたくなるものなり When one eats tempura, one naturally feels like talking back to others.

(56) **カチン** (onoma) argh; used when the particular word someone says triggers your anger.

(57) **お前ら【おまえら】** (n) (col) you scoundrel * お前 (see 第1章 コマ㉟) + ら (plural marker)

[Noun] みたいに (aux) –like ～; sort of ～; similar to ～

生意気（な）【なまいき】 (adj-na) sassy; smart-mouthed; smart-aleck

(58) **バンザイ** (int, n) banzai (a celebratory cheer); something worthy of celebration *Literally, it means "ten thousand years (of life)" and was used to express respect for the Emperor. After the Meiji Restoration until the end of World War II, banzai was used as a formal ritual to praise the Emperor, meaning "Long live the Emperor" or "Salute the Emperor."

やった！ (int) hooray (lit: I/we did it); yes!

(59) **騒動【そうどう】** (n) incident; uprising; revolt **続き【つづき】** (n) continuation; sequel

60. 温泉【おんせん】 (n) hot spring bath (house); onsen
通う【かよう】 (v5u, vi) to commute （〜に）
楽しみにする【たのしみにする】 (exp, vs) to look forward to something
61. 誰も〜ない【だれも〜ない】 (exp) no one (with negative predicate)
62. バシャバシャ (onoma) splish splash
63. 帰りに【かえりに】 (exp) on one's way home
色町【いろまち】 (n) red-light district
入口【いりぐち】 (n) entrance
団子【だんご】 (n) a sweet dumpling
寄る【よる】 (v5r, vi) to visit; to drop by （〜に）
64. 皿【さら】 (n) plate; dish; platter * 一皿【ひとさら】, 二皿【ふたさら】, 三皿【みさら】
65. [Number] 銭【せん】 (n) (ctr) hundredth of a yen
66. カア (onoma) Used when a person gets really upset.

(67)
次の教室でも——
色町の団子うまいうまい
(68)
ニヤ
ニヤ
(69)
俺は湯に入ってさっぱりしようといつものように温泉に行った。
(70)
道後温泉
(71)
今日も人がいなければ泳げるな。
(72)
ざくろ口をのぞいてみると、
(73)
湯の中で泳ぐべからず

(68) **ニヤニヤ** (onoma) smirk

(69) **湯【ゆ】** (n) hot spring; hot water **さっぱりする** (vs) to feel refreshed **いつものように** (exp) as always

(70) **道後温泉【どうごおんせん】** (n) a famous hot spring *Located in the city of Matsuyama, Ehime Prefecture on the island of Shikoku, 道後温泉 is one of the oldest onsen hot springs in Japan.

(71) **泳ぐ【およぐ】** (v5g, vi) to swim * 泳げる (potential form)

(72) **ざくろ口【ざくろぐち】** (n) the small, low entrance to the bathing pool *This was positioned within an enclosure inside the bathhouse. Customers entered this enclosure by bending over and going through the *zakuroguchi* (*zakuro* is pomegranate and *guchi* is entrance.) It was a common bathhouse structure during the Edo Period.

のぞく (v5k, vt) to peek (through a keyhole, gap, etc.)

㊆ いつもの通り【いつものとおり】 (adv) as always
㊅ つけ回す【つけまわす】 (v5s, vt) to follow around ＊つける (follow) ＋回す (to turn) => つけます [V (ます stem form)] ＋回す => つけ回す　　ピーピー (onoma) whistling light sound *The students are making fun of Botchan by making these noises.
㊆ カラ (onoma) rattle; sound of opening a sliding door ＊ガラ is commonly used to describe the sound of opening a sliding door; however, in this scene, Botchan is so tired that he opens the door slowly and feebly.
㊆ 茶器【ちゃき】 (n) tea utensils, used for Japanese tea ceremony
　　名品【めいひん】 (n) fine product; masterpiece
　　茶碗【ちゃわん】 (n) tea bowl ＊茶碗 in a wide range of sizes and styles are used for the Japanese tea ceremony. For example, shallow bowls, which allow the tea to cool rapidly, are used in summer; deep bowls are used in winter to keep the green tea hot for a longer time.
　　ズデン (onoma) thud; falling motion; faint

原文に挑戦しましょう

ウェブの練習問題（186ページ参照）をしてから、チャレンジしてみましょう。次の場面は、第3章のマンガのどのコマかわかりますか。引用文の後の質問に答えましょう。

原文❶

いよいよ学校へ出た。初めて教場へはいって高い所へ乗った時は、何だか変だった。講釈をしながら、おれでも先生が勤まるのかと思った。生徒はやかましい。時々図抜けた大きな声で先生と言う。先生には応えた。今まで物理学校で毎日先生先生と呼びつけていたが、先生と呼ぶのと、呼ばれるのは雲泥の差だ。何だか足の裏がむずむずする。

【原文❶の質問】坊っちゃんは先生と呼ばれた時、どんな気持ちになりましたか。

原文❷

翌日何の気もなく教場へはいると、黒板いっぱいぐらいな大きな字で、天麩羅先生とかいてある。おれの顔を見てみんなわあと笑った。おれは馬鹿馬鹿しいから、天麩羅を食っちゃ可笑しいかと聞いた。すると生徒の一人が、しかし四杯は過ぎるぞな、もし、と言った。四杯食おうが五杯食おうがおれの銭でおれが食うのに文句があるもんかと、さっさと講義を済まして控所へ帰って来た。十分たって次の教場へ出ると一つ天麩羅四杯なり。但し笑うべからず。と黒板にかいてある。さっきは別に腹も立たなかったが今度は癪に障った。冗談も度を過ごせばいたずらだ。

【原文❷の質問】どうして生徒たちは坊っちゃんをからかいましたか。

第4章を読む前に

生徒

新しく来た先生は、本当に早口じゃけれ、授業がわからん。また、天ぷらそばを四杯も食べるけれ、「天ぷら先生」とあだ名をつけたぞな、もし。それに、団子を食べたり、温泉で泳いだり、ちょっとおもしろそうな先生じゃけれ、初めての宿直の晩、みんなでいたずらをすることにしたぞな、もし。

早口　fast-talking　　じゃけれ＝だから　　わからん＝わからない　　食べるけれ＝食べるから
つけたぞなもし＝つけたんです　　団子【だんご】sweet dumplings　　宿直　night watch　　いたずら　prank

第４章 ❖ 宿直
Night Watch

① 中学校ー

② 今夜は初めての宿直ですね。ご苦労様です。

③ （画像）

④ "狸"と"赤シャツ"は宿直をしなくていいなんて、不公平だな。

⑤ 狸？ ああ！校長と教頭のことか！

⑥ 一人で不平を言っても通らんよ。「強者の権利」ってやつだ。

⑦ "狸"と"赤シャツ"が強者だなんて誰が承知するもんか！

② 今夜【こんや】 (n) this evening; tonight
　宿直【しゅくちょく】 (n) night duty; night watch
　ご苦労様です【ごくろうさまです】 (exp) thank you very much for your...; I appreciate your efforts *Literally, 苦労 means trouble, suffering, labor, and worries.

④ 不公平（な）【ふこうへい】 (adj-na, n) unfair

⑥ 通る【とおる】 (v5r, vi) to be heard; to be granted * 通る usually means "go through", but the idiomatic expression 不平が通らない means (your) complaints are not heard.
　強者【きょうしゃ】 (n) strong man; man of power
　権利【けんり】 (n) right; privilege * 強者の権利 Might makes right is a concept that many philosophers have debated, including Jean-Jacques Rousseau (1712 - 1778) in the Social Contract.
　〜ってやつだ（＝〜というものだ） * やつ refers to an idea or concept

⑦ 承知する【しょうちする】 (vs) to accept; to agree
　〜もんか・ものか (see 第３章 コマ⑱)

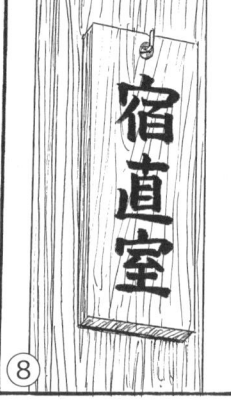

⑧ 宿直室

⑨ 飯は食ったが
日が暮れないから
寝るわけにいかないしー

⑩ よし！

⑪ 俺は日課にしている温泉に行くことにした。

⑫ いい湯だった。

⑬ あなた今日は宿直では？
狸……
おや……

⑭ さっきも同じことを言っただろう。

⑧ 宿直室【しゅくちょくしつ】 (n) night duty room
⑨ 飯【めし】 (n) (usually male) meals; food *飯を食う (vulg) to eat a meal
  暮れる【くれる】 (v1, vi) to get dark
  [V (plain form)] わけにはいかない (exp) impossible to do (although someone wants to)
  ～し (see 第2章 コマ⑬)
⑩ よし (int) Alright!; OK! *Used when one decides to do something. Botchan does not know if it is acceptable or not to go out during night duty, but decides to go to the bathhouse anyway.
⑪ 日課【にっか】 (n) daily routine *日課にしている温泉 a hot spring (visit), which is part of (my) daily schedule
⑬ おや (int) oh!; oh?; my!
⑭ さっき (n) (variant of 先：【さき】) some time ago
  同じ(な)【おなじ】 (adj-na) same; identical *同じ when modifying a following noun (e.g., 同じこと), but 同じな when followed by a particle such as の, ので, and のに (e.g., 同じなので).

⑮ きっぱり！

⑯ ええ宿直です！
ですからこれから帰って泊まりますよ。

⑰ ……

⑱ おい君！

⑲ 宿直じゃないのか？
うん宿直だ。

⑳ 宿直中に、出歩くなんてマズイだろう？
校長か教頭に会ったら面倒だぜ。
狸には会った。

㉑ 『暑い夜は散歩でもしないと宿直も大変でしょう』と言ってほめてくれたよ。
ハハッ

⑮ きっぱり　(adv) clearly; decisively　*Botchan was probably frustrated being asked twice; therefore, he responded to him firmly.
⑰ (exp) The principal is speechless (……) because he is probably shocked at Botchan's behavior. The phrase あきれてものが言えない is often used to describe this sort of situation.
⑲ **(plain form) のか**　(see 第2章 コマ⑬) *宿直じゃないのか？ Aren't you on night duty?
⑳ 出歩く【であるく】　(v5, vi) to go out; to take a stroll
　　マズイ・まずい　(adj-i) unwise; not a good idea　*The use of katakana マズイ emphasizes the poor judgment of leaving the dormitory while on night duty.
㉑ 大変（な）【たいへん】　(adj-na) difficult; hard　　ほめる　(v1, vt) to praise
　　ハハッ　(int) masculine laughter

その夜――

俺の癖は、寝る時に「とん」としりもちをつくことだ。

トン！

ああ、気持ちがいい。

？

ピョン

な、何だ!? こりゃ バッタ!?

ピョン

㉓ 癖【くせ】 (n) a habit (often a bad habit); peculiarity
　とん (onoma) tap; fairly quiet impact
　しりもちをつく (exp, v5k) to fall on one's backside *Used when skiing and falling in the snow. Literally, "to pound rice into mochi with one's butt"
㉔ 気持ちがいい【きもちがいい】 (exp, adj-i) to feel good; feel comfortable
㉖ ピョン (onoma) hopping; skipping
㉗ こりゃ (exp) (from これは) hey there; I say; see here
　バッタ (n) grasshopper; locust (of family Acridoidea)

㉘ ちくしょうめ！
蚊帳にたたきつけても死にゃしねぇ。

㉙ このやろーっ！

㉜ ハァ ハァ ハァ やっつけた……

㉝ 何事ですかい？

㉘ ちくしょうめ　(int) rats; dammit
　蚊帳【かや】　(n) mosquito netting *The Japanese *kaya* mosquito net has a spacious, box-like design, but the weave used for its netting impedes the flow of air, making it warm inside.
　たたきつける　(v1, vt) to smash; to smoosh; to slap something onto a surface *たたきます(to hit) + つける (to attach) => たたきつける (～を、～に)
　死にゃしねぇ　死にゃ＝死には；しねぇ＝しない
　バシ　(onoma) smack *sound for impact
　ブン　(onoma) swish of air; swoosh *Used when something is being swung around mid-air.
㉙ このやろーっ（＝このやろう）　(exp) this rascal *Used when one gets really upset.
㉛ バシ バシ　(onoma) smack, smack *sound for impact
㉜ ハァ　(int) pant ; out of breath　　やっつける　(v1, vt) to beat; to finish off
㉝ 何事【なにごと】　(n) what; something　　～かい　(see 第2章 コマ㉗)

61

㉞ ふとん　(n) futon; bed
　飼う【かう】　(v5u, vt) to keep; to raise (pets)
㉟ 存じる【ぞんじる】　(v1, hum) to know ＊ 存じません＝知りません
　寄宿生【きしゅくせい】　(n) boarding student
　代表【だいひょう】　(n) representative
㊱ 何で（＝どうして）　(adv) why?
　[Noun] なんか　(prt) things like 〜 ; or something like that 〜 (often derogatory)
　〜ぞな　(prt) (dialect) (pol) です；でございます
㊳ イナゴ　(n) locust (of family Catantopidae); rice grasshopper (of genus Oxya)
　〜ぞな、もし　(prt) (dialect) (pol)（イナゴというもの）でございます
㊴ 同じもん（＝同じもの）
　入れる【いれる】　(v1, vt) to put in（〜を、〜に）＊ いれてくれ (command form of いれてください)
　頼む【たのむ】　(v5m, vt) to request; to ask（〜を、〜に）

㊵ **入れんがな【いれんがな】** (dialect) 入れません
温い【ぬくい】 (adj-i) lukewarm; tepid * ぬくい is primarily used in Western Japan.
好きじゃけれ【すきじゃけれ】 (dialect) 好きだから　　**〜んじゃろ** (dialect) 〜でしょう *お入りになったんじゃろ [お (honorific) 入り (V ます stem form)] になる + の (explanation mode) + でしょう They probably got in (by themselves).

㊶ **[V (plain form)] な**　(prt) to indicate prohibition *言うな don't say 〜
[V (て form)] たまるもんか　(exp) cannot bear 〜 *たまる (to bear, often adds emphasis) + もんか・ものか (never do; how could 〜) お入りになられてたまるもんか It's impossible for honorable grasshoppers to have gotten into (my bed)!!

㊷ **いたずら**　(n) prank　　**説明する【せつめいする】**　(vs) to explain
できんじゃろ　(dialect) できないでしょう　　**そうじゃ**　(dialect) そうだ

㊸ **出て(行)く【でて(い)く】**　(v5k, vi) (い may be dropped, particularly in informal language) to leave and away *出て(い)け (command form)

㊹ **[Noun] のくせに**　(exp) and yet; though; in spite of *子供のくせに even though they are just kids (cunning disrespectful brats)
度胸がある【どきょうがある】　(exp) to have nerve; to be bold; to be daring
[V (ます stem form or て form)] やがる　(aux) indicates hatred, contempt, or disdain for another's action

㊽ やっと寝床に入った時は十時半になっていた。

㊻ 俺には教師なんて勤まりそうにないと考えていたら、清のことが頭に浮かんだ。

㊼ 親以上に世話をやいてくれたのに、そばにいる時はありがたいとも思わなかった……

でも、こうして遠く離れてみるとよくわかる。

坊っちゃんは欲がなくてまっすぐなご気性です。

㊽ 言ってる本人の方がずっと立派な人間だよ。

何だか清に会いたくなった。

㊾ どどん

㊺ やっと (adv) at last　　寝床【ねどこ】(n) bed　* 寝床に入る to go to bed
㊻ 勤まる【つとまる】(v5r, vi) to be fit for; to function properly
　　[V (ます stem form)] そうにない (exp) showing no signs of (verb); extremely unlikely to ～
　　頭に浮かぶ【あたまにうかぶ】(exp, v5b) to come to mind; to pop into one's head
㊼ 親【おや】(n) parent(s)　　～以上に【いじょうに】(adv) beyond ～ ; more than ～
　　世話をやく【せわをやく】(exp, v5k) to take care of; to meddle　　ありがたい (adj-i) grateful; thankful　　こうして (conj) thus
　　遠く離れて【とおくはなれて】(exp) at a distance　* 遠く離れてみると、よくわかる Now being far away from her, I understand (her kindness).　　[V (て form)] みると (exp) to see that ～ ; to find that ～　　欲【よく】(n) greed
　　まっすぐ（な）(adj-na) straightforward; honest　* 坊っちゃんは欲がなくてまっすぐなご気性です You are not greedy and you have a good straightforward temperament.
㊽ 本人【ほんにん】(n) the person oneself　* 言ってる本人＝清　　人間【にんげん】(n) human being; character (of a person)
㊾ どどん (onoma) ba-boom

な……何だ？

二階で——

ドドドドドンンン
ワァー

生徒のやつら——

ダダダダ

不思議なことに廊下は静まりかえっていた。

しーーん…

ハァハァ

㊼ ダダダ （onoma) dash; running sound
㊺ しーん （onoma) silence
不思議なことに【ふしぎなことに】 (adv) strangely; oddly enough
静まりかえる【しずまりかえる】 (exp, v5r) to fall silent

㊺ 夢【ゆめ】 (n) dream
寝ぼけ癖【ねぼけぐせ】 (n) a habit of being half asleep ＊寝ぼける (to be half asleep) ＋癖【くせ】
㊼ 夜中【よなか】 (n) midnight
うおおお (int) a very powerful scream
㊽ ガッ (onoma) impact of hitting something
㊿ 痛タタタ【いたたた】 (int) ouch-ouch-ouch

- ⑥¹ 程【ほど】 (n) degree; limit * ～にも程がある there is a limit to ～
- ⑥² 出て来る【でてくる】 (vk) to come out * 出て来い (command form)
- ⑥⁶ からかう (v5u, vt) to ridicule; to make fun of * からかわれる (passive form)
  - 泣き寝入り【なきねいり】 (exp, n) literally, crying oneself to sleep. It means giving up in frustration; accepting meekly; being compelled to accept a situation.
  - 恥【はじ】 (n) shame; embarrassment * ～と思われるのは江戸っ子の恥だ As an Edokko, it's shameful for me that (they think...).
- ⑥⁷ こうなれば (exp) If this is how it is　　謝る【あやまる】 (v5r, vt, vi) to apologize　　動く【うごく】 (v5k, vi) to move
- ⑥⁸ 血【ち】 (n) blood　　勝手に【かってに】 (adv) of its own accord; involuntarily
  - [V (ば form)] いい (exp) usually used for advice, but here conveys a nuance of letting something take its own course * 血なんて勝手に出ればいい I don't care if I'm bleeding.
- ⑥⁹ ブーンブーン (onoma) buzz; whirr; hum

67

翌朝

あ

さあ、宿直室まで来い！

ぐいっ

ズデン

⑦⓪ 翌朝【よくあさ】　(n) the next morning
⑦④ ぐいっ　(onoma) to yank (down)

(79) **知らんぞな【しらんぞな】** (dialect) 知らないです
(80) **豚【ぶた】** (n) pig
(82) **タヌー（＝狸）**
(83) **事情【じじょう】** (n) circumstances; conditions; situation; reasons
お [V (ます stem form)] する (exp) (hum) creates a humble form of a verb. * お聞きしましょうか Let me hear ～

㊻ 朝ごはん【あさごはん】 (n) breakfast
ぞろぞろ (onoma) in groups; in succession * This suggests a huge crowd or gathering and describes the dormitory students filing out of the room.
㊽ さぞ (adv) I am sure; no doubt 疲れる【つかれる】 (v1, vi) to get tired * お疲れでしょう is a humble expression.
㊾ これくらい・これぐらい (n, adv) this much; this amount; same as このくらい・このぐらい．
給料【きゅうりょう】 (n) salary いる (v5r, vi) to need
㊿ だいぶ (adv) considerably; greatly
はれる (v1, vi) to swell (from mosquito bites); to become swollen * はれている describes the state of being swollen.
かゆい (adj-i) itchy   [stem form] そう（だ） (aux) appearing that; seeming that. *It appears/seems that (someone will do something).
This is based on what the speaker sees or feels, and it is merely his or her guess. かゆい + そう = かゆそう（だ）(It) seems itchy.
㊼ ばん (onoma) used when showing something amazing to someone
㊾ ポリポリ (onoma) sound of scratching lightly
[V(plain form)] まい (aux) probably isn't (doesn't, won't, etc.) * ほめたんじゃあるまい He probably wasn't praising me.
ひやかす (v5s, vt) to banter; to make fun of

70

原文に挑戦しましょう

ウェブの練習問題（186ページ参照）をしてから、チャレンジしてみましょう。次の場面は、第4章のマンガのどのコマかわかりますか。引用文の後の質問に答えましょう。

原文❶

学校には宿直があって、職員が代る代るこれをつとめる。但し狸と赤シャツは例外である。何でこの両人が当然の義務を免かれるのかと聞いてみたら、＊奏任待遇だからと言う。面白くもない。月給はたくさんとる、時間は少ない、それで宿直を逃がれるなんて不公平があるものか。

＊奏任待遇（教頭以上への待遇）

【原文❶の質問】坊っちゃんは何が「不公平だ」と言っていますか。あなたも不公平だと思いますか。

原文❷

それを思うと清なんてのは見上げたものだ。教育もない身分もない婆さんだが、人間としてはすこぶる尊い。今まではあんなに世話になって別段難有いとも思わなかったが、こうして、一人で遠国へ来てみると、始めてあの親切がわかる。越後の笹飴が食いたければ、わざわざ越後まで買いに行って食わしてやっても、食わせるだけの価値は充分ある。清はおれの事を欲がなくって、真直な気性だと言って、ほめるが、ほめられるおれよりも、ほめる本人の方が立派な人間だ。何だか清に逢いたくなった。

【原文❷の質問】坊っちゃんは清のことをどんな人だと言っていますか。

第5章を読む前に

野だいこ

私は画学の教師をしている野田でげす。
実は私も江戸っ子でげす。
四国は海に囲まれているし、景色はいいし、いい所でげすよ。
さて、新しく来た「坊っちゃん先生」は、単純だから、生徒にからかわれるんでげすよ。
今日、教頭と釣りに誘って、あの宿直事件のいやがらせは、例の先生が生徒を扇動したって教えてあげたんでげすよ。
この陰謀、うまくいくかどうか。

囲まれる to be surrounded　　景色 scenery　　単純 simple-minded　　からかう to make fun of　　誘う to invite
事件 incident　　いやがらせ harassment; pestering　　例の〜 the ones referred to　　扇動する to agitate
陰謀 conspiracy

第5章 ❖ 陰謀(いんぼう)
Conspiracy

① 数日後、教頭の"赤シャツ"が俺に声をかけてきた。
「君、釣りに行きませんか?」

② 赤シャツは、気味の悪いようにやさしい声を出す男である。

③ 「そうですなあ……」

④ 「釣りをしたことはありますか?」

⑤ 「あります!」 ムッ

⑥ 「子供の頃、釣りぼりに行ったことがあります。それから、縁日で、コイを釣って逃してくやしい思いをしたことが――」

⑦ ホホホホ
「それじゃ、まだ釣りの味はわからんですな。」

陰謀【いんぼう】 (n) plot intrigue; conspiracy
① **数日後【すうじつご】** (adv, n) several days later　　**声をかける【こえをかける】** (exp, v1) to greet; to call out to someone
　釣り【つり】 (n) fishing
② **気味の（or が）悪い【きみの（or が）わるい】** (exp, adv) in a creepy manner; weirdly
　やさしい声【やさしいこえ】 (exp, n) soft voice
④ **[V (た form)] ことがある** (exp) someone has experienced doing something
⑤ **ムッ** (onoma) annoyed; offended; same as ム〜 (see 第3章 コマ㊻)
⑥ **[Noun] の頃【ころ】** (n) (approximate) time; around　　**釣りぼり【つりぼり】** (n) fishing pond
　縁日【えんにち】 (n) temple festival *A day believed to have a special relation（縁）with a particular Japanese deity. 縁 is fate; destiny, a mysterious force that binds people together.
　コイ (n) koi, carp * コイ is written as katakana here for emphasis, but it is usually written in Kanji or hiragana 鯉【こい】
　釣る【つる】 (v5r, vt) to fish　　**逃す【のがす】** (v5s, vt) to let escape　　**くやしい** (adj-i) regrettable; awful
　思い【おもい】 (n) a thought. *Used here to refer to an experience such as くやしい思い (awful, bitter experience).
⑦ **ホホホホ** (int) tee hee tee hee *It is laughter, specifically refined feminine laughter while アハハハ and ハハハハ is viewed more masculine laughter (see 第2章コマ㊻ Yama-Arashi's laughter)
　味【あじ】 (n) charm; style; flavor

⑧ お望みなら、手ほどきしましょう。

誰が手ほどきなんか受けるものか！

⑨ おひまなら、今日どうです？
吉川君と二人きりはさびしいし、ぜひ来たまえ。

⑩ "野だいこ"もいっしょか？

画学の教師の野だいこは、赤シャツの行く所なら、どこでもついて行く奴だ。

⑪ 二人がどうして俺に声をかけたのかわからない。

⑫ 断ったらヘタだから行かないと思われる。だから行くことにした。

⑧ 望む【のぞむ】　(v5m, vt) to desire; to wish for　＊お望みなら if you wish
　手ほどき【てほどき】　(n) learning the basics
　受ける【うける】　(v1, vt) to receive; to accept　＊誰が手ほどきなんか、受けるものか Who wants to be initiated by you! もんか・ものか (see 第3章 コマ⑱)
⑨ 二人きり　(exp) just two people　＊一人きり alone
　さびしい　(adj-i) lonely; lonesome
　ぜひ　(adv) by all means　＊This expresses a strong desire.
　[V (stem form)] たまえ　(see 第2章 コマ㊻)
⑩ どこでも　(adv) anywhere
⑫ 断る【ことわる】　(v5r, vt) to decline; to turn down
　ヘタ（な）　(adj-na, n) unskillful; poor (at fishing)

⑬ 舟は細長くて、東京では見たこともない形だった。

⑭ 船頭はゆっくりゆっくりこいでいたが、いつの間にか沖に出ていた。

いい景色だ。

ええ、絶景でげす。

⑮ あの松を見たまえ。ターナーの絵に、ありそうじゃないか?

まったくターナーでげす。

あの曲がりぐあいといったら、ターナーそっくりでげすよ。

⑯ ターナーって、何のことだ?

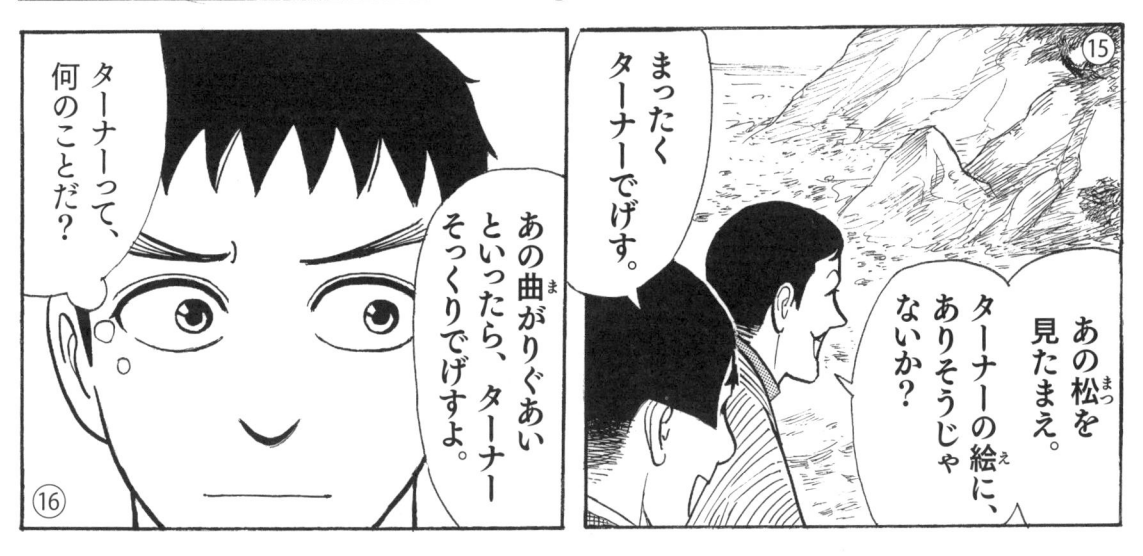

⑬ 舟【ふね】 (n) boat *舟 is often a small and hand-propelled boat while 船 is a large one.
　細長い【ほそながい】 (adj-i) long and narrow　　形【かたち】 (n) shape
⑭ 船頭【せんどう】 (n) boatman　　こぐ (v5g, vt) to row
　いつの間にか【いつのまにか】 (exp) before one knows or realizes it (something has happened)
　沖【おき】 (n) open sea　　景色【けしき】 (n) scenery　　絶景【ぜっけい】 (n) picturesque scenery
⑮ 松【まつ】 (n) pine tree
　ターナー (n) Joseph M. W. Turner (1775 - 1851) *Turner was a famous English Romantic landscape painter, watercolorist, and printmaker.
　[V (ます stem form)] そう(だ) (see 第4章 コマ⑰)
　まったく (adv) really; completely
⑯ 曲がる【まがる】 (v5r, vi) to curve; to bend　　[V (ます stem form)] ぐあい (n) condition; manner
　〜といったら (exp) speaking of 〜; talking of 〜 *This emphasizes feelings and emotions of surprise or disappointment.
　そっくり(な) (adj-na) just like 〜; the spitting image of 〜

⑰ ま、いいか。これから、あの島をターナー島と名付けてはどうげす？

⑱ そいつはおもしろい！あの岩の上に、マドンナを立たせちゃどうげす？

⑲ いい絵ができますぜ。

⑳ ホホホ マドンナの話は、よそうじゃないか。何、誰もいないから、大丈夫でげすよ。

㉑ マドンナだろうが、小旦那だろうが、立たせるがいい。どうせ赤シャツのなじみの芸者のあだ名か何かだろう。

㉒ やがて船頭が舟を止めていかりをおろした。

⑰ ま（あ）(int) well　名付ける【なづける】(v1, vt) to name (someone)（〜を、〜と）
⑱ そいつ (pn) (col) that (person)　岩【いわ】(n) rock
　マドンナ (n) Madonna *Nodaiko referred to two meanings of Madonna: the Madonna drawn by the Italian artist, Raphael (Raffaello Sanzio da Urbino, 1483 – 1520) and the Madonna who is the object of adoration and longing in town and who has some relationship with Red Shirt.
　立たせちゃ（＝立たせては）(exp) たたせる (causative form) + ちゃ (contracted form of ては) +（どうですか）How about having Madonna stand there?
⑳ よす (v5s, vt) to cease; to give up
㉑ 小旦那【こだんな】(n) young master * こだんな is a pun based on the word マドンナ.
　どうせ (adv) anyhow; in any case　なじみ (n) intimacy; friendship; familiarity
　芸者【げいしゃ】(n) geisha; a professional female entertainer who is hired to create a lively atmosphere at social gatherings by singing, dancing, and conversing.
㉒ やがて (adv) before long; soon; at length　いかり (n) anchor　おろす (v5s, vt) to drop

㉓ 釣りざおが一本もないがどうするんですか。
沖釣には糸だけでげす。

㉔ こうやっておもりをつけた糸を投げ入れるんでげす。

㉕ この深さじゃ、鯛はむずかしいだろう。

㉖ 教頭だったら、大丈夫ですよ。

おべっか使いめ。

㉗ そら来た！
さすが教頭！

㉘ ピシャ

㉙

㉚

㉓ 釣りざお【つりざお】 (n) fishing rod
   [Counter] も〜ない (exp) there is no * 一本もない there isn't even one fishing pole.
   沖釣【おきづり】 (n) offshore fishing
   糸【いと】 (n) fishing line; string
㉔ 投げ入れる【なげいれる】 (v1, vt) to throw into
㉕ 深さ【ふかさ】 (n) depth *Drop い of an adj-i and add さ. ふかい => ふかさ
   鯛【たい】 (n) *tai* (species of reddish-brown Pacific sea bream)
㉖ おべっか使い【おべっかづかい】 (n) flatterer; someone who sucks up to another
㉗ そら (exp) look!; look out!
   さすが (adv) (with affirmative sentence) as one would expect (e.g., That's just what one would expect of a vice principal.)
㉘ ピシャ (onoma) splashing sound

㉛ 今のは、確かに大物に違いなかったでげす。残念なことをしましたね。

㉝ しめた！かかった！

㉞ でかいぞ！

㉟ 一番のりはお手がらだが、ゴルキーじゃ……

㊱ "ゴルキ"とは、ロシア文学者のような名だね。

㉛ 確かに【たしかに】 (adv) surely; certainly
　大物【おおもの】 (n) important person; big-shot; big game (animal, fish)
　違いない【ちがいない】 (exp) to be sure; no mistaking it (〜に)
㉝ しめた (exp) I've got it; all right
　かかる (v5r, vi) to be caught (on a hook); be hooked ＊（魚が）かかった I caught one!
㉞ でかい (adj-i) (col) huge; gargantuan
㊱ 一番のり (n) the first person to do (e.g., catch a fish)
　手がら【てがら】 (n) achievement; feat; meritorious deed
　ゴルキー (n) a kind of fish, similar to wrasse (ベラ in Japanese) *In the Matsuyama region of Shikoku, people call wrasse gizo. Soseki felt that the name sounded like the French historian, François Guizot (1787-1874), but for this story he decided to use gorugi instead, as it sounded like the Russian author, Maxim Gorky (1868-1936). Gorky founded the Socialist Realism literary style and was also a political activist.
　文学者【ぶんがくしゃ】 (n) literary person

㊲ そうでげすね。まるでロシアの文学者のようでげすね。

ゴルキはまずくて、とても食べられんし、肥料にしかならんぞな、もし。

㊳ ポチャン

㊴ 釣りをするより、大空をながめてるほうがずっといい。

㊵ 赤シャツと野だいこは、一時間ばかり一生懸命に釣っていたが、

㊶ トホホ

㊷ おかしなことに二人が釣ったのは、みんなゴルキだった。

㊲ まるで (adv) as if *Used with the expression よう（だ）.
  ～よう（だ） (aux) seeming to be; appearing to be. This expression is usually based on what the speaker sees or saw, and involves the speaker's reasoning process based on firsthand, reliable information and his or her knowledge.
  肥料【ひりょう】 (n) fertilizer
  [Noun] にしかならん (exp) X can/will only become ～
㊳ ポチャン (onoma) plopping; splashing sound（～と）
㊴ 大空【おおぞら】 (n) heavens; sky
  ながめる (v1, vt) to view; to gaze at
㊵ [Number/Quantifier] ばかり (see 第2章 コマ⑤)
  一生懸命に【いっしょうけんめいに】 (adv) very hard; with utmost effort; with all one's might
㊶ トホホ (int) boo-hoo; boo-hoo-hoo
㊷ おかしなことに (exp) oddly enough; the odd thing is that ～

㊸ 清を連れて、こんなきれいな所に遊びに来たら、さぞ楽しいだろう。

㊹ 野だいこなんかと一緒じゃ、どんなに景色がよくてもつまらない。

野だいこは俺が教頭だったら、やっぱり俺にお世辞を使うに違いない。

㊺ ヒソヒソ
クスッ

㊻ クスクス
まったくでげす……知らないんでげすから。
——まさか

㊼ バッタを……？
また例の堀田が？

㊸ さぞ (adv) I am sure; certainly; no doubt
㊺ ヒソヒソ (onoma) in hushed whispering tones; conspiratorial
　クスッ (onoma) a little laugh
㊻ クスクス (onoma) giggling
　まさか (int) by no means; never!; you don't say!
㊼ 例の [Noun]【れいの】 (adj-pn) the usual (culprit); as it always is; (the one) in question　＊例の堀田が As usual, Hotta did…

㊽
天ぷら……
そそのかして
……団子も?
㊾
言葉はとぎれとぎれだったが、俺についての内緒話に違いなかった。
(50)
おしはかると、バッタ騒動は〝山嵐〟が生徒をそそのかして起こした——ととれた。
(51)
もう、帰ろうか?
ええ、ちょうど時間でげすね。
(52)
今夜は、マドンナの君にお会いでげすか?
ばか言っちゃいけない!
まちがいになる。
大丈夫ですよ。

㊽ **そそのかす** (v5s, vt) to instigate; to coax
㊾ **とぎれとぎれ** (exp) broken; intermittent **内緒話【ないしょばなし】** (n) secret talk
(50) **おしはかる** (v5r, vt) to guess **起こす【おこす】** (v5s, vt) to cause **とれる** (v1, vi) to be interpreted (as) (〜と)
(51) **ちょうど** (adv) just; right; exactly
(52) **[Noun]の君【きみ】** (n) poetic second person, used to express one's longing and affection towards the person ＊君 was formally polite. Nodaiko used マドンナの君 to elevate マドンナ as someone who is longed for and to show respect to Red Shirt. On the other hand, if 君 is used alone to address "you," this usage is not polite. It is rude when used with superiors, elders, or strangers.
ばか(なこと)を言う (exp) to talk nonsense.
言っちゃいけない(＝言ってはいけない)
まちがい (n) mistake ＊ばか言っちゃいけない!まちがいになる Don't talk nonsense! That would be a mistake.

(53)
聞いたって……
(54)
カッ
聞こえてるよ！
(55)
ヘヘヘッ
(56)
君、釣りはあまり好きでないようですね。
ええ、空を見てる方がいいですね。
(57)
君が来て生徒も大変喜んでいるから、がんばってくれたまえ。
あんまり喜んでいないでしょう。
(58)
いや、お世辞じゃない。喜んでますよ。
ね、
吉川君。
喜んでいるどころじゃない、大騒ぎでげす。

(53) **って（＝としても）** (prt) assuming ～ ; even if ～ *Actually, 大丈夫ですよ (コマ(52) on previous page) is the predicate of this inverted sentence. 聞いたって（聞いたとしても）、大丈夫ですよ It'll be fine even if he heard.

(54) **カッ** (onoma) motion of opening eyes wide in rage or alarm

(57) **喜ぶ【よろこぶ】** (v5b, vi) to be delighted; to be glad; to be pleased
がんばる (v5r, vi) to persist; to insist on; to try one's best

(58) **～どころ／ところじゃない** (exp) It's not the time/condition/situation for ～
大騒ぎ【おおさわぎ】 (n, vs) clamour; uproar; tumult *喜んでいるどころじゃない、大騒ぎでげす They're not just glad, they're falling over themselves and making such a fuss.

⑤⑨ 生徒は君を歓迎しているが、学校というところはいろいろな事情があって……

いろいろな事情とは、何ですか？

⑥⑩ あなたは失礼ながら、教師として経験にとぼしい。

思わぬことで、つけこまれることがあるというんです。

⑥② 正直に生きていれば、誰につけこまれても恐くはないです。

だが、自分だけが正しくても、人が悪いのがわからなくちゃ、ひどい目にあうでしょう？

⑥③ むろん 恐くない。

⑥④ 世の中には親切にして下宿の世話などしてくれても、油断のできない人がいるから、気をつけなさいと言うんです。

---

⑤⑨ 歓迎する【かんげいする】 (vs) to welcome
事情【じじょう】 (n) circumstances; reasons（see 第4章 コマ⑧③）
⑥⑩ 失礼ながら (exp) Perhaps I shouldn't say so [this], but…　　[Noun]として (prt) as (i.e., in the role of)
経験【けいけん】 (n, vs) experience　　とぼしい (adj-i) limited; lacking（〜が／に）
思わぬ [Noun]【おもわぬ】 (adj-pn) unexpected; unforeseen　　つけこむ (v5m, vi) to take advantage of（〜に）* つけこまれる (passive form)
⑥② 正直（な）【しょうじき】 (adj-na) honest; straight-forward　　恐い【こわい】 (adj-i) scary; frightening * 正直にしていれば、誰につけこまれても、恐くはないです　I am not afraid of being taken advantage of so long as I am doing my job honestly.
⑥③ むろん (adv) of course; naturally
⑥④ だが (conj) but; however; (and) yet; nevertheless　　〜なくちゃ（＝なくては）(exp) if 〜 not
ひどい目にあう【ひどいめにあう】 (exp) to have a bad time　　世の中【よのなか】 (n) the world; society
油断【ゆだん】 (n, vs) negligence; unpreparedness * 油断のできない人がいる the person around whom you cannot let down your guard
気をつける【きをつける】 (exp) to be careful; to pay attention（〜に）

83

⑥ もう秋ですね。

⑥ 吉川君、いいね あの浜の景色は。

なるほど。
惜しいですね。時間があったら、写生するんでげすが。

⑥ 赤シャツははっきり言わないが、山嵐が悪い奴だから気をつけろと言いたいらしい。

⑥ 虫の好かない赤シャツが親切で、気の合った山嵐に裏表があるなんて――

⑥ 世の中は不思議だと思った……。

---

⑥ **なるほど** (adv) I see; that's right
　惜しい【おしい】 (adj-i) regrettable; disappointing
　写生する【しゃせいする】 (vs) sketching; drawing from nature
⑥ [V/adj-i) plain, (adj-na) stem] らしい　(see 第2章 コマ⑤)
⑥ **虫の好かない【むしのすかない】** (exp) unpleasant; disagreeable
　気の合った【きのあった】 (exp) congenial
　裏表【うらおもて】 (n) both sides; double-dealing; literally "back" and "front" * 裏表のある人 a double-dealer; a two-faced person
⑥ **不思議（な）【ふしぎ】** (adj-na, n) strange; mysterious

原文に挑戦しましょう

ウェブの練習問題（186ページ参照）をしてから、チャレンジしてみましょう。次の場面は、第5章のマンガのどのコマかわかりますか。引用文の後の質問に答えましょう。

【原文①】
君釣りに行きませんかと赤シャツがおれに聞いた。赤シャツは気味の悪いように優しい声を出す男である。まるで男だか女だか分りゃしない。男なら男らしい声を出すもんだ。ことに大学卒業生じゃないか。物理学校でさえおれくらいな声が出るのに、文学士がこれじゃ見っともない。

【原文①の質問】坊っちゃんは赤シャツの話し方について何と言っていますか。

【原文②】
「無論悪いことをしなければ好いんですが、自分だけ悪い事をしなくっても、人の悪るいのが分らなくっちゃ、やっぱりひどい目に逢うでしょう。世の中には磊落なように見えても、淡泊なように見えても、親切に下宿の世話なんかしてくれても、めったに油断の出来ないのがありますから……。大分寒くなった。もう秋ですね、浜の方は靄でセピヤ色になった。いい景色だ。おい、吉川君どうだい、あの浜の景色は……」と大きな声を出して野だ（いこ）を呼んだ。

【原文②の質問】赤シャツはどんな時、ひどい目にあうと言っていますか。

第6章を読む前に

山嵐

俺は、数学の主任だ。
今朝、学校へ来たら、あの新米教師は、俺がおごってやった氷水の代金を返してきた。失敬なやつだ。
下宿先でも、迷惑をかけているっていう話じゃないか。
ただし、宿直事件では、あの教師に非はない。
あれは寄宿生が新米教師をばかにしてやったことだ。

新米教師　a new teacher　　迷惑をかける　to trouble　　非はない　no wrongdoing

第6章 ❖ 山嵐との決裂(けつれつ)
The Falling Out with Yama-Arashi

① 俺はあくる日早めに学校に行って、山嵐を待っていた。

② 山嵐のやつ遅(おそ)いな。

③ 家を出る時から握(にぎ)りしめていた一銭(いっせん)五厘(ごりん)が汗(あせ)をかいてる。

④ フーッ

⑤ 教頭―― 昨日は失敬(しっけい)。

⑥ 帰りに舟(ふね)の中で話したことだが、まだ、誰(だれ)にも話してないだろうね?

決裂【けつれつ】 (n, vs) breakdown; rupture * 山嵐との決裂 falling out with Yama-Arashi
① あくる日【あくるひ】 (n) the next day; same as 次の日【つぎのひ】and 翌日【よくじつ】
早めに【はやめに】 (adv) ahead of time
③ 握りしめる【にぎりしめる】 (v1, vt) to grasp tightly
[Number] 厘【りん】 (n) (ctr) old monetary unit (0.001 yen)
汗をかく【あせをかく】 (exp, v5k) to perspire; to sweat * 一銭五厘が汗をかいて（い）る The one and a half *sen* coins are all sweaty.
④ フーッ (int) blowing sound
⑤ 昨日は失敬【きのう／さくじつはしっけい】 (exp) Thanks for yesterday. This expression literally means "I am sorry to have detained you yesterday," which sounds as though Botchan had been held against his wishes. 失 means a wrong action attributable to bad judgment, ignorance, or inattention. 敬 means respect. 失敬 is the same as 失礼, but 失敬 is used by male speakers towards their colleagues or juniors.
⑥ 誰にも〜ない【だれにも〜ない】 (exp) not anyone (with negative predicate)

⑦ これから堀田君に話すつもりです。

⑧ それは困る。
僕は堀田君だと、君にはっきり言った覚えはないんだから。

⑨ もし君が乱暴など働くと、僕は非常に迷惑する！
君も学校で騒動を起こすつもりはないだろう？

⑩ 当たり前です！

⑪ それじゃ、昨日のことは決して話さないでくれたまえ！

⑫ そんなに迷惑なら、よしましょう。

⑬ 大丈夫だろうね？

⑧ 困る【こまる】　(v5r, vi) to be troubled; to be worried（〜に）
　はっきり　(adv) clearly; plainly
　覚え【おぼえ】　(n) memory; experience *[V (past form)] 覚えはない I don't recall that I did 〜.
⑨ 乱暴を働く【らんぼうをはたらく】　(exp, v5k) to act violently; to resort to violence
　非常に【ひじょうに】　(adv) very * 僕は非常に迷惑する You could cause me so much trouble (if you resorted to violence).
　起こす【おこす】　(v5s, vt) to cause; to wake someone * 騒動を起こすつもりはないだろう Surely you're not planning on instigating any disturbances at school, right?
⑩ 当たり前（な）【あたりまえ】　(adj-na, n) normal; natural; reasonable

⑭ 今日は君のせいで遅くなった。

⑮ 罰金を出したまえ。

⑯ カチン

⑰ これを取っておけ。
チャリーン

⑱ 先日おごってもらった氷水の代金だ。

⑲ ……何を言ってる……

⑳

㉑ ……

⑭ [Noun] のせいで　(exp) because of (Noun)'s fault; to blame something on someone (or on something)
⑮ 罰金【ばっきん】　(n) fine * 罰金を出したまえ Pay me the fine (for being late to school).
⑯ カチン　(onoma) a clink sound; used when something "triggers your anger."
⑰ 取っておく【とっておく】　(exp, v5k) to set aside; to keep in reserve * 取っておけ (command form) means "Take it (and keep it)," or "(I'll) let you take it."
　チャリン　(onoma) jingle; sound of coin(s) falling
⑱ 先日【せんじつ】　(n) the other day
　代金【だいきん】　(n) cost; payment * おごってもらった氷水の代金だ Here is the money for treating me to shaved ice.

89

㉒ つまらない　(adj-i) insignificant; trifling
　　冗談【じょうだん】　(n) jest; joke *つまらない冗談を言うな！ Don't be ridiculous! Don't talk nonsense! (see 第4章 コマ㊶)
㉓ 本当【ほんとう】　(n) truth; reality
㉔ 筋合い【すじあい】　(n) reason; logic *君におごられる筋合いはない I have no reason to be treated by you / for you to pay for me.
㉕ 気になる【きになる】　(exp, v5r) to be bothered by; to feel uneasy
　　受け取る【うけとる】　(v5r, vt) to receive; to get
㉖ 嫌（な）【いや】　(adj-na, n) disagreeable; unpleasant *Here Botchan did not want to be in debt to Yama-Arashi even though it was a small amount of money.
㉗ フン　(int) hmph
㉘ [V (volitional, plain form)]が [V (negative stem form)]まいが　(exp) whether V or not *出ようが出まいが、俺の勝手だろう Whether I leave or not is my own business.

㉙ ところが勝手ではない。いか銀の亭主が君に出て行ってもらいたいと言ってきた。

㉚ その話で今日遅くなったんだ。いくら下宿屋の女房でも、足をふかせるなんていばりすぎだ。

㉛ 俺がいつ足をふかせた？

㉜ とにかく、向こうじゃ君に迷惑しているんだ。

㉝ 出てやれ。当たり前だ！！

㉞ いてくれと手を合わせられてもいてやるもんか！だいたい そんな言いがかりをつける下宿屋を紹介するとは、君もけしからん奴だ！

㉙ **ところが** (conj) even so; as a matter of fact　　**亭主【ていしゅ】** (n) landlord; master; husband
出て行く【でていく】 (v5u, vi) to go out and away; to leave ＊出てく (col)
㉚ **[Noun]で** (prt) indicates means of action; cause of effect ＊その話で because of that talk　　**いくら[V（て form)]も** (see 第1章 コマ②)
下宿屋の女房【げしゅくやのにょうぼう】 (n) innkeeper's wife
ふく (v5k, vt) to wipe; to dry ＊女房に足をふかせる (You) made her wipe your feet
いばる (v5r, vi) to behave arrogantly ＊[(V ます stem form)] ＋すぎ => いばりすぎる too arrogant
㉜ **とにかく** (adv) anyhow　　**向こう【むこう】** (n) the other party (i.e., いか銀 and his wife).
迷惑する【めいわくする】 (vs) to be troubled; be inconvenienced
㉞ **手を合わせる【てをあわせる】** (exp) to beg ＊いてくれと手を合わせたって、いてやるもんか！ I wouldn't stay even if you begged me to.
だいたい (adv) generally; for the most part
言いがかり【いいがかり】 (n) false accusation ＊〜をつける make a false accusation
けしからん (exp) outrageous; inexcusable ＊君もけしからんやつだ　It was inexcusable of you also to 〜.

91

俺がけしからんか、君が温厚じゃないかの、どちらかだ！！

㉟ 温厚（な）【おんこう】 (adj-na) gentle; mild-mannered; easy-going
　〜か、〜か (prt) either 〜 or not ＊俺がけしからんか、君が温厚じゃないかのどちらかだ Either I'm outrageous or you're short-tempered!
㊲ ギロ (onoma) stare ＊It means a momentary glare intended to intimidate an opponent.
㊴ トテチテタ (see 第2章 コマ㉟)

㊷ 午後はバッタ騒動を起こした寄宿生の処分についての会議だった。

古賀君がまだですが。

㊸ 少々用事がありまして、遅刻いたしました。すみません。

㊹ どういうわけか、俺は唐茄子のようなうらなり君が顔をしたうらなり君が気になって仕方がない。

㊺ うらなり君ほど、温厚な紳士はいない。

㊻ 彼のような人物を「君子」と言うのだろう。

職員や生徒の過失はみんな私の不徳のいたすところです。

今回の騒動もまた深くおわびします。

㊷ 処分【しょぶん】 (n, vs) punishment
㊸ 少々【しょうしょう】 (n, adv) small quantity　　用事【ようじ】 (n) errand; business (to take care of)
　遅刻する【ちこくする】 (vs, n) lateness; tardiness * 遅刻いたしました (いたす is a humble expression of します).
㊹ どういう [Noun] (adj-pn) somehow　　唐茄子【とうなす】 (n) squash; pumpkin
　気になる【きになる】 (exp, v5r) to be on one's mind; to care about * どういうわけか〜が気になって仕方がない For some reason I cannot help but think about 〜 .
㊺ [Noun] ほど (prt) as; to the extent. * うらなり君ほど〜いない No one is as (gentle) as Uranari.
　紳士【しんし】 (n) gentleman
㊻ 人物【じんぶつ】 (n) character; person　　君子【くんし】 (n) man of virtue
　職員【しょくいん】 (n) staff member; personnel
　過失【かしつ】 (n) error; accident; negligence
　不徳【ふとく】 (n) lacking virtue; immoral * 私の不徳のいたすところです (with an apologetic tone) undesirable state brought about by (my) lack of virtue
　深く【ふかく】 (adv) deeply; profoundly
　おわび (n) apology * 深くおわびします (お + [V(ます stem form)] + する , to apologize, humble expression)

93

㊼ しかし、起こってしまった以上は処分しなければなりません。

㊽ 参考のためのご意見をお述べください。

㊾ 私も―あの騒動の責任は学校にあるかもしれないと考えます。

㊿ 学生の元気が余ってやったいたずらをきびしく罰するのは、少年の未来によくないと思われます。

㊱ なるべく寛大な処分をお願いします。

㊲ 狸が狸なら、赤シャツも赤シャツだ。生徒があばれるのは生徒が悪いんじゃない、教師が悪いんだと言っている。

㊼ 〜以上【いじょう】 (adv) once 〜 ; since 〜 ; seeing that 〜 (commonly 'and more')
  [V(ます stem form)] なければならない (exp) have to do; should do
  参考【さんこう】 (n) reference; consultation　　意見【いけん】 (n) opinion; view; comment
  述べる【のべる】 (v1, vt) to state * お述べください (お + [V(ます stem form)] + ください , please do 〜 ; polite request)
㊾ 責任【せきにん】 (n) liability (for the incident); duty; responsibility * 〜かもしれない (see 第 1 章 コマ ㊽)
㊿ 余る【あまる】 (v5r, vi) to be in excess * 元気余ってやったいたずら Just a harmless prank committed out of an excess of youthful energy.
  きびしく (adv) severely; strictly　　罰する【ばっする】 (vs, vt) to punish; to penalize　　少年【しょうねん】 (n) boys
  未来【みらい】 (n) the future (usually distant)
㊱ なるべく (adv) as much as possible　　寛大（な）【かんだい】 (adj-na) lenient; tolerant
㊲ [Noun1] が [Noun1] なら、[Noun2] も [Noun2] （だ） (exp) both of them are equally horrible (something negative) * 狸が狸なら、赤シャツも赤シャツだ This statement implies Botchan is surprised that both Tanuki and Red Shirt lack common sense.
  あばれる (v1, vi) to act violently; to act up

㊅ ガタ　(onoma) rattle
㊄ ただいま　(adv) presently; just now　　および　(conj) and; as well as
　述べる【のべる】　(v1, vt) to state　* お述べになった (お + [V(ます stem form)] + になる , honorific expression)
　ご [Noun]　* ご意見【ごいけん】ご処分【ごしょぶん】(see 第 1 章 コマ㉜)
　賛成【さんせい】　(n, vs) approval; agreement（～に）*（～の）ご意見にまったく賛成です (I) wholeheartedly agree with ～ .
　どうか　(adv) please; somehow or other
㊎ 反対【はんたい】　(n, vs) opposition; disagreement（～に）
㊐ とんちんかん（な）　(adj-na, n) absurdity; contradiction
㊱ かえって　(adv) on the contrary; instead
　反動【はんどう】　(n) backlash; reaction　* あまりきびしく罰するとかえって反動を起こすでしょうね If you punish them too severely it may cause a backlash.

㊿ ガタ

㊲ 山嵐の野郎も赤シャツの肩を持つ気か！

㊱ 私は教頭および先生方のお考えにはまったく反対であります！

㊴ 教育とは単に学問を与えるばかりではなく、高尚、正直、そして、武士的な精神をきたえることであります。

来たばかりの新米教師をばかにするような生徒を見逃してはなりません。

私は寄宿生一同をきびしく処分すべきだと考えます！

㉒ 野郎【やろう】 (n) (vulg) rascal　　肩を持つ【かたをもつ】 (exp, v5t) to side with; to support
㉓ [Noun]方【がた】 (suf) (hon) honorific pluralizing suffix (used only for people)
　　お考え (see 第１章 コマ㉜)　　〜である (v5r) to be (formal, literary style)
㉔ 単に【たんに】 (adv) merely; only　　学問【がくもん】 (n) study; learning
　　与える【あたえる】 (v1, vt) to give (to someone of lower status)　　[V (plain form)] ばかりでなく (exp) not only 〜 but (also)
　　高尚(な)【こうしょう】 (adj-na, n) noble; refined　　武士【ぶし】 (n) warrior; samurai
　　〜的(な)【てき】 (adj-na, suf) -like; typical　　精神【せいしん】 (n) mind; spirit　　きたえる (v1, vt) to train; to discipline
　　[V (た from)] ばかり (prt) have just done ＊来たばかり have just arrived
　　新米【しんまい】 (exp, n) newcomer; beginner (coming from new rice) ＊Literally 新米 means new rice crops.
　　ばかにする (exp, vs) to make fun of　　見逃す【みのがす】 (v5s, vt) to overlook
　　[V (て form)] はならない (exp) must not do ＊新米教師をばかにするような生徒を見逃してはなりません We shouldn't overlook the pranks of students who make fun of our newly arrived teacher.
　　一同【いちどう】 (n) all present; all concerned　　〜すべき (exp) should do 〜 (abbr. of する + べき); ought to do 〜

㊻ 俺は何だか非常にうれしかった。

㊺ 俺の言いたかったことを俺の代わりに山嵐がすっかり言ってくれた。

㊼ 言い忘れましたが、宿直中の教師が外出して温泉に行かれたようだが、この点については校長からのご注意を希望します。

㊽ 私は確かに宿直中に温泉に行きました。これはまったく私が悪いです。あやまります。

㊾ ——それから、生徒への影響を考え、教師はあまり上等でない場所へ行かないことです。

㊿ そうですね。例えば——

㋀ そば屋だの、団子屋だの。

- ㊹ 代わりに【かわりに】 (adv) instead of　　すっかり (adv) completely
- ㊺ 言い忘れる【いいわすれる】 (exp, v1) to forget to say; to forget to mention 言う + 忘れる => 言い忘れる
  〜中【ちゅう・じゅう】 (suf) during (a certain time when one did or is doing something)
  外出する【がいしゅつする】 (vs) to go out
- ㊻ 点【てん】 (n) point　　注意【ちゅうい】 (n, vs) caution; attention * ご注意 polite expression
  希望する【きぼうする】 (vs) to hope; to wish * 希望する to hope
- ㊾ 上等(な)【じょうとう】 (adj-na, n) superior; first-class　　場所【ばしょ】 (n) place; location; spot; position
- ㋀ [Noun1]だの、[Noun2]だの (prt) and the like; and so forth *This indicates an explanation or emotive emphasis * そば屋だの、団子屋だの。
  例えば【たとえば】 (adv) for example

㉒ 文学を読むとか俳句を作るとか――物質的な快楽ばかり求めず、高尚で精神的な楽しみを求めなくてはいけない。

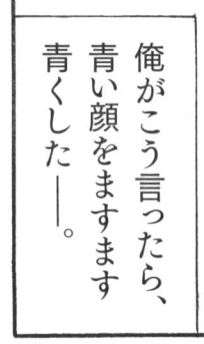

㉓ マドンナに会うのも精神的な楽しみですか。

㉖ それ見ろ！こたえたか！

㉗ うらなり君は

㉘ 俺がこう言ったら、青い顔をますます青くした――。

㉒ 文学【ぶんがく】　(n) literature
　俳句【はいく】　(n) haiku poetry　*Haiku is a 17-syllable poem usually in 3 lines of 5, 7, and 5 syllables)
　〜とか　(prt) among other things; such things as
　物質的（な）【ぶっしつてき】　(adj-na) material or physical (as opposed to spiritual, intangible); materialistic
　〜的【〜てき】（な）　(adj-na, suf) -like; typical　*It creates adjectives such as 物質的 and 精神的.　　快楽【かいらく】　(n) pleasure
　求める【もとめる】　(v1, vt) to seek; to pursue (pleasure)　　精神的（な）【せいしんてき】　(adj-na) mental; emotional
　楽しみ【たのしみ】　(n) pleasure; amusement　* 物質的な快楽ばかり求めず、高尚で精神的な楽しみを求めなくちゃいけない (Teachers) should not seek out material pleasures but must pursue refined and spiritual pleasures.
㉖ それ見ろ【それみろ】　(exp) Look at that; I told you so.　*Used when someone ignores your advice and ultimately fails at something.
　こたえる　(v1, vi) to take its toll; to have an effect on

原文に挑戦しましょう

ウェブの練習問題（186ページ参照）をしてから、チャレンジしてみましょう。次の場面は、第6章のマンガのどのコマかわかりますか。引用文の後の質問に答えましょう。

原文❶

ここへ来た時第一番に氷水を奢ったのは山嵐だ。そんな裏表のある奴から、氷水でも奢ってもらっちゃ、おれの顔に関わる。おれはたった一杯しか飲まなかったから一銭五厘しか払わしちゃない。しかし一銭だろうが五厘だろうが、詐欺師の恩になっては、死ぬまで心持ちがよくない。あした学校へ行ったら、一銭五厘返しておこう。

【原文❶の質問】どうして坊っちゃんは山嵐に一銭五厘返すことにしましたか。

原文❷

すると今までだまって聞いていた山嵐が奮然として、起ち上がった。野郎また赤シャツ賛成の意を表するな、どうせ、貴様とは喧嘩だ、勝手にしろと見ていると山嵐は硝子窓を振わせるような声で「私は教頭及びその他諸君のお説には全然不同意であります。というもこの事件はどの点から見ても、五十名の寄宿生が新来の教師某氏を軽侮してこれを翻弄しようとした所為とより外には認められんのであります。教頭はその源因を教師の人物いかんにお求めになるようでありますが失礼ながらそれは失言かと思います。

【原文❷の質問】赤シャツと山嵐の声を比べてみましょう。山嵐は何が「失言」だと言っていますか。

第7章を読む前に

マドンナ

私は遠山と申します。
この町の人々は私のことを「マドンナ」と呼んでいますが、イタリア語の「ma donna」からきた言葉で「あこがれの人」という意味らしいです。
実は、私は古賀先生の婚約者でした。
でも、先生のお父様がお亡くなりになってから、生活が大変になり、結婚式がのびていました。
今、教頭先生にお嫁に来てほしいと言われています……。

あこがれ longing 　亡くなる to die 　のびる to be postponed 　嫁 bride

第７章 ❖ うらなりとマドンナ
Uranari and Madonna

① その夜、俺はさっそくいか銀の下宿を出た。

お客さん、どちらへ？

② だまってついて来い。今にわかる。

③ とはいうものの行くあてはない。

④ そのうち下宿が見つかるだろうと車屋に荷物をひかせぐるぐる町を歩いていた。

⑤ そう言えばうらなり君はこのあたりに住んでいたな。

⑥

---

① さっそく　(adv) immediately; without delay
② だまる　(v5r, vi) to become silent
　今に【いまに】　(adv) before long; even now
③ とはいうものの　(exp) having said that * 〜ものの is a conjunction meaning "although" and tends to be used in writing.
　あては（or が、も）ない　(exp) aimless; no definite object (e.g., place) in view
④ そのうち　(adv) eventually; sooner or later
　車屋【くるまや】　(n) rickshaw man
　荷物【にもつ】　(n) luggage; baggage
　ひく　(v5k, vt) to pull * ひかせる a causative form
　ぐるぐる　(onoma) turning round and round; going around in circles（〜と）
⑤ そう言えば【そういえば】　(exp) which reminds me; come to think of it
　あたり　(n) neighborhood; vicinity
　〜な　(see 第２章 コマ⑰)

101

⑦ 古賀

⑧ 彼なら地元の人だから下宿を紹介してくれるかもしれない。

⑨ ごめん！ごめん！

⑩ ——それは、さぞお困りでしょう。
そう言えば——

⑪ 萩野という老夫婦から、確かな人なら貸してもいいと頼まれたことがあります。

⑫ 一緒に行って聞いてみましょう。

⑬ 萩野邸

⑭ その夜から俺は萩野の家の下宿人になった。

⑧ 地元【じもと】 (n) home area; home town; local
⑨ ごめん (int, n) your pardon; permission * ごめん（ください）May I come in?
⑪ 萩野【はぎの】 (n) Hagino, family name of Botchan's new landlord　　老夫婦【ろうふうふ】 (n) an old couple
　確か（な）【たしか】 (adj-na) reliable *Often used with 身元 (【みもと】, identity). 身元が確かな人 means a
　person with good references (who comes well recommended).
　貸す【かす】 (v5s, vt) to rent out; to lend （～を、～に）
　頼む【たのむ】 (v5m, vt) to request; to ask * 頼まれる is a passive form.
　～ことがある　(see 第5章 コマ④)
⑬ ～邸【てい】 (n) ～'s house; residence; estate

⑮
驚いたのは、あくる日から入れちがいに、野だいこがいか銀の俺がいた部屋を占領したことだ。
⑯
さすがの俺もこれにはあきれた。
⑰
こうして田舎に来てみると、清はやっぱり善人だ。
こんなことなら、数学なんて芸を覚えるより東京で牛乳屋でも始めればよかった。
⑱
そうすれば、清をそばにおいてやれたのに……
それにしても、手紙の返事が来ないな……
⑲
お茶をお持ちしましたぞなもし。

⑮ **驚く【おどろく】** (v5k, vi) to be surprised; to be astonished（～に）＊驚いたのは～こと（だ）What surprised me was that ～.
入れちがい【いれちがい】 (n) passing each other **占領する【せんりょうする】** (vs, vt) to occupy

⑯ **さすがの [Noun] も** (exp) even (Noun) ＊さすがの俺も～ Even someone like me
あきれる (v1, vi) to be amazed; to be shocked; to be disgusted（～に）

⑰ **善人【ぜんにん】** (n) good person; virtuous person
芸を覚える【げいをおぼえる】 (exp, v1) to master an art/a technique/a performance (through personal experience)
牛乳屋【ぎゅうにゅうや】 (n) dairy; milkman **[V(ば form)] よかった** (exp) I wish I had done; I should have done

⑱ **そうすれば** (exp) if so; in that situation
おく (v5k) to put; to place; to keep（～を、～に）＊そばにおいてやれたのに (If I had done that) I could have kept Kiyo by my side.
それにしても (see 第２章 コマ(55))

⑲ **～ぞなもし** This dialect is no longer used, but is the most famous sentence-final particle of Iyo dialect because it is used in *Botchan*. Soseki expresses this dialect as ～ぞな、もし and ～ぞなもし. (see 第３章 コマ㊺)

㉠ 先生はどうして奥さんと一緒においでなんだぞなもし。

㉑ 僕はまだ二十四ですよ。
どうして奥さんがいると思ったんですか？

㉒ どうしてって、東京から便りはないかと毎日待ちこがれておいでるぞなもし。

㉓ こいつあ驚いた！
よく見ているね。

㉔ けれど、今時の女子は油断ができんけれ、お気をつけた方がええぞなもし。

㉕ 僕の奥さんが東京で男でもこしらえてるかい？

---

⑳ おいでなんだ ぞなもし　(dialect) おいでにならなかったんですか　　おいでになる　(v5r) (hon) to come; to go; to be (〜に)
㉒ 〜って（＝〜というのは）　(exp) presents a topic that is to be defined or explained
　便り【たより】　(n) letter; news　　待ちこがれる【まちこがれる】　(v1, vt) to long for; to wait longingly for something or someone
　〜おいでるぞなもし　(dialect) 〜いらっしゃいます
㉓ こいつあ（＝こいつ）　(pn) (col) usually refers to a person, but here to the fact that Hagino noticed a lot about Botchan. This can be used in a friendly or derogatory manner; Botchan uses it in a friendly manner here.
㉔ 今時【いまどき】　(adv, n) recently; nowadays　　女子【おなご】　(n) (arch) (dialect) woman
　できんけれ　(dialect) できないので　* 油断できんけれ (women these days) are not faithful
　[V (た form)] 方がいい　(exp) had better 〜
　ええぞなもし　(dialect) いい／よろしいでございます（よ）
㉕ [Noun] でも　(prt) or something　　こしらえる　(v1,vt) to make　* 男／女をこしらえる to find a lover

104

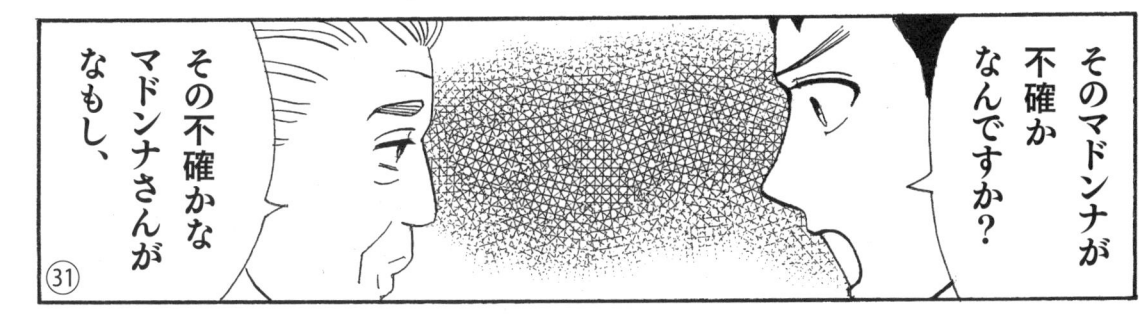

㉖ いえ、いえ。あなたの奥さんは確かじゃけれど。誰が不確かなんですか。

㉗ 遠山のお嬢さんてご存知がなもし。

㉘ ここらで一番のべっぴんさんで、先生方は皆、『マドンナ』『マドンナ』言うとるぞなもし。

㉙ ……マドンナか——ぼくは芸者の名かと思った。

㉚ マドンナというと唐人の言葉でべっぴんさんのことじゃろうがなもし。

㉛ そのマドンナが不確かなんですか？ その不確かなマドンナさんがなもし、

㉖ 〜じゃけれど (dialect) 〜ですが
　不確か（な）【ふたしか】 (adj-na) unreliable; uncertain　*In this context, 不確かな人 refers to an unfaithful person and 確かな人 to a faithful person. 不〜 is a negative prefix (un-; non-).
㉗ 遠山【とおやま】 (n) Madonna's family name
　お嬢さん【おじょうさん】 (n) (term of respect for) someone else's daughter; daughter of a high-class or wealthy family
　ご存知がなもし【ごぞんじがなもし】 (dialect) ご存知でしょうか
㉘ ここら (pn) around here　*Same as このあたり and このへん.
　べっぴんさん (n) beautiful woman　　言うとるぞなもし (dialect) 言っていらっしゃいます（よ）
㉚ 唐人【とうじん】 (n) (arch) foreigner (e.g., Europeans), originally Chinese people because Japanese used to call China as 唐土【とうど】 and its people as 唐土の人【とうどののひと】 or 唐人【からびと】.
　言葉【ことば】 (n) language　　〜じゃろうがなもし (dialect) 〜でしょう
㉛ マドンナさんがなもし (dialect) マドンナさんですね

あの古賀先生の所にお嫁に行くことになっていたんぞなもし。

ところが、去年、先生のお父さんがお亡くなりになってから、急に暮らし向きが悪うなって……

お輿入れがのびているところに、

あの教頭さんが、お嫁に欲しいと出てきたんぞなもし。

——どうもあの赤シャツはただのシャツじゃないと思ってた……

赤シャツさんも赤シャツさんだが、お嬢さんもお嬢さんじゃって。

㉜ 嫁に行く【よめにいく】 (exp, v5k) to marry（〜に）
 [V (plain form)] ことになっている (exp, v1) to be arranged that * 〜ことになっていた it has been arranged 〜
 去年【きょねん】 (n) last year　　亡くなる【なくなる】 (v5r, vi) to die
 急に【きゅうに】 (adv) suddenly　　暮らし向き【くらしむき】 (n) one's (living) circumstances; standards of living
 悪うなって【わるうなって】 (dialect) 悪くなって
㉝ お輿入れ【おこしいれ】 (n, vs) (arch) marriage (into a family); wedding; bridal possessions. *In the feudal times, 輿 (bridal possessions) were brought to the bride's residence by palanquin (a closed litter carried on the shoulders of two to four bearers). These days お輿入れする is not commonly used, but 嫁ぐ【とつぐ】 and 嫁に行く【よめにいく】, which mean marrying into a family, are still used.
 のびる (v1, vi) to be postponed; to be prolonged　　[V (plain form)] ところ（に） (n) the moment; just at that time 〜
 嫁【よめ】 (n) wife; bride　　欲しい【ほしい】 (adj-i) want; wish for
 出てきたんぞなもし (dialect) 出てきたんでございますよ
 [Verb (て form)] くる (aux) to come to 〜 *It describes a motion of coming towards the speaker or of appearing at an event.
㉟ どうも (adv) somehow　　ただの [Noun] (adj-pn) common; ordinary * ただのシャツじゃない (He) is not an ordinary shirt (person).
 [Noun1] も [Noun1] だが、[Noun2] も [Noun2] だ (exp) emphasis on the degree of an action; implies a sense of condemnation for both X and Y.
 * 赤シャツさんも赤シャツさんだが、お嬢さんもお嬢さんじゃって What Red Shirt did was wrong, but what Toyama's daughter did was also wrong.

萩野のばあさんの話だと、
うらなり君を気の毒に思った山嵐が赤シャツに意見しに行ったそうだ。
赤シャツは
私は婚約者を横取りするつもりはありません。
ま、破談になれば別ですけどね。
と言ったそうだ。
それ以来、赤シャツと山嵐は仲が悪いらしい。
これじゃどっちが悪者で、
どっちを味方にしていいかわからない。

㊳ **ばあさん** (n) grandmother figure; female senior citizen *Botchan omits the honorific prefix お because this is the first-person narrative and he speaks casually.
気の毒（な）【きのどく】 (adj-na, n) pitiful; unfortunate *～を気の毒に思う to feel sorry for ～
意見する【いけんする】 (vs) to comment; give one's opinion（～に）

㊴ **婚約者【こんやくしゃ】** (n) fiancé; fiancée **横取りする【よこどりする】** (vs) to snatch; to seize
破談【はだん】 (n) cancellation; breaking off (one's engagement) **別【べつ】** (n) difference; distinction *別の another
[V (plain form)] そう（だ） (see 第1章 コマ㊺)

㊵ **それ以来【それいらい】** (exp) since then; from that time
仲が悪い【なかがわるい】 (exp, adj-i) on bad terms; at loggerheads（～と）

㊷ **悪者【わるもの】** (n) bad fellow; scoundrel **味方【みかた】** (n, vs) friend; ally
味方にする (exp) gain [win] (a person) over to one's side（～を）
[WH+ か] わからない (exp) I don't know WH (question words).

㊸ ただいま

学校から帰ると、清からの便りが届いていた。

㊹ 山城屋からいか銀の方へ回り、いか銀から萩野へ回って来たのである。

㊺ 山城屋で一週間ばかり留まっている。宿屋だけに手紙まで泊めていたのだろう。

㊻ 長い手紙だ。

㊼

㊽ ぼっちゃんのてがみをいただいてからすぐへんじをかこうとおもいましたがあいにくかぜをひいてしゅかんばかりねていたものですからおそくなってすみません

㊸ 届く【とどく】 (v5k, vi) to be delivered; to arrive
㊹ 回る (v5r, vi) to go around; to visit several places （～へ・に）
㊺ [Number] ばかり (see 第２章 コマ⑤)
　留まる【とまる】 (v5r, vi) to stop; to remain; to stay (in the one place) （～に）
　[Noun] だけに (exp) being the case; (precisely) because ～ ; as might be expected (from ～)
　泊める【とめる】 (v1, vt) to give shelter to; to lodge ＊手紙まで泊めていたのだろう even the letters stay there
　あいにく (adv,n) unfortunately; sorry, but

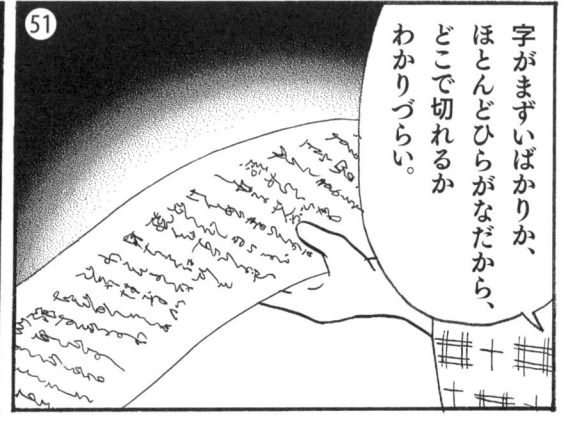

㊾ よみかきがうまくないので おいにかいてもらおうと おもいましたが じぶんで かかなくちゃ ぼっちゃんに すまないとおもって 下がきに四日 せいしょに二日 かけてかきました

㊿ ——なるほど……読みにくい。

よみにくいかも しれませんが いっしょうけんめい かいたので どうぞ おしまいまで よんでください まし

㊼ 字がまずいばかりか、ほとんどひらがなだから、どこで切れるか わかりづらい。

㊽ ぼっちゃんは竹をわったようなごきしょうですがただかんしゃくがつよすぎるのがしんぱいです。

㊾ よみかき (n) reading and writing 読み書き　うまい (adj-i) skillful *Same as 上手.
　おい (n) nephew　かかなくちゃ（=書かなくては）　すまない (exp) inexcusable; sorry
　下がき【したがき】(n,vs) rough copy; draft 下書き
　せいしょ (n, vs) clean copy 清書　かける (v1,vt) to take (time, money); to expend (money, time, etc.)
㊿ [V(ます stem form)]にくい　(aux, adj-i) hard (to do) *This indicates that because of some reason or situation, something cannot be done easily. The cause, in many cases, is due to an external situation.　おしまい (n) end
　〜まし　(aux)(pol) (used to make a polite request or demand) please *Same as 〜ませ.
㊼ まずい (adj-i) unskillful * 字がまずい (Her) penmanship is poor. Same as 下手.
　〜ばかりか (exp) not only 〜 , but also *Same as 〜ばかりでなく (see 第6章 コマ㊹)
　ほとんど (adv) mostly; almost　切れる【きれる】(v1,vi) to be disconnected
　[V(ます stem form)]づらい　(aux, adj-i) difficult (to do) *This indicates doing something is troublesome or difficult and suggests a stronger degree of difficulty than 〜にくい. わかりづらい difficult to understand
㊽ 竹【たけ】(n) bamboo
　わる (v5r, vt) to cut; to break 竹をわったようなご気性 (You have) a refreshingly direct and frank temperament like split bamboo.
　ただ (conj) but; however　かんしゃく (n) temper; irritability * かんしゃくが強すぎる (You are) too impulsive.

まだ見ておいでるのかもし。
よっぽど長いお手紙ぞなもし。
夕飯はまた、さつまいものにつけか。
生卵でも食べて栄養をとらなくっちゃあ。
カチッ
週に二十一時間の授業ができるもんか。
清の手紙を読んでいて湯に行くのが遅くなったので、汽車に乗って出かけることにした。
汽車は発車したばかりか。

㊾ **見ておいでるのかもし** (dialect) 見ていらっしゃるのですか
よっぽど（＝よほど） (adv) very; quite
㊿ **夕飯【ゆうはん／ゆうめし】** (n) evening meal ＊ゆうめし (male, informal)
さつまいも (n) sweet potato
につけ (n) vegetables or fish boiled in soy sauce
55 **生卵【なまたまご】** (n) raw egg
栄養【えいよう】 (n) nutrition; nourishment
とらなくっちゃあ（＝とらなくては［ならない］）
56 **～に** (prt) per ＊一週間に二十一時間 21 hours per week
カチッ (onoma) click; the sound of cracking eggs（～と）
58 **発車する【はっしゃする】** (vs) to depart; to set off

(59)
(60)
古賀先生もお湯ですか？
こっちにすわりませんか。
(61)
いえ、おかまいなく。
少し待たなくちゃいけないから、くたびれますよ。
どうぞ。
(62)
それではおじゃましましょう。
(63)
あなたはどこか悪いんじゃありませんか？
いえ、別に持病もありませんが。
(64)
うらなり君が気の毒でたまらなかった。
そりゃ結構です。
こんないい男を捨てて赤シャツになびくなんてマドンナはおきゃんだと思った。
(65)
ホホホホ

(61) **おかまいなく** (exp) please don't fuss over me; don't go out of your way
待たなくちゃ（＝待たなくては）
くたびれる (v1, vi) to get tired; to wear out（～に）
(62) **おじゃまします** (exp) excuse me for disturbing (interrupting) you * I'll have a seat.
(63) **別に【べつに】** (adv) not particularly; nothing **持病【じびょう】** (n) chronic disease
(64) **結構（な）【けっこう】** (adj-na, n) sufficient; fine * そりゃ結構です That's good.
たまらない (exp, adj-i) cannot help (doing/feeling) **捨てる【すてる】** (v1, vt) to break up with (someone)
なびく (v5k, vi) to flutter; to be swayed by（～に）
おきゃん (n) (arch) girl with "attitude" ; lively minx. This word is no longer used; in this context, equivalent to 軽薄な女性（【けいはく】, a fickle girl).

俺は美人の形容などができる男ではないが、これが美人というものだろうか。

なんだか水晶の珠を香水であたためて、手のひらで握ってみたような気がした。

⑱ 美人【びじん】　(n) beautiful person (woman)
　形容する【けいようする】　(vs) to describe
　〜というもの　(exp) something like 〜 ; something called 〜
⑲ 水晶【すいしょう】　(n) crystal
　珠【たま】　(n) bead
　香水【こうすい】　(n) perfume
　あたためる　(v1, vt) to warm; to heat
　手のひら　(n) the palm (of one's hand)
　握る【にぎる】　(v5r, vt) to grasp; to seize
　〜ような気がする【ようなきがする】　(exp) to have a certain mood or feeling

これがマドンナかー？

やがてピューッと汽笛が鳴って、汽車が入ってきた。

や、君も湯ですか？

赤シャツまで登場だ。

⑦⓪ **スクッ** (onoma) standing up quickly
⑦④ **[Noun] まで** (prt) even; to the extent of
　　登場【とうじょう】 (n, vs) entry (on stage); appearance (on screen)
⑦⑦ **やがて** (adv) before long; soon; at length
　　ピューッ (onoma) toot toot *sound of the whistle of a steam-operated train（〜と）
　　汽笛【きてき】 (n) whistle of a steam-operated train
　　鳴る【なる】 (v5r, vi) to sound; to ring; to resound

⑦⑧ 道後温泉

⑦⑨ 湯の中でまた、うらなり君に会ったので慰めようと思っていろいろ話しかけた。

ところが何を言っても、『え』とか『いえ』と答えるだけだった。

⑧⑩

⑧① おっ、この前の団子屋だ。食いたいな。

⑧② がまん　がまん。

狸からまた、会議の時にしかられる。

⑧③ 食いたい団子の食えないのは情けない。

⑦⑨ **慰める【なぐさめる】** (v1, vt) to comfort; to console
　話しかける【はなしかける】 (v1, vt) to accost a person; to talk (to someone) (〜に)
　何を言っても【なにをいっても】 (exp) no matter what I said
⑧① **この前【このまえ】** (n) last; the other day ＊この前の団子屋　It's the dango-ya where I stopped the other day.
⑧② **がまん** (n,vs) patience; endurance; will power
　しかる (v5r, vt) to scold (a person with the intention of correcting wrong behavior)
⑧③ **情けない【なさけない】** (adj-i) miserable; pitiable; regrettable

しかし

許嫁が他人に心を移したのは、もっと情けないだろう。 ⑧④

あのうつくしい顔を見ると、そんな不人情なことをしそうには思えないんだが、 ⑧⑤

本当に人間とはわからないものだ。

ここに来てからまだ一カ月たつかたたないかなのに、急に世の中が物騒に思えた。 ⑧⑥

そして自分が五つ六つ年を取ったような気がした。

ぶらぶら土手を歩いていたら向こうに人影が見えてきた。 ⑧⑦

…！ ⑧⑧

⑧④ 許嫁【いいなずけ】 (n) fiancé; fiancée *The term 許嫁 is not commonly used these days because it originally meant that parents chose their child's marriage partner. 婚約者【こんやくしゃ】 is more equivalent in meaning to fiancé/fiancée.
　　他人【たにん】 (n) another person　　心【こころ】 (n) heart
　　移す【うつす】 (v5s, vt) to move or change the object of one's interest or focus（〜に、〜を）
⑧⑤ 不人情（な）【ふにんじょう】 (adj-na, n) unkindness; inhumanity; heartlessness
　　思える【おもえる】 (v1, vi) to seem, to appear likely　* 〜そうには思えない it does not seem likely 〜
⑧⑥ たつ (v5t, vi) to pass; pass by [away]　* 一ヶ月たつかたたないか It's been hardly a month.
　　物騒（な）【ぶっそう】 (adj-na, n) disturbed; insecure; dangerous　　年を取る【としをとる】 (exp, v5r) to grow old; to age
⑧⑦ ぶらぶら (onoma) leisurely; aimlessly（〜と）　　土手【どて】 (n) embankment; bank
　　向こう【むこう】 (n) over there; far away　　人影【ひとかげ】 (n) figure(s) or shadow of a person (persons)

町が狭くて困っているのは俺だけではなかった。

あ……

⑨⓪ ダッ　(onoma) charge; sound of footsteps
⑨④ 〜だけではなかった　(exp) It was not only 〜

原文に挑戦しましょう

ウェブの練習問題（186ページ参照）をしてから、チャレンジしてみましょう。次の場面は、第7章のマンガのどのコマかわかりますか。引用文の後の質問に答えましょう。

原文❶

――ほかの人にむやみに渾名なんか、つけるのは人に恨まれるもとになるから、やたらに使っちゃいけない、もしつけたら、清だけに手紙で知らせろ。――田舎者は人がわるいそうだから、気をつけてひどい目に遭わないようにしろ。――気候だって東京より不順にきまってるから、寝冷えをして風邪を引いてはいけない。坊っちゃんの手紙はあまり短過ぎて、容子がよくわからないから、この次にはせめてこの手紙の半分ぐらいの長さのを書いてくれ。――宿屋へ茶代を五円やるのはいいが、あとで困りゃしないか、田舎へ行って頼りになるはお金ばかりだから、なるべく倹約して、万一の時に差支えないようにしなくっちゃいけない。――お小遣がなくて困るかも知れないから、為替で十円あげる。――先だって坊ちゃんからもらった五十円を、坊っちゃんが、東京へ帰って、うちを持つ時の足しにと思って、郵便局へ預けておいたが、この十円を引いてもまだ四十円あるから大丈夫だ。――なるほど女というものは細かいものだ。

【原文❶の質問】清が心配していることをリストにしてみましょう。清と坊っちゃんはどんな関係だと思いますか。

原文❷

ところへ入口で若々しい女の笑声が聞えたから、何心なく振り返ってみるとえらい奴が来た。色の白い、ハイカラ頭の、背の高い美人と、四十五六の奥さんとが並んで切符を売る窓の前に立っている。おれは美人の形容などが出来る男でないから何にも言えないがまったく美人に相違ない。何だか水晶の珠を香水で暖ためて、掌に握ってみたような心持ちがした。年寄の方が背は低い。しかし顔はよく似ているから親子だろう。

【原文❷の質問】坊っちゃんは誰について書いていますか。その人の身体的特徴（physical appearance）は何ですか。坊っちゃんがその人にもった第一印象（first impression）は何でしたか。

第8章を読む前に

萩野

坊っちゃん先生の下宿先の萩野でぞなもし。
先日、坊っちゃん先生にマドンナさんが古賀先生と婚約していたこと、教頭先生がお嫁にほしいと言っている話をしたぞなもし。
今晩、夕食の時、古賀先生が希望して他の学校に行くなんておかしいことを言うけれ、古賀先生のお母さんから聞いた話を坊っちゃん先生にしたんぞなもし。
そしたら、坊っちゃん先生怒って、また教頭先生の家に走っていかれたぞなもし。

希望 wish　**怒る** to get mad

第8章 ❖ 増給話の裏
The Other Side of the Salary Increase Story

① 山嵐に返した一銭五厘は、ほこりだらけになって机の上に乗っている。

②

③ 俺はもちろん手が出せない。

④ 山嵐は決して持って帰らない。

⑤ この一銭五厘が壁になって、俺は話そうと思っても話せない。

⑥ しまいには見るのも苦になった。

⑦ 君、今度の下宿はどうですか？

増給【ぞうきゅう】　(n) salary increase
話【はなし】　(n) story * はなし becomes ばなし when it is the second part of a compound ～話．
裏【うら】　(n) out of sight; behind the scenes
① ほこり　(n) dust
　[Noun] だらけ　(suf) covered all over
　乗る　(v5r, vi) to mount; to board（～に）* 机の上に乗っている sitting on a desk
③ もちろん　(adv) of course
　手を出す【てをだす】　(exp) to make a move * 手が出せない I cannot take it back/claim it.
⑤ 壁【かべ】　(n) wall; barrier
⑥ しまいに　(adv) at the end
　苦になる【くになる】　(exp, v5r) to be bothered (by something); to suffer
⑦ 今度【こんど】　(n) this time * 今度の下宿 the new boarding house

⑧ 夕べ、お会いしましたね？

⑨ ええ、駅で。

⑩ 土手でも、お目にかかりましたね？

いいえ、僕はあっちへは行きませんでした。湯に入って、すぐに帰りました。

⑪ うそつきめ。

⑫ これで中学校の教頭が勤まるなら、俺なんか大学の総長が勤まるはずだ。

⑬ 俺はこの時から、ますます赤シャツを信用しなくなった。

⑭ 信用しなくなった赤シャツとは口をきいて、感心している山嵐とは話をしないとはずいぶん妙なものだ。

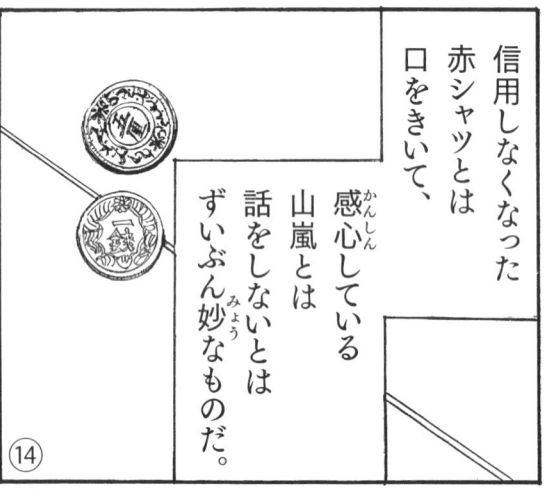

⑧ 夕べ【ゆうべ】　(n) last night
⑩ お目にかかる【おめにかかる】　(exp, v5r) (hum) to meet (someone of higher status)　*Botchan is using humble forms お会いする／お目にかかる in a conversation with Red Shirt.
　あっち　(pn) that place (somewhere physically distant from both speaker and listener, or somewhere not visible but known by both speaker and listener)
⑪ うそつき　(n) a liar　* うそつき＋め (derogatory suffix) => うそつきめ "What a liar!"
⑫ 勤まる【つとまる】　(v5r, vi) to be fif for; to function properly　　総長【そうちょう】　(n) (university or college) president
　[plain form] はず（だ）　(n) expected to be; must be　* 勤まるはずだ (I) should be able to serve or work as ～．
⑬ 信用する【しんようする】　(vs) to trust
⑭ 口をきく【くちをきく】　(exp, v5k) to speak; to utter　　感心する【かんしんする】　(vs) to admire

⑮ ある日赤シャツに呼ばれて、俺は家へ訪ねて行った。

頼む！

⑯ 兄を呼んできます。

⑰ 赤シャツの弟は俺が数学を教えているが、いたってデキが悪い。

⑱ それにしても、立派な玄関だ。

⑲ これで家賃が九円五十銭なら、俺もこんな家を借りて東京から清を呼びよせ、喜ばせてやりたいものだと思った。

⑳ 君が来てくれてから、前任者の時より生徒の成績が上がって、校長も喜んでいます。

へえ、そうですか。

⑮ 訪ねる【たずねる】 (v1, vt) to visit
　頼む【たのむ】 (v5m) to ask; to order; (arch) to ask for assistance at the entrance. * 頼む！ Is anyone home!? Same as ごめんください．
⑰ いたって (adv) very much; extremely
　デキが悪い【できがわるい】 (exp, adj-i) (having) bad marks or results (e.g., in school) *Katakana, デキ, is used here for emphasis.
⑱ 玄関【げんかん】 (n) entranceway
⑲ 家賃【やちん】 (n) rent　呼びよせる【よびよせる】 (v1, vt) to invite; to have (Kiyo) come (to Shikoku)
　喜ばす【よろこばす】 (v5s, vt) to please; to satisfy * 喜ばせる (causative form) have (her) be delighted
⑳ 前任者【ぜんにんしゃ】 (n) predecessor　成績【せいせき】 (n) results; record; grades * 成績が上がる　grades go up
　喜ぶ【よろこぶ】 (v5b, vi) to be delighted; to be glad; to be pleased　　へえ (int) oh, yes?; really?

㉑ ただ、この前話したことを、忘れないでください。

㉒ 下宿の世話なんてする奴は、あやしいってことですか。
……そう ろこつに言われると——

㉓ 僕が言いたいのは、もう少ししたら君が昇給する可能性があるということです。

㉔ へえ……昇給ですか。
そりゃあ上がった方がいいですけど。

㉕ 幸い、転任者がいますからね。
え？誰が転任するんですか？

㉖ 実は、古賀君です。

㉑ [V（ない form）]でください (exp) please do not ～ ; without doing
㉒ 世話する【せわする】 (vs) to look after; to help
　あやしい (adj-i) suspicious; dubious ＊あやしい奴 someone who should not be trusted
　～って（＝～という） (prt) the one you say is ～ ; called thus　　ろこつに (adv) bluntly; plainly; outspokenly
㉓ もう少ししたら【もうすこししたら】 (exp) soon
　昇給する【しょうきゅうする】 (vs) to get a (salary) raise　　可能性【かのうせい】 (n) possibility
㉕ 幸い【さいわい】 (adv, n) fortunately　　転任者【てんにんしゃ】 (n) a person who is transferred
　転任する【てんにんする】 (vs) to be transferred
㉖ 実は【じつは】 (adv) as a matter of fact; actually

㉗ 古賀さんは土地の人じゃありませんか！

㉘ ……ですが、少し事情があって——半分は本人の希望です。

㉙ どこへ行くんです？
日向の延岡です。
そんな遠くに——！？

㉚ これから君にもっと働いてもらおうと思っています。
今より時間が増すんですか？
いいえ。つまり、もっと重大な責任を持ってもらうという意味です。

㉛ 重大な責任——と言えば、数学主任だが……

㉜ 主任は山嵐で、彼は辞職するつもりはない——
わからん。

㉗ 土地の人【とちのひと】 (n) locals; natives
㉘ 半分【はんぶん】 (n) half
㉙ 日向【ひゅうが】 (n) place name *This is located in present-day Miyazaki prefecture, Kyushu, Hyūga was an old administrative division used during the Meiji period.
　延岡【のべおか】 (n) Nobeoka, place name *Nobeoka is the northernmost city in Miyazaki. In the Meiji period, it was considered a backward place. The original text reads, "Nobeoka is situated in the heart of the most mountainous area of the country."
㉚ [V (て form)] もらう　(aux) to get somebody to do something　　増す【ます】 (v5s, vi) to increase
　つまり　(adv) in other words　　重大（な）【じゅうだい】 (adj-na) serious; important
㉛ 〜と言えば【〜といえば】 (exp) speaking of
㉜ 辞職する【じしょくする】 (vs) to resign from (work or position)

㉝ (panel)
㉞ 今日は豆腐か。さつまいもも豆腐も似たようなものだ。
㉟ 古賀さんは延岡に行くそうですね。
　もぐ
㊱ 本当にお気の毒じゃなもし。
㊲ 好きで行くんだから、仕方ないですね。
　ズッ
㊳ 誰が延岡なんぞに好きで行くんでなもし。
�439 だって赤シャツがそう言っていましたぜ。
　教頭さんがそうおっしゃるのも古賀さんの行きたくないのももっともぞなもし。
㊵ それは一体どういう訳なんです？

㉞ 豆腐【とうふ】　(n) tofu; bean-curd　＊さつまいもも豆腐も似たようなものだ Sweet potatoes and tofu are much the same.
㉟ [V (plain form)] そう（だ）　(see 第 1 章 コマ㊺)
㊱ お気の毒じゃなもし【おきのどくじゃなもし】　(dialect) お気の毒でございませんか It's truly pitiful, isn't it?
㊲ ズッ　(onoma) sip
㊳ なんぞ　(prt) and [or] the like ＊Same as など , but emphasizes the negation. 誰が延岡なんぞに好きで行くんでなもし Who would want to go to a place like Nobeoka?
�439 だって　(conj) (col) but; however
　もっとも（な）　(adj-na, adv) quite right; plausible　＊教頭さんがそうおっしゃるのも、古賀さんの行きたくないのも、もっともぞなもし It is plausible for the Vice Principal to say that, and also plausible that Koga doesn't want to go.
㊵ 一体【いったい】　(adv) 〜 the heck (e.g., "what the heck?"); 〜 in the world (e.g., "why in the world?"); 〜 on earth (e.g., "who on earth")
　訳【わけ】　(n) reason

今朝、古賀先生のお母さんが見えて、訳を話されたがなもし。

あそこはお父さんがお亡くなりになってから暮らし向きが悪くなってお困りじゃけれ、お母さんが校長さんにお頼みて、

うちの息子の月給をどうぞもう少し増やしておくれんかなもし。

では、考えておきましょう。

それで安心して待っておいでたところ

古賀先生が校長さんに呼ばれて……

気の毒ですが、うちの学校には予算が足りません。

しかし延岡の学校なら毎月五円余分にもらえるそうだから、手続きしておきました。

月給は元のままでよいので、ここにいられませんか？

㊶ **今朝【けさ】** (n) this morning;
　見える【みえる】 (v1, vi) (hon) to come *Similar to いらっしゃる、おいでになる．
　暮らし向き【くらしむき】 (n) one's (living) circumstances
　お困りじゃけれ【おこまりじゃけれ】 (dialect) 困っていらっしゃるので　　**お頼みて【おたのみて】** (dialect) お頼みになって
㊷ **息子【むすこ】** (n) a son
　増やす【ふやす】 (v5s, vt) to increase　　**〜おくれんかなもし** (dialect) 〜いただけませんでしょうか
㊸ **安心する【あんしんする】** (vs) to feel relieved; to stop worrying
　待っておいでたところ【まっておいでたところ】 (dialect) 待っていらっしゃったところ
㊹ **予算【よさん】** (n) estimate; budget　　**足りる【たりる】** (v1, vi) to be sufficient; to be enough
　余分【よぶん】 (adj-na, n) surplus; excess * 余分に excessively　　**手続きする【てつづきする】** (vs) to follow the necessary procedures
　〜まま (prt) condition; state; as is/was * 元のまま as it was before

㊺ もうあなたの代わりの先生も決まったあとなので、仕方ないですね。

㊻ それじゃ命令じゃありませんか!?

㊼ まったく人をバカにした話だ！赤シャツの策略だよ！まるでだましうちだ！

㊽ それで俺の月給を上げてやるなんて言われても、誰がもらうもんか——お断りだ！

㊾ カッ

㊿ 赤シャツ邸

㊺ [Noun] の代わりに 【〜のかわりに】 (exp) in place of 〜
　決まる 【きまる】 (v5r, vi) to be decided
㊻ 命令 【めいれい】 (n, vs) order; command; decree; directive
㊼ 策略 【さくりゃく】 (n) scheme; tactic
　まるで (adv) as if; just like
　だましうち (n) surprise attack; sneak attack
㊽ 上げる (v1, vt) to raise
　お断り 【おことわり】 (n) (pol) declining; refusal
㊾ カッ (onoma) clack *the sound of running/walking in 下駄 (げた see コマ㊾)

126

また、弟が取り次ぎに出て来て、また来たかという顔をした。
お待ちください。
野だいこが来てるのか……
こんな芸人じみた下駄をはくのはあいつしかいない。
まあ、上がりたまえ。
吉川君も来てる。
いえ、ここでいいです。
野だ公と飲んでたな。
さっきの僕の月給を上げてやるというお話ですが、お断りにきました。

⑤① **取り次ぎに出る【とりつぎにでる】** (exp, v1) answer the door [knock, bell]
顔をする【かおをする】 (exp, vs) have an expression on the face like ～
⑤④ **[Noun] じみる** (suf, v1) to have a touch of; to look like
下駄【げた】 (n) *geta* (Japanese footwear); wooden clogs
あいつ (pn) (col) that guy; that person
⑤⑤ **上がる** (v5r, vi) to enter (from outdoors) ＊上がりたまえ Please come in.
⑤⑦ **[Noun] 公【こう】** (suf) familiar or derogatory suffix (after a name, etc.)
⑤⑧ **断る【ことわる】** (v5r, vt) to turn down; to decline

㉕ あの時承知したのは、古賀さんが自分の希望で転任すると聞いたからです。

㉖ そうです。古賀君の希望です。

㉖ そうじゃないんです。ここにいたいんです。

㉖ 古賀さんは元の月給でいいから郷里にいたいんです！

㉖ 君は古賀君から直接そう聞いたのですか？

—いえ

㉖ 古賀さんのお母さんが僕の下宿のばあさんにそう話したそうなんです。

あなたの言い方だと、下宿のばあさんの言うことは信じるが、教頭の言うことは信じない—というように聞こえるが—？

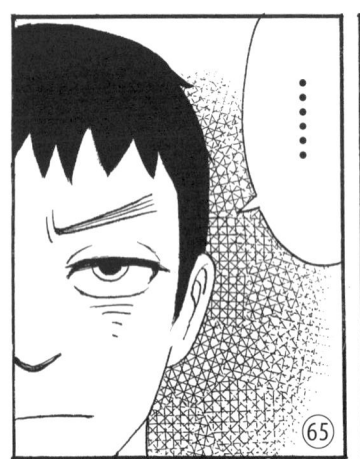

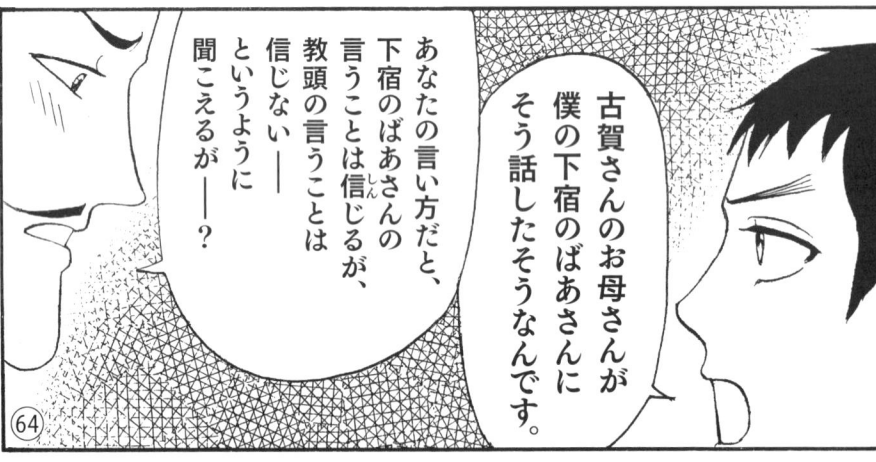

㉖ ……

⑩ 承知する【しょうちする】 (vs) to consent; to accept
⑫ 元【もと】 (n) former; original
　郷里【きょうり】 (n) birthplace; hometown
⑬ 直接【ちょくせつ】 (adv, n) direct; firsthand
⑭ 信じる【しんじる】 (v1, vt) to believe; to believe in; to place trust in
　聞こえる【きこえる】 (v1, vi) (can) hear ＊下宿のばあさんの言うことは信じるが、教頭の言うことは信じない—というように聞こえるが It seems that you believe what the boarding house landlady says but you don't believe the Vice Principal, is that what I'm hearing?

66 あなたの言う通りかもしれないが、とにかく増給はけっこうです。

67 それはますますおかしいですね。君が増給を断る理由はないのに、なぜ拒むのかわかりませんね。

68 わからないかもしれませんが、とにかく断ります。

69 そんなにいやなら、しいてとは言いませんが、二、三時間のうちにそう考えが変わっては、君の信用にかかわりますね。

70 かかわっても、かまわないです。

71 いいですか？

72 君の増給は古賀君の給料をけずるからではありません。

---

66 **言う通り【いうとおり】** (exp) as (you) say
   とにかく (adv) anyhow; in any case * あなたの言うとおりかもしれないが、とにかく増給はけっこうです What you say may be true but, in any case I decline my salary increase.

67 **理由【りゆう】** (n) reason　　**拒む【こばむ】** (v5m, vt) to refuse; to decline

69 **しいる** (v1, vt) to force; to compel; to coerce * しいてとは言いませんが I won't force it on (you), but...
   [Noun] のうちに (exp) within ~ * 二、三時間のうちにそう変わっては changing your mind within two to three hours
   信用にかかわる【しんようにかかわる】 (exp, v5r) to reflect (badly) on one's trustworthiness; to affect people's confidence in one; to damage one's standing/credit

70 **かまわない** (v5u) no problem; it doesn't matter *Negative form of かまう

72 **けずる** (v5r, vt) to reduce; to curtail

㉓ 古賀君の代わりは最初からの約束で低給で来てくれる。

その差額を君の増給に回す。そして、古賀君は延岡で今より昇給する——

㉔ 君が彼を気の毒がる必要はないはずです。

㉕ あなたの言うことはもっともですが、いやなものはいやなので、お断りします。

人間は好き嫌いで動くものだ。論法で動くものじゃない——！

㉖ 赤シャツがどんなに論理的に俺をやりこめようと、今夜だけは引き下がらなかった。

さようなら！

㉗ 頭上に天の川が一筋かかっていた。

㊂ 最初【さいしょ】 (n, adv) beginning　　約束【やくそく】 (n, vs) arrangement
低給【ていきゅう】 (n) low salary ⇔ 高給 (n) high salary　　差額【さがく】 (n) the difference in amount; the balance
昇給する【しょうきゅうする】 (vs) to get a salary raise

㊃ [Adj-stem] がる (suf, v5r) to feel *Used to describe a third person's apparent emotion or feeling.　　必要【ひつよう】 (n) necessity, need

㊄ いやなものはいや (exp) dislike *I dislike things which I dislike; What stinks, stinks.

㊅ 論理的に【ろんりてきに】 (adv) logically　　やりこめる (v1, vt) to talk down; to corner someone in an argument
引き下がる【ひきさがる】 (v5r, vi) to withdraw; to leave

㊆ 好き嫌い【すききらい】 (n) likes and dislikes; taste * 人間は好き嫌いで動くものだ People are moved by their emotion, but not so much by logic and reason.
論法【ろんぽう】 (n) logic; reasoning
頭上【ずじょう】 (n) overhead; high in sky　　天の川【あまのがわ】 (n) Milky Way
一筋【ひとすじ】 (n) one long straight object (e.g., beam of light)
かかる (v5r, vi) to hang * 頭上に天の川が一筋かかっていた。 The single straight line of the Milky Way hung high in the sky. Here Botchan is able to see beyond the pettiness of his situation for the first time.

130

原文に挑戦しましょう

ウェブの練習問題（186ページ参照）をしてから、チャレンジしてみましょう。次の場面は、第8章のマンガのどのコマかわかりますか。引用文の後の質問に答えましょう。

原文❶

赤シャツに勧められて釣に行った帰りから、山嵐を疑ぐり出した。無い事を種に下宿を出ろと言われた時は、いよいよ不埒な奴だと思った。ところが会議の席では案に相違して滔々と生徒厳罰論を述べたから、おや変だなと首を捻った。萩野の婆さんから、山嵐が、うちなり君のために赤シャツと談判をしたと聞いた時は、それは感心だと手を拍った。この様子ではわる者は山嵐じゃあるまい、赤シャツの方が曲ってるんで、好加減な邪推を実しやかに、しかも遠廻しに、おれの頭の中へ浸み込ましたのではあるまいかと迷ってる矢先へ、野芹川の土手で、マドンナを連れて散歩なんかしている姿を見たから、それ以来赤シャツは曲者だと極めてしまった。曲者だか何だかよくは分らないが、ともかくも善い男じゃない。表と裏は違った男だ。人間は竹のように真直でなくっちゃ頼もしくない。

【原文❶の質問】

原文を読んで、坊っちゃんの赤シャツと山嵐に対する考え・気持ちをまとめましょう。（例）この章で、坊っちゃんは赤シャツのことを［…］だと思い始めた。なぜかというと、［…］からだ。その反面、山嵐のことを［…］

原文❷

議論のいい人が善人とはきまらない。遣り込められる方が悪人とは限らない。表向きは赤シャツの方が重々もっともだが、表向きがいくら立派だって、腹の中で惚れさせる訳には行かない。金や威力や理屈で人間の心が買える者なら、高利貸でも巡査でも大学教授でも一番人に好かれなくてはならない。中学の教頭ぐらいな論法でおれの心がどう動くものか。人間は好き嫌いで働くものだ。論法で働くものじゃない。

【原文❷の質問】

坊っちゃんは、高利貸し、巡査、大学教授はどんな人たちだと言っていますか。人間の心を動かすものは何だといっていますか。

第9章を読む前に

うらなり

私は英語を教えている古賀と申します。
本日は私のために盛大な送別会を開いていただくことになりました。
私は地元の人間なのでここにいたいですが、やはり無理なようです。
私がしっかりしていないので、暮らし向きが悪くなってしまいました。
これから、母のことをどうしたらいいのか。
もう、遠山のおじょうさんともお別れです……。

盛大な送別会　grand farewell party　　無理　impossible　　しっかりしている　to be strong; to be stable

第9章 ❖ さらばうらなり君
Farewell to Uranari

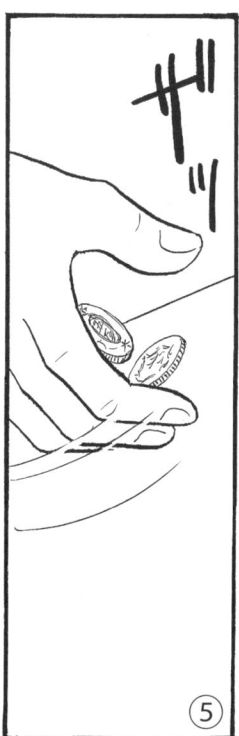

①君には大変失敬した！

②あとから聞いたが、いか銀は偽物の骨董を売りつける悪い奴らしい。
君が骨董を買わないから、乱暴を働くなどと作り話をしたんだ。

③いか銀がそんな奴とは知らず、奴の言葉を信じて、君に下宿を出ろなどと言って
どうか勘弁したまえ！

⑥君におごられるのは嫌だと思ったが、やっぱりおごってもらった方がいいようだ。

---

① 大変 失敬した【たいへんしっけいした】 (exp) I owe you a big apology! (Lit. I was extremely rude to you)
② あとから (adv) afterward
  偽物【にせもの】 (n) imitation; faked antiques
  売りつける【うりつける】 (v1, vt) to palm off; to force a sale * 売ります [V (ます stem form)] ＋つける (to attach; to load) => 売りつける
  乱暴を働く【らんぼうをはたらく】 (exp, v5k) to commit an act of violence
  作り話【つくりばなし】 (n) made-up story * 作ります [V (ます stem form)] ＋話す => 作り話
③ 勘弁する【かんべんする】 (vs) to pardon; to forgive * どうか勘弁したまえ！ Can you find it in your heart to forgive me?
⑤ ザッ (onoma) sound made when knocking or swiping things (e.g., coins) off a table with one's hand.
⑥ おごる (v5r, vt) to treat (someone) ; to pay for someone * 〜におごられる to be treated (by Yama-Arashi) (passive form)

⑦ もっと早く受け取ればいいのに、君はよほど負け惜しみの強い奴だ。

⑧ 君はよほど強情っぱりだ。

⑨ うらなり君の送別会に行く前に、俺は山嵐を下宿に呼んだ。

⑩ ふふん なるほど——

⑪ 赤シャツは君を数学主任にして、俺を免職にする考えだな。
もちろん俺は断ったぜ。
さすが江戸っ子だ。

⑫ うらなり君の転任は、赤シャツがマドンナを手に入れるためなんだろうね?
そうに違いない。

⑦ 受け取る【うけとる】 (v5r, vt) to take; to get; to accept * もっと早く受け取ればいいのに You should have taken (the money) sooner.
よほど (adv) very; really * よほど denotes that something is of a much higher degree or greater extent than was expected or is usually considered possible.
負け惜しみが強い【まけおしみがつよい】 (exp) sore loser; unwilling to admit defeat 負けます [V (ます stem form)] (to lose) + 惜しむ (to regret) => 負け惜しみ
強情っぱり(な)【ごうじょうっぱり】 (adj-na, n) obstinate; stubborn 強情 (stubborn) + 張る (to insist) => 強情っぱり
⑨ 送別会【そうべつかい】 (n) farewell party
⑪ 免職【めんしょく】 (n, vs) dismissal; discharge   考え【かんがえ】 (n) thinking; ideas; intention
断る【ことわる】 (v5r,vt) to refuse; to reject
さすが江戸っ子 (exp) By using さすが, the speaker (Yama-Arashi) expresses his admiration for Botchan because Botchan's action measures up to or is worthy of the reputation of an Edokko, who is believed to have high moral convictions.
⑫ 手に入れる【てにいれる】 (v1, vt) to obtain   [V (plain form)] ため (n) purpose; objective

⑬ うらなり君も人がいいから、赤シャツの弁舌にごまかされてしまったのだ。

⑭ あんな奴は痛い目にあわせないとだめだ。 どうだ？送別会の後、赤シャツと野だいこを殴ってやらないか？

⑮ いや……今夜はよしておこう。 ピキピキ

⑯ あいつらが悪いという証拠をつかんで殴らないとこっちが悪者になる。 …それもそうだ。

⑰ じゃあ、俺は演説をしてうらなり君をほめてやれ。肝心な所で言葉がつまるから君にゆずる。

⑱ それは困った病気だな。 何、そんなに困りゃしないさ。

⑬ **人がいい**【ひとがいい】(exp, adj-i) generous; having a good personality　　**弁舌**【べんぜつ】(n) eloquence; speech
　ごまかす　(v5s, vt) to deceive; to falsify　*（〜に）ごまかされてしまったのだ (I was) completely deceived by 〜
⑭ **痛い目にあわす**【いたいめにあわす】(exp) to make a person sweat　　**殴る**【なぐる】(v5r, vt) to strike; to hit
⑮ **ピキピキ**　(onoma) muscles flexing; muscle vein popping
　よす　(v5s, vt) to cease; to give up　* よしとこう (same as よしておこう) we should not do it (after considering the consequence of the action).
⑯ **証拠**【しょうこ】(n) evidence; proof　　**つかむ**　(v5m, vt) to seize; to catch　　**それもそうだ**　(exp) It may be so
⑰ **演説**【えんぜつ】(n, vs) speech; address　　**肝心(な)**【かんじん】(adj-na) crucial; essential
　つまる　(v5r, vi) to be choked; to be blocked　*言葉がつまる I get all tongue-tied.　　**ゆずる**　(v5r, vt) to turn over; to hand over（〜を、〜に）
⑱ **[V (ます base form)] はしない**　(exp) express a strong negative intention.　* そんなに困りゃしないさ（＝困りはしない）It's not that much of a problem.　　**〜さ**　(prt) (sentence end, mainly male) indicates assertion.

⑲ 送別会 ——料亭にて

花菱亭

⑳ 送別会の挨拶で、皆うらなり君をほめたたえた。

え〜 これより古賀君の……

㉑ 狸は彼が学校を去るのは大変惜しいが、本人が転任を希望したので仕方ないと嘘を述べた。

㉒ えー 古賀君のような良友を失うのは学校だけでなく、

㉓ 私個人としても大いに不幸であります。

良友?

㉔ 赤シャツだけに真っ赤なウソか!

このやさしい口調にマドンナもだまされたのだろう。

---

⑲ 料亭【りょうてい】 (n) (Japanese-style) restaurant　　〜にて (prt) indicates location of action (formal literary form of で)
⑳ 挨拶【あいさつ】 (n) speech; greeting
　ほめたたえる (v1, vt) to praise; to admire ほめます [V (ます stem form)] (to praise) ＋ たたえる (to give high praise to 〜)
㉑ 去る【さる】 (v5r, vi) to leave; to go away (place of departure を)
　惜しい【おしい】 (adj-i) regrettable; disappointing
　仕方ない【しかたない】 (exp, adj-i) it cannot be helped; there is nothing to do but　　嘘【うそ】 (n) lie
㉒ 良友【りょうゆう】 (n) good friend　　失う【うしなう】 (v5u, vt) to lose; to part with　　〜だけでなく (exp) not just 〜 (but also 〜)
㉓ 個人【こじん】 (n) individual * 私個人としても for me　　大いに【おおいに】 (adv) very; much; greatly
　不幸(な)【ふこう】 (adj-na, n) unhappiness; misfortune
㉔ 真っ赤(な)【まっか】 (adj-na) bright red * 真っ赤な嘘 a downright lie 赤シャツだけに真っ赤なウソか! (I) thought just his shirts were red, but now he's telling a big fat "red" lie.　　口調【くちょう】 (n) tone of voice; (verbal) expression
　だます (v5s, vt) to trick; to cheat * マドンナもだまされたのだろう Madonna was probably deceived, too.

㉕ スクッ

㉖ よっ 待ってました！
パチパチ

㉗

㉘ ただ今校長をはじめ、ことに教頭は、古賀君の転任を残念がられていましたが、私は少々反対です。

㉙ 延岡はへき地で不便はあるでしょうが、人柄は大変純朴誠実であると聞いています。

心にもない世辞を言ったり、

㉖ よっ（＝よう）　(int) hello; hey; yes ＊ よっ待ってました！ Yes! This is what I've been waiting for.
　パチパチ　(onoma) clapping; sound of applause
㉘ 〜をはじめ　(exp) starting with 〜　　ことに　(adv) especially; particularly
　[Adj-stem] がる　(see 第8章コマ㉔) *Here, Yama-Arashi is using an honorific expression (towards Tanuki and Red Shirt who expressed their regrets) using a passive form of 残念がる.
㉙ へき地【へきち】　(n) remote place; backwoods　　不便（な）【ふべん】　(adj-na, n) inconvenient; inconvenience
　人柄【ひとがら】　(n) personality; character　　純朴（な）【じゅんぼく】　(adj-na, n) rustic simplicity; honest
　誠実（な）【せいじつ】　(adj-na, n) sincere　　心にもない【こころにもない】　(exp) (something) one does not really mean; insincere
　世辞【せじ】　(n) flattery; compliment

㉛ 美しい顔をして君子をおとしいれたりするハイカラ野郎は、一人もいないと信じております。

㉚ 古賀君のような温厚な紳士は、きっとその地方の歓迎を受けるに違いありません。

㉝ 最後になりましたが、私は一日も早く古賀君が君子に、ふさわしい淑女と円満な家庭を作られることを願います。

㉞ エヘン！エヘン！ 以上！

㉟ よっ 名演説！

㊱ と…

㉚ おとしいれる (v1, vt) to hatch a plan and deceive someone
　ハイカラ（な）(adj-na, n) refers to people dressed in a western style; it derives from the English word, "high-collar." * ハイカラ野郎 means a fellow dressed in the latest western fashion (i.e., Red Shirt).
㉜ 地方【ちほう】(n) area; countryside　　歓迎【かんげい】(n) welcome; reception
㉝ 最後【さいご】(n) end; conclusion * 最後になりましたが In conclusion
　一日も早く【いちにちもはやく】(exp) lose no time (in) doing　　ふさわしい (adj-i) suitable; appropriate
　淑女【しゅくじょ】(n) lady　　円満（な）【えんまん】(adj-na, n) perfect; harmonious; peaceful * 〜にふさわしい淑女と円満な家庭を作る to make a happy home with a suitable lady (unlike Madonna)
　願う【ねがう】(v5u, vt) to desire; to wish
㉞ 以上 (adv) this is all; the end　　エヘン (int) ahem; attention-drawing cough
㉟ 名演説【めいえんぜつ】(n) great speech; fine speech
㊱ （おっ）と (int) uh-oh; oops; sorry

�37 この度は私のために このような盛大な 送別会をお開きくださり

�38 その上、皆様からの送別のお言葉をいただき、誠にありがたく思います。

�39 うらなり君はどこまで人がいいのかわからない。

�40 どうやら自分がこんなにバカにされてる校長や教頭に

�41 心から感謝しているようだ。

�42 お今晩は〜〜

�37 この度【このたび】 (n) this occasion; at this time　　盛大（な）【せいだい】 (adj-na, n) grand; magnificent
開く【ひらく】 (v5k, vt) to hold * お開きくださり humble expression　　私のために (exp) on my behalf
�38 その上【そのうえ】 (conj) in addition; on top of (that)　　誠に【まことに】 (adv) indeed; really
ありがたい (adj-i) grateful; thankful
�39 [WH+ か] わからない （see 第7章コマ㊷）* どこまで人がいいのかわからない I don't understand how Uranari can be so kind-hearted.
ow or other *Used together with expressions such as 〜よう（だ）／〜らしい．
�40 どうやら (adv) it seems like; somehow or other *Used together with expressions such as 〜よう（だ）／〜らしい．
�41 感謝する【かんしゃする】 (vs) thanks; gratitude * 心から感謝しているらしい It seems that he is giving thanks (to the principal and vice
principal) from the bottom of his heart.
�42 お今晩は【おこんばんは】 (exp) (arch) (dialect) a polite way to say good evening. Here, geisha use the greeting when entering the room. It is
not a commonly used expression.

㊸ 芸者が来て酒が回り始めると急ににぎやかになった。

㊹ (panel)

㊺ (panel)

㊻ (panel)

㊼ 狸はいつの間にかいなくなって

赤シャツも出て行った。

㊽ (panel)

㊸ **回る【まわる】** (v5r, vi) pass around; go around ＊酒が回る the sake has taken effect. ＊芸者が来て酒が回り始めると When the geisha came and sake began to be passed around and people became drunk...
急に【きゅうに】 (adv) suddenly
㊼ **いつの間にか【いつのまにか】** (adv) before one knows; before one becomes aware of

(49)
(50)
この送別会は、うらなり君の転任を惜しむためじゃない。
(51)
皆が酒を飲んでバカ騒ぎをするためだ。
(52)
こんな送別会なら開いてもらわない方がよっぽどマシだ。
(53)

(49) **惜しむ【おしむ】** (v5m, vt) to regret (e.g., a loss); to feel sorry (for) ＊惜しむためじゃない (This farewell party) is not for showing regret for/at ～

(52) **バカ騒ぎ【ばかさわぎ】** (vs) to get drunk and horse around

(53) **マシ／まし（な）** (adj-na) better; preferable

Panel 54
あんた何か唄いなはれ。

Panel 55
いや俺は唄わない。

Panel 56
鈴ちゃーん。

Panel 57
せっかく会いたい人に会ったのに、すぐ帰っちゃってお気の毒でげすね。

Panel 58
知りまへん。
プイ

Panel 59
僕、踊るから何かひいてちょうだい。

Panel 60
俺はうらなり君が気の毒でたまらなかった。
スコン

⑤⑤ あんた (pn, fam) you (familiar form of あなた)   何か【なんか／なにか】 (exp) something
唄う【うたう】 (v5u,vt) to sing traditional Japanese songs such as *nagauta* (long epic song) and *kouta* (Japanese ballad) accompanied on the *shamisen* (three-stringed Japanese guitar).   【V (ます stem form)】なはる (aux)(pol)(dialect) to do * 唄いなはれ is a command form, but it is more tentative, something like お唄いになったら.

⑤⑥ 鈴【すず】 (n) Suzu, given name
〜ちゃん (suf, fam) an endearing way to refer to usually females of equal or lower social position. *Nodaiko calls her 鈴ちゃーん Suzu-chan, which indicates that Nodaiko is familiar with this person. Typically used to address children when calling them by their given names. Also used like お嬢ちゃん (*ojōchan*, polite, used for other people's daughters) and お坊っちゃん (*obotchan*, polite, used for other people's sons).

⑤⑦ せっかく (adv) with trouble; at great pains; long-awaited   すぐ (adv) immediately

⑤⑧ 知りまへん【しりまへん】 (dialect) 知りません *I don't know what you're talking about.
プイ (onoma) movement of looking away

⑤⑨ 【V (て form)】ちょうだい (aux) (fam) (fem) please do 〜 for me *Nodaiko talks like a woman when he is drunk.

⑥⓪ スコン (onoma) clunk   たまらない (see 第7章 コマ ⑥④)

古賀さん、もう帰りましょう。
いえ。
今日は私の送別会ですから、先に帰るのは失礼です。
どうぞご遠慮なく。
何、かまうもんですか。
こんなの送別会じゃないです。
行きましょう。
主役が先に帰るとはひどい。
帰しませんぞ。

61 **もう** (adv, int) used to show emotional overtone (often exasperation)

62 **先に【さきに】** (adv) before; earlier than

失礼(な)【しつれい】 (adj-na, n) impolite; rude

63 **遠慮【えんりょ】** (n, vs) diffidence; thoughtfulness ＊どうぞご遠慮なく Please don't worry about me.

64 **かまう** (v5u) to mind; to be concerned about ＊かまうもんですか You don't have to worry about the others.

67 **主役【しゅやく】** (n) leading part

ひどい (adj-i) awful; severe

〜ぞ (prt) (male) (sentence end) adds force/assertion; may indicate a command ＊帰しませんぞ You're not leaving!

⑱ どく (v5k, vi) to step aside * どけ Step aside!
⑲ 酔っ払い【よっぱらい】 (n) drunkard; someone who is drunk　　ポカ (onoma) Pow! Impact of hitting with one's fist.
㉑ ぶつ (v5t, vt) to hit (a person); to strike * おぶちになる This is a polite expression, but it is the way Nodaiko usually talks and does not mean that he respects the act of being hit.
いよいよ (adv) at last; finally
日清戦争【にっしんせんそう】 (n) First Sino-Japanese War (1894-1895) * いよいよ日清戦争だ Alright then, Sino-Japanese War time!
㉓ 何やら【なにやら】 (adv) something; for some reason　　わめく (v5k, vi) to shout; to cry out

原文に挑戦しましょう

ウェブの練習問題（186ページ参照）をしてから、チャレンジしてみましょう。次の場面は、第9章のマンガのどのコマかわかりますか。引用文の後の質問に答えましょう。

原文 ❶

「君は一体どこの産だ」「おれは江戸っ子だ」「うん、江戸っ子か、道理で負け惜しみが強いと思った」「きみはどこだ」「僕は会津だ」「会津っぽか、強情な訳だ。今日の送別会へ行くのかい」「行くとも、君は？」「おれは無論行くんだ。古賀さんが立つ時は、浜まで見送りに行こうと思ってるくらいだ」「送別会は面白いぜ、出て見たまえ。今日は大いに飲むつもりだ」「勝手に飲むがいい。おれは肴を食ったら、すぐ帰る。酒なんか飲む奴は馬鹿だ」「君はすぐ喧嘩を吹き懸ける男だ。なるほど江戸っ子の軽佻な風を、よく、あらわしてる」「何でもいい、送別会へ行く前にちょっとおれのうちへ寄り、話しがあるから」

【原文❶の質問】誰と誰の台詞かわかりますか。会津と江戸出身の人はどんな性格だと言われていますか。

原文 ❷

ところへお座敷はこちら？　と芸者が三、四人はいって来た。おれも少し驚ろいたが、壁際へ圧し付けられているんだから、じっとしてただ見ていた。すると今まで床柱へもたれて例の琥珀のパイプを自慢そうに啣えていた、赤シャツが急に起って、座敷を出にかかった。向うからはいって来た芸者の一人が、行き違いながら、笑って挨拶をした。その一人は一番若くて一番奇麗な奴だ。遠くで聞えなかったが、おや今晩はぐらい言ったらしい。赤シャツは知らん顔をして出て行ったぎり、顔を出さなかった。大方校長のあとを追懸けて帰ったんだろう。

【原文❷の質問】「おや今晩は」と言ったのは誰が誰に言いましたか。芸者が部屋に入って来た後の赤シャツの様子はどうでしたか。それはなぜだと思いますか。

第10章を読む前に

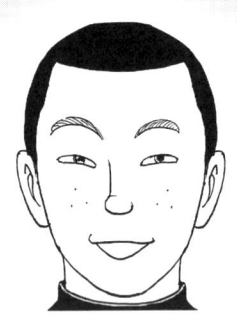

赤シャツの弟

僕は教頭の弟です。
日本は戦争に勝ったので、今日は祝勝会で、学校が休みです。
朝は式典で、午後は祝勝会の催しがありますが、
そこには僕たちと仲の良くない師範学校の生徒も来るでしょう。
けんかになるかもしれません。
ところで、僕は堀田先生を祝勝会の催しに誘いました。
どうしてかって？ とても珍しい踊りだし、それに……

戦争に勝つ　to win a war　　祝勝会　victory celebration　　催し　events
師範学校　normal school (= teachers' college)　　けんか　fight　　珍しい　rare

第10章 ❖ 祝勝会のわな
The Victory Celebration Trap

① 今日は祝勝会で学校は休みだ。

教師は八百人の生徒を引率して式典に行かなければならない。

だまって行進しろ！

静かに！

② 天ぷらが列を乱すな！

団子……

③ 列の中から絶えず俺の悪口が聞こえるが、誰だかわからない。

④ こんな卑劣な奴らを相手にしていると、俺も人間がダメになる。

⑤ やっぱり東京に帰って、新聞配達をしてでも、清と暮らした方がいい。

バンザーイ　バンザイ

祝勝会【しゅくしょうかい】 (n) victory celebration *There were two wars: the Sino-Japanese War in 1894-95 and the Russo-Japanese War in 1904-05. Soseki observed the victory celebration for the Sino-Japanese War in Shikoku, and he observed the victory celebration for the Russo-Japanese War during the writing of Botchan. This victory celebration was probably a combination of his experiences of these two historical events.　**わな** (n) trap; snare

① **静かに【しずかに】** (exp) be quiet　**だまる** (v5r, vi) to be silent
　行進する【こうしんする】 (vs) to march; to parade　**引率する【いんそつする】** (vs) to lead; to supervise (students)
　式典【しきてん】 (n) ceremony
② **列【れつ】** (n) line; row　**乱す【みだす】** (v5s, vt) to throw out of order; throw into disarray
③ **絶えず【たえず】** (adv) constantly; always　**悪口【わるぐち】** (n) abuse; insult
④ **卑劣（な）【ひれつ】** (adj-na) mean; cowardly　**相手にする【あいてにする】** (exp, vs) to deal with
　ダメになる (exp, v5r) to be spoiled; to be ruined
⑤ **新聞配達【しんぶんはいたつ】** (n) (newspaper) carrier　**〜でも** (prt) even 〜 ; even if 〜
　バンザイ (see 第3章 コマ㊳)

⑥ 式のあと、俺は下宿に帰って清への手紙を書くことにした。

⑦ 今度はもっと詳しく書いてくれと言ってたな……

⑧ 書くことはたくさんあるが、何から書いていいかわからない。

⑨ ……

⑩ コト

⑪ ゴロリ

⑫ こうやって遠くから清を思うだけで、俺の真心は清に通じるに違いない。

⑥ 式【しき】 (n, suf) ceremony
⑦ もっと (adv) more; even more　　詳しく【くわしく】 (adv) in detail; fully
⑧ [WH+か] わからない (see 第７章コマ㊷) (exp) don't know whether 〜 *何から書いていいかわからない I don't know where to start.
⑩ コト (onoma) clink *sound of putting something down softly
⑪ ゴロリ (onoma) rolling around
⑫ こうやって (conj) thus; in this way　　真心【まごころ】 (n) sincerity; devotion
　 通じる【つうじる】 (v1, vi) to make oneself understood; to lead to (〜に) *俺の真心は清に通じるに違いない I'm sure she understands my heartfelt sincerity.

⑬ みかんの木か……

あと三週間で食えるなあ……

⑭ よお

⑮ 今日は祝勝会だから、君とスキヤキでも食おうと思って、牛肉を買って来た。

⑯ グツ グツ

⑰ 君は赤シャツが芸者と関係を持ってることは知ってるか？

ああ。うらなり君の送別会に来た芸者の一人だろ？

そうだ。よくわかったな。

⑬ **みかん** (n) mandarin orange *Ehime Prefecture, the setting of this novel, is known for producing sweet mandarin oranges.
  あと (adv) remaining; further * あと三週間で in three more weeks...
⑮ **スキヤキ** (n) thin slices of beef, cooked with various vegetables in a table-top cast-iron pan, written as すきやき and すき焼 *すきやき became popular in Japan during the Meiji Period, when beef first became available to the general population.
  牛肉【ぎゅうにく】 (n) beef
⑯ **グツ** (onoma) boiling sound *It is used when something is boiling or being simmered.
⑰ **関係【かんけい】** (n) relation; connection * 芸者と関係を持つ to have a relationship with a geisha.
  〜な (prt) (sentence end) (mainly masc.) indicates emphasis. * よくわかったな I see you already figured that out.

⑱ 君には団子屋に行くのも非難するくせに、自分が裏で芸者と関係を持つとはけしからんやつだ。

⑲ それが精神的娯楽というなら、もっと堂々とやればいい。

⑳ なじみの芸者が入ってきたら、逃げるなんて男じゃないよ。奴は角屋という宿屋で、あの芸者に会っているそうだ。

㉑ あいつをやっつけるには、芸者と角屋に入る現場をおさえればいいんだよ。

寝ずの見張りでもするのかい？

㉒ ああ。

⑱ 〜も　(prt) about (emphasizing an upper limit); even 〜　＊ 〜に行くのも even going to 〜
　非難する【ひなんする】　(vs) to blame; to criticize
　〜くせに　(conj, prt) though; in spite of
⑲ 堂々と【どうどうと】　(adv) boldly; confidently
　ハフ　(onoma) blowing sound
⑳ なじみ　(n) intimacy; friendship ＊なじみの芸者 Botchan refers to the geisha in 第9章コマ㊽．
　角屋【かどや】　(n) name of a Japanese inn (where Red Shirt and the geisha meet)
㉑ 現場をおさえる【げんばをおさえる】　(exp, v1) to catch in the act (of)
㉒ 見張り【みはり】　(n) keeping watch ＊寝ずの見張り nightwatch; stakeout

㉓ 角屋の前にある宿屋の二階を借りて、二週間ばかり見ているのさ。きっとやってくる。

㉔ あんな奴を放っておくのは、日本のためにならないから、俺が天に代わって、罰してやる。

㉕ いいね。俺も加勢する。先生―

㉖ 生徒さんが堀田先生を訪ねておいでたぞなもし。お宅へ行って、お留守じゃけれここじゃろうて。

㉗ よくここにいるとわかったな。ペコリ

㉘ 祝 勝会の催しの珍しい踊りを見に来ませんか？

㉙ 赤シャツの弟が何で……？

㉓ 借りる【かりる】 (v1, vt) to rent　～さ (prt) (see 第9章コマ⑱)
　やってくる (vk) to come along; to come around
㉔ 放っておく【ほおっておく】 (exp, v5k) to leave alone; to ignore
　[Noun] のためになる (exp, v5r) to be of benefit for; to be useful for　* 日本のためにならないから because it is not good for Japan
　代わる【かわる】 (v5r, vi) to take the place of　* 天に代わって on behalf of heaven
㉕ 加勢する【かせいする】 (vs, n) assistance; reinforcements
㉖ 訪ねておいでたぞなもし (dialect) 訪ねていらっしゃいましたが
　お宅【おたく】 (n) (hon) your house　　留守【るす】 (n) absence; being away from home
　～じゃけれ、ここじゃろうて (dialect) ～なので、ここにいらっしゃるだろうと思って
㉗ ペコリ (onoma) action of quickly bowing or lowering one's head
㉘ 催し【もよおし】 (n) event; festivities　　珍しい【めずらしい】 (adj-i) unusual; rare

㉚ ドン　(onoma) boom, boom
㉛ 人出【ひとで】　(n) crowd; turnout　　舞台【ぶたい】　(n) stage (theater)
㉜ けんか　(n) quarrel; fight
㉝ 師範学校【しはんがっこう】　(n) normal school; teacher training school　*In the Meiji Period, a new educational system was established, with elementary schools, middle schools, high schools, normal schools, and an imperial university. Normal schools provided training for students to become teachers.　One type of middle school educated students for the imperial university and a second type educated entrepreneurs.
㉞ またか　(exp) again?　　*This suggests that the middle school students have fought before with the normal school students.

まったく！

世話のやける小僧たちだ。

やめろー

㉟ ガッ　　(onoma) thump; impact of geta stepping hard on the ground
㊱ 世話のやける【せわのやける】　(exp) to be annoying; to be troublesome
　小僧【こぞう】　(n) youngster
　やめる　(v1, vt) to end; to stop　やめろ (command form)

㊲ けんかはやめろ！

㊳ よせと言ってるんだ。

㊴ ガッ

㊵ ズガッ

㊶ ぐり

㊷ この野郎（やろう）どけっ！

㊳ よす　(v5s, vt) to cease; to give up　＊よせ (command form)
㊵ ズサッ　(onoma) sound of something heavy falling
㊶ ぐり　(onoma) grinding sound
㊷ 野郎【やろう】　(n) guy (vulg)　＊この野郎　this rascal
　　どく　(v5k, vi) to step aside; to move (i.e., out of the way)　＊どけっ (command form) Step aside!

154

㊸ 教師のくせに 教師は二人だ。やっつけろ。

㊹ ぶて！

石を投げろ

ぶて

㊺ ㊻ ㊼

㊽ 巡査だ！ 巡査が来た！逃げろ！

㊸ 投げる【なげる】 (v1,vt) (1) to throw; to cast away ＊投げろ (command form)
　　 ぶつ (v5t, vt) to hit (a person); to strike
㊹ やっつける (v1,vt) to beat; to attack (an enemy) ＊やっつけろ (command from)
㊽ 巡査【じゅんさ】 (n) police; policeman

㊾ コラーッ！

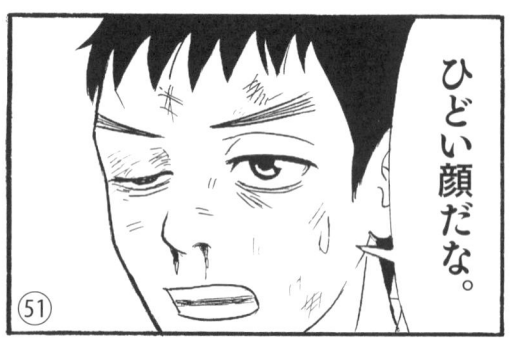

やめろーっ

いてて……大丈夫か？

㊿

㉛ ひどい顔だな。

㉜ 君こそ、だいぶ出血してるぜ。

㉝ 巡査は十五、六名来たが、生徒は逃げ足が早く、つかまったのは山嵐と俺だけだった——

㊾ コラーッ　(int) loud shouting (see 第１章 コマ⑮) *The small っ indicates strong feelings, astonishment, or loud shouting and is often followed by an exclamation mark（！）.
㉜ 〜こそ　(prt) for sure (to emphasize a preceding word)
　出血する【しゅっけつする】(vs) to bleed
㉝ 逃げ足【にげあし】(n) running away; escaping on foot * 逃げ足が早い to be quick at running away
　つかまる　(v5r, vi) to be caught; to be arrested

原文に挑戦しましょう

ウェブの練習問題（186ページ参照）をしてから、チャレンジしてみましょう。次の場面は、第10章のマンガのどのコマかわかりますか。引用文の後の質問に答えましょう。

原文❶

おれが蜜柑の事を考えているところへ、偶然山嵐が話しにやって来た。今日は祝勝会だから、君といっしょにご馳走を食おうと思って牛肉を買って来たと、竹の皮の包を袂から引きずり出して、座敷の真中へ抛り出した。おれは下宿で芋責め豆腐責めになってる上、蕎麦屋行き、団子屋行きを禁じられてる際だから、そいつは結構だと、すぐ婆さんから鍋と砂糖をかり込んで、煮方に取りかかった。

【原文❶の質問】なぜ山嵐は牛肉を買って来ましたか。どうして、坊っちゃんはその料理をうれしがっていますか。

原文❷

ひゅうと風を切って飛んで来た石が、いきなりおれの頬骨へ中ったなと思ったら、後ろからも、背中を棒でどやした奴がある。教師の癖に出ている、打て打てと言う声がする。教師は二人だ。大きい奴と、小さい奴だ。石を抛げろ。という声もする。おれは、なに生意気な事をぬかすな、田舎者の癖にと、いきなり、傍にいた師範生の頭を張りつけてやった。石がまたひゅうと来る。今度はおれの五分刈の頭を掠めて後ろの方へ飛んで行った。山嵐はどうなったか見えない。こうなっちゃ仕方がない。始めは喧嘩をとめにはいったんだが、どやされたり、石をなげられたりして、恐れ入って引き下がる*うんでれがんがあるものか。おれを誰だと思うんだ。身長は小さくっても喧嘩の本場で修行を積んだ兄さんだと無茶苦茶に張り飛ばしたり、張り飛ばされたりしていると、やがて巡査だ逃げろ巡査だ逃げろと言う声がした。

*うんでれがん（おろかもの）

【原文❷の質問】坊っちゃんがけんかに参加した理由を二つ述べてください。

第11章を読む前に

また私の策略はうまくいったね。
新聞社に手を回して記事を書いてもらったんですよ。
古賀君はもういない。
堀田君も乱闘事件で、ここを出ていかなければならない。
これで、邪魔者はいなくなったわけです。
坊っちゃん先生ですか。
あれは単純だから、学校にいても害はないでしょう。

僕の弟が堀田先生を祝勝会の催しものに誘いに行ったから、こんなことになってしまった。まったくけしからん新聞ですよ。
お二人は本当にお気の毒だ。

うそをついている赤シャツ | **戦略家の赤シャツ**

| 手を回す | use one's influence (to write an article) | 乱闘事件 | fighting incident |
| 邪魔者 | someone who is a nuisance or a burden | 害 | harm | けしからん | outrageous |

第11章 ❖ 天誅(てんちゅう)
Heaven's Punishment

① 何だと〜〜

② 中学の教師堀田某と近頃東京から赴任した生意気なる某が生徒をけしかけて……

③ 俺と山嵐が生徒のけんかを先導したって……!?

④ よくこんなデタラメを書いたな。
くしゃくしゃ

⑤ 新聞のウソツキめ！
こんちくしょう！

---

① 師範生【しはんせい】 (n) students at a teacher training school (normal school)　　乱闘【らんとう】 (n) brawling
　何だと【なんだと】 (int) What?!
② 某【ぼう・なにがし】 (suf, pref) one; a certain *堀田某（ほったぼう）means a certain Mr. Hotta. 某 can be also used as a prefix like 某堀田 and 某氏（Mr. So-and-so）.
　近頃【ちかごろ】 (adv, n) lately　　赴任する【ふにんする】 (vs) to arrive at [leave for] one's new post
　〜なる (suf) (arch) who is called *生意気なる某 means a certain impertinent someone. This expression is similar to 〜たる：教師たるもの, he who is a teacher, and 学生たるもの, he who is a student.
　けしかける (v1, vt) to instigate (a fight)
③ 先導する【せんどうする】 (vs) to lead (the way)
　〜って（＝〜と） (prt, informal) indicates a quotation.
④ デタラメ【な】 (adj-na, n) nonsense　　くしゃ (onoma) sound of crumpling a piece of paper
⑤ こんちくしょう (int) dammit *この＋ちくしょう => こんちくしょう

⑨ 名誉【めいよ】 (n) honor
　負傷【ふしょう】 (n, vs) injury; wound * 名誉のご負傷でげすか？ Are those wounds of honor? Nodaiko is being sarcastic about the wounds received from breaking up the fight.
⑩ よけい（な） (adj-na) unnecessary * よけいなこと言わずに without saying unnecessary things
　絵筆【えふで】 (n) paintbrush　　なめる (v1, vt) to lick
⑫ とんだ (adj-pn) unthinkable; terrible *Used as an intensifier.
　災難【さいなん】 (n) disaster

⑬ 僕の弟が堀田君を誘いに行ったから、こんなことになってしまった。

⑭ 記事については校長と相談して訂正の手続きをしておきましたから。

実に申しわけありません。

⑮ まったくけしからん新聞ですよ。

二人は実にお気の毒だ。

⑯

⑰

⑱ トテチテター

⑲ 気がついたか？

⑳ 赤シャツが俺たちをはめたんだ。

⑬ 誘う【さそう】　(v5u, vt) to invite
　　こんなことになる　(exp) to turn out be like this
⑭ 実に【じつに】　(adv) indeed; truly
　　相談する【そうだんする】　(vs) to consult （〜について、〜と・に）
　　訂正【ていせい】　(n, vs) correction; amendment
　　手続き【てつづき】　(n) procedure
⑲ 気がつく【きがつく】　(exp, v5k) to notice （〜に）
⑳ はめる　(v1, vt) to set someone up (i.e., frame someone for a crime)

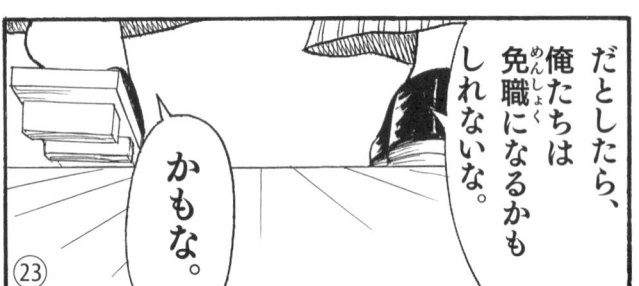

㉑ 弟を使って俺たちをケンカの中に誘い出し、巡査を呼んで新聞屋に手を回し、あんな記事を書かせたのさ。

㉒ 新聞屋まで赤シャツの味方か——

違いない！

㉓ だとしたら、俺たちは免職になるかもしれないな。

かもな。

㉔ 赤シャツの奴めどうやってやっつけたらいいんだ？

㉕ もう二、三日様子を見ていざとなったら、例の宿で芸者と会う現場をおさえるしかないな。

㉖ わかった。俺は策略はヘタだから、君に任せるよ。

㉑ 誘い出す【さそいだす】 (v5s, vt) to lure（〜を、〜に）
手を回す【てをまわす】 (exp, v5s) use one's influence（〜に） 記事【きじ】 (n) article; news article
㉓ （そう）だとしたら (exp) if it's the case 免職になる【めんしょくになる】 (exp, v5r) to be dismissed; to be fired
かもな (exp) maybe *（そう）かもな That may be the case.
㉔ どうやって (exp) in what way
㉕ 様子【ようす】 (n) situation; circumstances *もう二、三日様子を見て (I will wait and) see what happens for a couple more days.
いざとなったら (exp) if one has to; when the occasion demands it
例の [Noun]【れいの】 (see 第5章 コマ㊼)
現場をおさえる【げんばをおさえる】 (exp, v1) to catch in the act
〜しかない (see 第2章 コマ⑬)
㉖ 策略【さくりゃく】 (n) scheme
任せる【まかせる】 (v1, vt) to entrust (e.g., a task) to another（〜を、〜に）

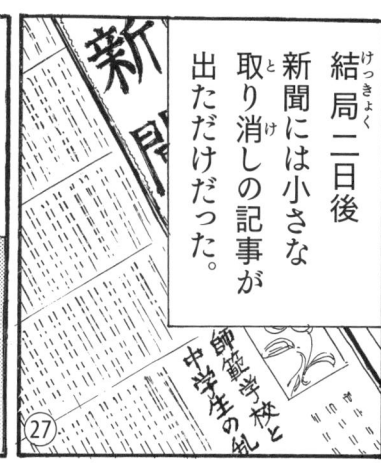

㉗ 結局二日後新聞には小さな取り消しの記事が出ただけだった。

㉘ それから三日後

㉙ 今日校長に辞表を出せと言われた。俺は言われなかったぜ。

㉚ もともと俺と赤シャツは相いれない人間なんだ。君は単純だから、いても害はないと思っているんだろう。失敬だ！

㉛ 俺だってあいつとは相いれないよ！まあ、二人共追い出したら、数学の授業ができなくなるからな。

㉜ 誰がその手にのるものか！バカにしやがって。

㉗ 結局【けっきょく】 (adv, n) in the end　　取り消し【とりけし】 (n) cancellation
㉙ 辞表【じひょう】 (n) letter of resignation
㉚ 相いれない【あいいれない】 (exp, adj-i) impossible to reconcile; incompatible
　　単純（な）【たんじゅん】 (adj-na, n) simple-minded　　害【がい】 (n) harm; evil influence
　　失敬（な）【しっけい】 (adj-na) rude　*Botchan got upset with Red Shirt and others, not with Yama-Arashi.
㉛ [Noun] だって (prt) also; even ～　　追い出す【おいだす】 (v5s, vt) to expel
㉜ 手にのる (exp, v5r) to be fooled by somebody's trick　* その手にのらない None of your tricks; you can't fool me with a trick like that.

㉝ 何で私に辞表を出せと言わないんですか？

㉞ へえ？

私と堀田はいっしょに祝勝会に出て、いっしょにけんかを止めに入ったんです。

㉟ 堀田には出せ、私には出さなくてもいいというのは、間違っているでしょう!?

㊱ それは学校の都合で——

㊲ 私一人だけが学校に留まるなんて、そんな不人情なことはできません。

㊳ しかし、一カ月もたたないうちに辞めたら、君の経歴に傷がつきますよ。

経歴より義理が大切です。

㊴ 君の言うことはごもっともだが、どうかもう一度考え直してください。

㉞ へえ　(onoma) huh
㊱ 都合【つごう】　(n) circumstances
㊲ 留まる【とどまる】　(v5r, vi) to remain
　　不人情（な）【ふにんじょう】　(adj-na, n) unkind; heartless　＊ 不 (negative prefix) ＋ 人情（emotion or compassion) A true Tokyoite is known to have a strong sense of moral ground such as *giri* (duty, obligation) and *ninjō* (feeling).
㊳ [V(ない form)] うちに　(exp) within; while　＊一カ月もたたないうちに辞めたら resign after (working) for less than a month
　　経歴【けいれき】　(n) career　　傷がつく【きずがつく】　(exp, v5k) to damage; to harm
　　義理【ぎり】　(n) sense of duty; social obligation
㊴ ごもっとも　(exp) You are quite right.
　　どうか　(adv) please; somehow or other　＊Used to express wholehearted wishes and present a stronger feeling of desire than どうぞ．
　　考え直す【かんがえなおす】　(v5s, vt) to reconsider　＊ 考えます [V (ます stem form)] (to think) ＋ 直す (to amend) => 考え直す

俺は狸がかわいそうになってひとまず学校に残ることにしたが、山嵐は学校を去った。

そして、赤シャツが芸者と会う現場をおさえるために、角屋の向かいの宿屋の二階に身をひそめた。

来る気配が全然ないな。

まだ三日目だ。

必ず来る！

その日は山嵐に代わって九時から十時半まで見張り、下宿に帰った。

---

⑩ かわいそう【な】 (adj-na) pitiful ＊かわいそうになる I felt sorry for Tanuki.
ひとまず (adv) for the present ＊It is implied that the action or condition will resume after a short time.
残る【のこる】 (v5r, vi) to remain（〜に）
去る【さる】 (v5r, vi) to leave (place of departure を)
向かい【むかい】 (n) across the street; the other side
身をひそめる【みをひそめる】 (exp, v1) to hide oneself ＊向かいの宿屋の二階に身をひそめた (Yama-Arashi) hid on the second floor of the inn across the street (from Kadoya).
㊹ 気配【けはい】 (n) indication; sign; hint
[Number] 目【〜め】 (n) ordinal number suffix (e.g., 三日目 the third day)
㊺ 必ず【かならず】 (adv) surely
㊻ 見張る【みはる】 (v5r, vt) to watch; to look out

㊼
そして五日が過ぎ……
もし来なかったらどうなる？
㊽
……
来るさ。
㊾
八日目
㊿
卵買って来た。
どうだ？
(51)
いい知らせだ。
(52)
七時半頃あの芸者が角屋に入った。
(53)
赤シャツはいっしょか？
いや芸者二人だ。
だが、あとから来るかもしれんだろ？

㊼ 過ぎる【すぎる】 (v1, vi) to pass by
㊿ どうだ (exp) How's it going? Botchan is asking for an update on the situation.
(51) 知らせ【しらせ】 (n) notice ＊いい知らせ good news

㊺ オイ、ランプを消せ。

㊋ 障子に、男が二人で頭を寄せて映っていては、あやしすぎる。

㊌ 見ろ、見ろ！

㊍ 大丈夫でげすね、邪魔者は追っ払ったから。強がるばかりで、策がないからね。

㊎ あのべらんめいの方は威勢のいい坊っちゃんで、かわいいもんですがね。増給がいやだの、辞表を出したいだの、どこか神経がおかしいに違いないよ。

㊏ まあ、待て。抑えろ！

㊐ まったくでげす。

㊺ 障子【しょうじ】 (n) shoji (paper sliding door)　　寄せる【よせる】 (v1, vt) to come near; to gather * 頭を寄せる put (our) heads close together　　映る【うつる】 (v5r, vi) to be reflected; to be projected

㊌ 邪魔者【じゃまもの】 (n) someone who is a nuisance or a burden
追っ払う・追い払う【おっぱらう・おいはらう】 (v5u, vt) to chase away; to drive away * 追います [V (ます stem form)] (follow) + 払う (pay)　　強がる【つよがる】 (v5r, vi) to bluff; to pretend to be tough　　策【さく】 (n) plan; strategy

㊎ べらんめい (n) (arch) moron; idiot *Nodaiko refers to Botchan as べらんめい because Botchan often uses べらんめい (a variation of べらぼうめ). (see 第3章コマ⑰)
威勢のいい【いせいのいい】 (exp) vigorous; full-blooded * あのべらんめいの方は 威勢のいい坊っちゃんで、かわいいもんですがね As for that young idiot, he is a vigorous, inexperienced "young master" and absolutely darling.

㊏ 〜だの、〜だの (suf, prt) and; or * 増給がいやだの辞表を出したいだの He refuses his salary increase, wants to submit his resignation, and the like.　　神経【しんけい】 (n) nerve; sensitivity　　おかしい (adj-i) strange; odd * 神経がおかしい crazy.
抑える【おさえる】 (v1, vt) to hold back one's anger; to restrain 抑えろ (command form) Calm down!

167

(61)
それから俺たちは、赤シャツが出てくるのをじっと待った。
(62)
これほど退屈で、大変な思いをしたのは初めてだった。
(63)
そして、とうとう朝の五時——
(64)
出て来たぞ。
升屋
角
(65)
(66)
(67)
待て！

(61) **じっと** (adv) fixedly (e.g., to stare); patiently
(62) **これほど** (adv) this much
退屈（な）【たいくつ】 (adj-na, n) tedium; boredom
大変な思いをする (exp, vs) to have a terrible experience
(63) **とうとう** (adv) finally; at last (after all that waiting)

⑥⑧ 教師のくせに、芸者と角屋に泊まるとは、何事だ!?

⑥⑨ 何か証拠でもあるんですか? 私は吉川君と泊まったんです。

⑦⓪ べらんめえの坊っちゃんとは何だ!?

⑦① いえ、君のことじゃないんです。

⑦② 俺の晩めしだ。食らえ！

⑦③ [ベシャッ]

⑦④ [ぐい] 理屈がたたないからって、乱暴するのは、ただの無法ですよ。

⑥⑧ [Noun] のくせに　(exp) in spite of ～
⑥⑨ 証拠【しょうこ】　(n) evidence; proof
⑦① [Noun] こと　(n) a matter of ～　* 君のこと the matter concerning you
⑦② 晩めし【ばんめし】　(n) (col) evening meal　*Same as 夕食, 夕ご飯, and 晩ご飯.
　　食らう【くらう】　(v5u, vt) (vulg) to eat　* 食らえ Eat it! / Have it!
⑦③ ベシャッ　(onoma) splat
⑦④ ぐい　(onoma) sound of grabbing and pulling hard
　　理屈【りくつ】　(n) logic
　　無法【むほう】　(n) outrageous, unlawful act

(75) **どりゃあ～** (int) hayaa *a loud yell; a war cry
(76) **乱暴者【らんぼうもの】** (n) roughneck; a thug
ズザッ (onoma) heavy thud
(77) **貴様【きさま】** (pn) (vulg) you *Historically formal, but by this time extremely hostile and rude.
くさる (v5r) to rot
こたえる (v1, vi) to take its toll; to have an effect on *殴らないとこたえないんだ (You) can't really be made to understand unless it's beaten into you.
(78) **天誅【てんちゅう】** (n) heaven's (well-deserved) punishment
(79) **ポカポカ** (onoma) pow, pow

参ったか?

参らないなら もっと殴ってやる。

参りました! 助けて…… ひぇ

いくらたくみな言葉で言い訳したって、正義は許さん!

俺たちは逃げも隠れもしない。

今夜五時までは港屋にいるから、文句があるなら、巡査でも何でも呼んで来い。

⑧⓪ 参る【まいる】 (v5r, vi) to give up [in] （〜に）
⑧① 助ける【たすける】 (v1, vt) to rescue　ひぇ (int) eep
⑧② いくら [V(て form)] も　(see 第1章 コマ②)
　たくみ（な）(adj-na, n) skillful; dexterous　言い訳【いいわけ】(n) excuse; explanation; defense　正義【せいぎ】(n) justice
⑧③ 逃げ隠れ【にげかくれ】(n) fleeing and hiding　* 逃げ隠れしない We won't run away or hide. / We have no intention of trying to escape from justice.
　港屋【みなとや】(n) Minatoya, the name of a Japanese inn　文句【もんく】(n) complaint
　何でも【なんでも】(exp) whatever one likes　* 巡査でも何でも 呼んで来い You can call the police or whatever (and come get us).

やったな。
ああ、やった。
俺は下宿を引き払い、辞表を郵便で送り、
ボーボー
その夜、六時の船に乗って四国を離れた。

(84) **やった** (see 第３章コマ (58))
(87) **引き払う【ひきはらう】** (v5u, vt) to vacate; to move out
ボー (onoma) echo of a large ship's air horn
(88) **離れる【はなれる】** (v1, vi) to leave; to go away (place of departure を)

⑨ 山嵐とは東京の新橋駅で別れ、それっきり会ってない。

⑩ …あれ、まあ、…坊っちゃん！

清のことを話すのを忘れていた。

⑪ 帰ったよ、清。

⑫ 早く帰って来てくださった……

⑬ もう田舎へは行かない。東京で清と暮らすんだ。

⑭ その後俺は人の紹介で市電の運転手になった。

⑮ 立派な玄関付きの家は借りられなかったが、清はとても満足そうだった。

⑧⑨ **新橋駅【しんばしえき】** (n) Shinbashi station located in Tokyo. Shimbashi is the original terminus of Japan's first stretch of railway, the Tokaido Main Line, and is one of Japan's oldest stations.
　別れる【わかれる】 (v1, vi) to bid farewell (〜と)
　それっきり (adv) (stronger version of それきり) since then
⑩ **あれ、まあ** (exp) oh my; my goodness; expression of surprise
⑭ **紹介【しょうかい】** (n) referral
　市電【しでん】 (n) municipal railway; city streetcar
　運転手【うんてんしゅ】 (n) driver
⑮ **[Noun] 付き【つき】** (suf) furnished with 〜 ＊立派な玄関付きの家 a home with a fine entryway
　満足（な）【まんぞく】 (adj-na, n) satisfied; satisfaction

(96)
だが、今年の二月
肺炎になった。
(97)
清は俺を
呼んで言った。
坊っちゃん……
(98)
お願いですから
私が死んだら、
坊っちゃんのお寺へ
埋めて下さい。
(99)
養源寺
(100)
だから、清の墓は
小日向の養源寺にある。
完

(96) **肺炎【はいえん】** (n) pneumonia

(98) **寺【てら】** (n) temple *Kiyo refers to a temple (i.e., Yōgenji) which, for generation after generation, has taken care of Botchan's family grave, performing commemorative ceremonies for the deceased.

埋める【うめる】 (v1, vt) to bury (e.g., in the graveyard)

(100) **小日向【こびなた】** (n) a place in Tokyo. *Kobinata is also pronounced as Kohinata (the administrative pronunciation), but the locals pronounce it Kobinata. Since the Edo period, the Natsume family had their family temple 本法寺（ほんぽうじ）in 小日向.

養源寺【ようげんじ】 (n) Yōgen temple. *Yōgenji does exist in Tokyo. It is not the Natsume's family temple, but Soseki's friend Yasusaburō Yoneyama (1869-1897) and his family were buried there. The name of his grandmother was Kiyo. It is said that Soseki used the name Kiyo in his novel out of respect for Yoneyama.

完【かん】 (n) The End

原文に挑戦しましょう

ウェブの練習問題（186ページ参照）をしてから、チャレンジしてみましょう。次の場面は、第11章のマンガのどのコマかわかりますか。引用文の後の質問に答えましょう。

原文 ❶

「ああやって喧嘩をさせておいて、すぐあとから新聞屋へ手を廻してあんな記事をかかせたんだ。実に奸物だ」

「新聞までも赤シャツか。そいつは驚いた。しかし新聞が赤シャツの言う事をそう容易く聴くかね」

「聴かなくって。新聞屋に友達がいりゃわけはないさ」

「友達がいるのかい」

「いなくってもわけはないさ。嘘をついて、事実これこれと話しゃ、すぐ書くさ」

「ひどいもんだな。本当に赤シャツの策なら、僕らはこの事件で免職になるかも知れないね」

「わるくすると、やられるかも知れない」

【原文 ❶ の質問】山嵐の台詞はどれですか。山嵐によると、赤シャツの「策（plot）」は何だと言っていますか。

原文 ❷

清の事を話すのを忘れていた。——おれが東京へ着いて下宿へも行かず、革鞄を提げたまま、清や帰ったよと飛び込んだら、あら坊っちゃん、よくまあ、早く帰って来て下さったと涙をぽたぽたと落した。おれもあまり嬉しかったから、もう田舎へは行かない、東京で清とうちを持つんだと言った。

その後ある人の周旋で*街鉄の技手になった。月給は二十五円で、家賃は六円だ。清は玄関付きの家でなくってもしごく満足の様子であったが気の毒な事に今年の二月肺炎に罹って死んでしまった。死ぬ前日おれを呼んで坊っちゃん後生だから坊っちゃんのお寺へ埋めて下さい。お墓のなかで坊っちゃんの来るのを楽しみに待っておりますと言った。だから清の墓は小日向の養源寺にある。

＊街鉄（東京市街鉄道株式会社の略）

【原文 ❷ の質問】坊っちゃんが東京に戻ってからの仕事や生活はどうなりましたか。簡単にまとめてください。

175

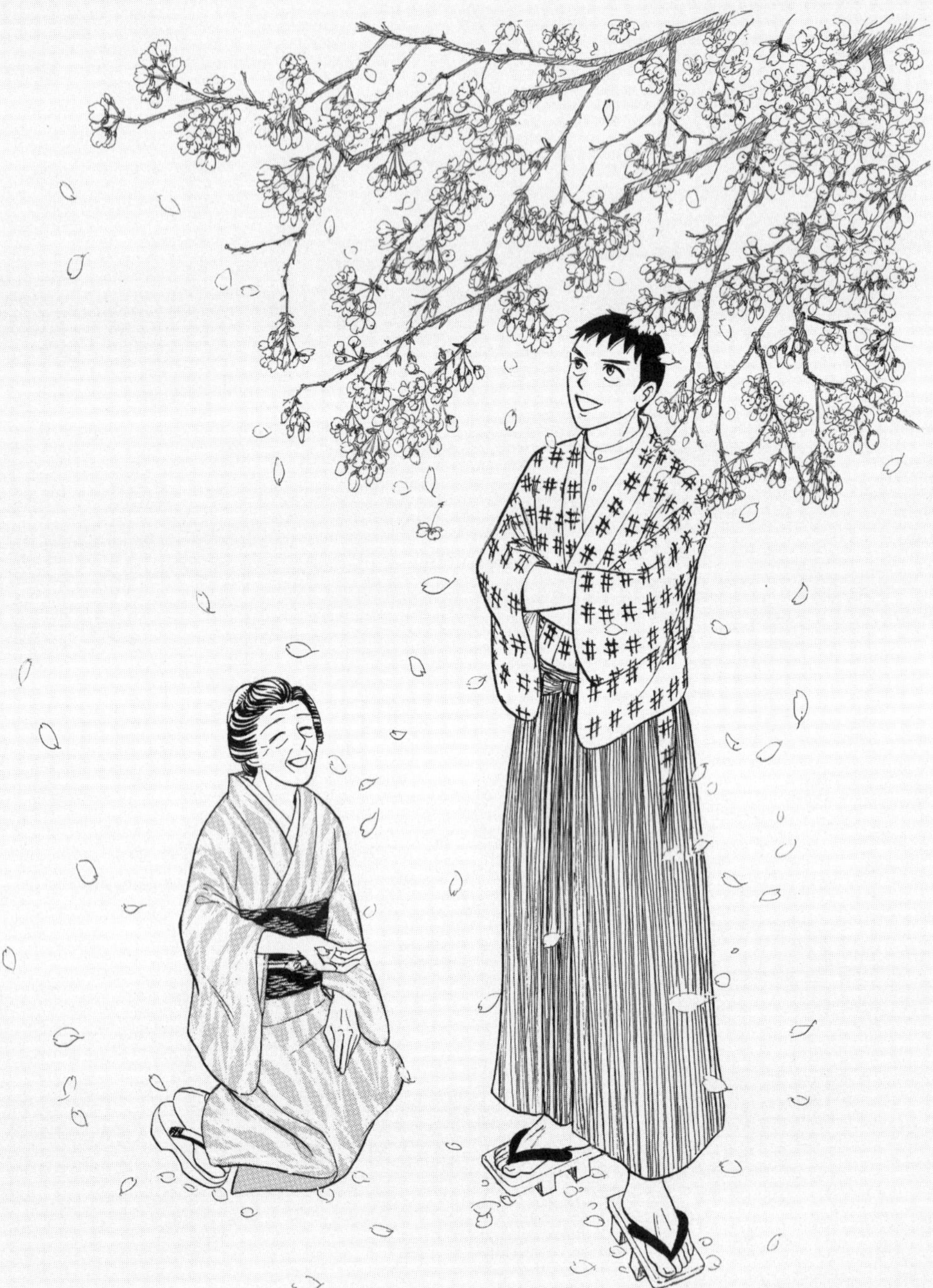

練習問題の構成
The Structure of the Exercises

マンガを読みましょう　Let's Read Manga

マンガは各章 10 ページから 16 ページで構成してあります。
Each chapter is composed of 10 to 16 pages of manga.

ことば・文化ノート　Language and Culture Notes

その章の大切なことば・文化について学習し、知識を深めます。
In this section, you will learn about important language and cultural elements that appear in the chapter.

読む前に　Before Reading

登場人物の一人がその章の簡単な紹介をします。マンガを読む前に質問に答えましょう。
One of the main characters briefly introduces each chapter. Before reading the manga, answer the questions.

理解しましょう　Let's Understand

時、場所、登場人物、出来事、原因、理由を整理してあらすじをつかみ、登場人物の気持ち・性格を理解し、主題を考える練習をします。
This section aims to help you grasp the storyline, the feelings and personal traits of the main characters, and the main points of the chapter by identifying elements such as when, where, who (main characters), what (events), and why (cause and reasons).

表現しましょう　Let's Express Ourselves

場面の様子や登場人物の気持ちや行動を描写し、自分の意見・考えを相手にわかるように表現する練習をします。
In this section, you will learn to describe the setting and the main characters (their feelings and actions) and then express your own opinions.

原文に挑戦しましょう　Be Challenged by the Original Text

原文の一部を読んで、質問に答えます。
After reading an extract of the original text, you will answer some questions based on the text.

ことば・文化ノート

登場人物の性格や気持ちのつかみ方
（とうじょうじんぶつ　せいかく）

```
          表情
          Facial
        Expressions
              ↓
発言・発話  →  登場人物   ←  行動・態度
Utterances    性格・気持ち    Actions・
              Character       Attitudes
              Traits
              Revealed
外見的特徴  →              ←  他者の評価
Physical                       Others' Views of
Appearance                     the Person
```

物語を読む時、登場人物の外見的特徴（がいけんてきとくちょう）をつかみ、言ったこと、顔の表情、行動・態度（ひょうじょう　こうどう　たいど）、そして他者（た）からの評価（ひょうか　かんさつ）を観察し、登場人物の性格や気持ちを理解（りかい）します。例えば、主人公の坊っちゃんが「何を言い、どんな表情をし、どんな行動・動作・態度をとったか」、それについて、「他の人はどう思ったか」を深（ふか）く読んでいくことで、登場人物の性格や気持ちをつかんでいきます。

How to understand the personality and feeling of the main characters.
When we read the story, we need to understand the personalities and feelings of the main characters by observing their distinctive physical features, utterances, facial expressions, actions and attitudes, and comments by others. For example, the readers understand Botchan's personality and feelings by observing what Botchan said, looked like, did, and what others thought of Botchan's speech and actions.

気持ちや様子を表す言葉

喜　よろこび Happiness	怒　いかり Anger	哀　かなしみ Sorrow	怖　おそれ Fear
うれしい 幸せ（な）（しあわ） 幸福（な）（こうふく） 楽しい ありがたい わくわくする 安心する	くやしい ばかばかしい 腹が立つ（はら） むかつく イライラする	かなしい　さびしい つらい　心苦しい かわいそう（な） 気の毒（な）（どく） 情けない みじめ（な） 孤独（な）（こどく）　むなしい 後悔する（こうかい）　くやむ	おそろしい こわい 不安（な） 心配（な）（する） おそれる とまどう ひやひやする あせる

179ページへ

178

気持ちや様子を表す言葉

驚　おどろき Suprise	恥　はじ Shame	愛　あい Love	嫌　にくしみ Hatred
あっけにとられる あきれる おどろく びっくりする まごつく	はずかしい てれる はじらう	いとしい かわいい 好き（な） 愛しむ（いと） 感謝する（かんしゃ） 好む（この）	憎い（にく） いや（な） きらい（な） うらむ うんざりする むかつく 嫉妬する（しっと）

❶ 178、179 ページ（上）の表は、気持ちや様子を表す表現です。意味を調べてみましょう。

The words listed above express feelings and appearances. Let's look into the meaning of these words.

例：うれしい！(I am happy!)　ちょっとイライラしている。(I am a little bit irritated.)　大変感謝します。(I really appreciate [something].)　好きでたまらない。(I cannot help loving.)　みじめな気持ちになった。(I started feeling miserable.)

❷ 感情・気持ちを間接的に表したり、推測したりする時に使う文末表現の例

Examples of sentence-final expressions to describe indirect statements or conjecture.

Pattern	Meaning	Usage
・い -adjective ・な -adjective ・Verb	Direct Statement	・うらなりはやさしい。Uranari is gentle. ・清は心配だ。Kiyo is worried. ・坊っちゃんはおどろく。Botchan will be surprised.
(plain)+ と思う	(I) feel; think	（私は）うらなりはやさしいと思う。I think that Uranari is gentle. （私は）清は心配だと思う。I think that Kiyo is worried. （私は）坊っちゃんはおどろくと思う。I feel that Botchan will be surprised. ＊思う is used for your thoughts and feelings. It is often used at the end of a sentence expressing conjecture, hope, opinion, or argument in order to make the statement softer.
(plain)+ と考える	(I) consider; think	（私は）うらなりはやさしいと考える。I consider Uranari to be gentle. （私は）清は心配だと考える。I think that Kiyo is worried. （私は）坊っちゃんはおどろくと考える。I think that Botchan will be surprised. ＊考える refers to the action of thinking, which is the intellectual and mental process of making judgments or forming logical ideas based on reason or sense.

(plain)+ そう（だ）	People say that~; I hear that~	うらなりはやさしいそうだ。I hear that Uranari is gentle. 清は心配だそうだ。I hear that Kiyo is worried. 坊っちゃんはおどろいたそうだ。People say that Botchan was surprised.
(stem)+ そう（だ）	It seems to be~; it seems that~; I guess that ~	うらなりはやさしそうだ。Uranari seems to be gentle. 清は心配そうだ。I guess that Kiyo will be worried. 坊っちゃんはおどろきそうだ。I guess that Botchan will be surprised. *そうだ is based on what the speaker sees or feels, and it is merely his or her guess.
(plain negative, drop い) + さそう（だ）	It does not seem to be~; it does not seem that~	うらなりはやさしくなさそうだ。Uranari does not seem to be gentle. 清は心配じゃなさそうだ。Kiyo does not seem to be worried. 坊っちゃんはおどろかなさそうだ。It does not seem that Botchan is surprised.
(plain)+ らしい * Drop な for な-adjective	It seems to be~; it seems that~	うらなりはやさしいらしい。From what I hear Uranari is gentle. 清は心配らしい。It seems that Kiyo is worried. 坊っちゃんはおどろいたらしい。From what I hear, Botchan was surprised. *らしい expresses judgment based on evidence, reason or trustworthy hearsay.
(plain)+ よう（だ） * Keep な for な-adjective	It seems/appears to be~; it seems/appears that~	うらなりはやさしいようだ。It appears that Uranari is gentle. 清は心配なようだ。It seems that Kiyo is worried. 坊っちゃんはおどろいたようだ。Botchan appears to have been surprised. *ようだ is usually based on what the speaker sees or saw, and involves the speaker's reasoning process based on firsthand, reliable information and his or her knowledge.
(plain)+ だろう * Drop な for な-adjective	(I) think; guess; wonder; hope; probably	うらなりはやさしいだろう。I guess that Uranari is gentle. 清は心配だろう。Kiyo is probably worried. 坊っちゃんはおどろくだろう。I think that Botchan will be surprised. *だろう (でしょう = a formal form of だろう) is used when guessing.
(plain)+ かなあ * Drop な for な-adjective	(I) wonder; hope; Could it be?	うらなりはやさしいかなあ。I wonder if Uranari is gentle. 清は心配かなあ。Could Kiyo be worried? 坊っちゃんはおどろくかなあ。I wonder if Botchan is surprised.
(plain or stem)+ に + ちがいない * Drop な for な-adjective	must be	うらなりはやさしいにちがいない。There's no doubt that Uranari is gentle. 清は心配にちがいない。Kiyo must be worried. 坊っちゃんはおどろくにちがいない。There's no doubt that Botchan is surprised.

❸ A. 今、あなたはどんな気持ちですか。

どんな時に喜 (happiness)、怒 (anger)、哀 (sorrow)、怖 (fear)、驚 (surprise)、恥 (shame)、愛 (love)、嫌 (hatred) の感情を持ちますか。3つの場面を考えて、その時の気持ちをリストの言葉を使って表現してみましょう。

例：玄関でペットが迎えてくれる時、とてもうれしくて、ありがたい気持ちになります。
(When my pet welcomes me at the entrance, I feel very happy and thankful.)

B. 同じ場面を使って、家族や友だちの気持ちを推測してみましょう。

第1章を読む前に

第1章を読む前に、下記の質問❶—❹に答えましょう。

❶ この物語は明治時代に書かれました。明治時代はいつですか。どんな時代でしたか。

❷ あなたの子供の頃を思い出してください。どんな子供でしたか。どんな性格だと言われましたか。

❸ 坊っちゃんの吹き出し(balloon)の台詞(lines)(p.14)を読みましょう。坊っちゃんについて書いてあることを箇条書き(list)にしてみましょう。

❹ 「無鉄砲」な人とは、どんなことをする人だと思いますか。あなたには無鉄砲なところがありますか。

理解しましょう

❶ **登場人物と場面を理解しましょう。**

A. 登場人物を書き出しましょう。『坊っちゃん』は1906年に書かれました。登場人物の服装、髪型は今と比べて、何が同じですか、何が違いますか。

B. 第1章は、坊っちゃんが (a. 小学校 b. 中学校 c. 高校) から (a. 東京 b. 四国 c. 箱根) に出発するまでの話です。

C. 門（コマ⑦）、玄関（コマ⑧）、茶の間（コマ㉑）、寝室（コマ㉖）、台所（コマ㉘）、縁側（コマ㊲）を見てください。坊っちゃんの家は、あなたが住んでいる所と比べて何が同じですか、そして、何が違いますか。

❷ **出来事が起こった順 (order) に下記 (the following) の文を並べてください。**

坊っちゃんが大学を卒業した／父が死んだ／坊っちゃんが人参畑で相撲をとった／清が甥の家に住んだ／母が死んだ／家が売られた／坊っちゃんが四国に出発した／坊っちゃんが学校の二階から飛び降りた

❸ **これは坊っちゃんの行動ですが、どのマンガのコマですか。**

坊っちゃんの「無鉄砲」な行動に○をつけて、どうしてそんな無鉄砲な行動をしたのか考えましょう。

( ) 学校の二階から飛び降りた　　( ) 畑で相撲をとった
( ) 台所で宙返りをした　　　　　( ) 授業中けんかした
( ) 四国へ行った

❹ **坊っちゃんと両親との関係 (relationship) について考えましょう。**

A. お父さんは坊っちゃんのことをどう思っていますか。

B. 坊っちゃんのお母さんは「行く先が心配です」（コマ㉔）と言いました。どうしてですか。

❺ **AからDの場面での登場人物の気持ちを表す言葉が右の欄 (column) に書いてあります。この中に一つだけ違う言葉が入っていますが、どれですか。**

A. 子供たちが学校で坊っちゃんをからかっている場面	登場人物の気持ち
	〈坊っちゃん〉 くやしい　イライラする はずかしい　腹がたつ ばかにされた　頭にきた

182

183ページへ

B. 坊っちゃんが宙返りしてお母さんを起こした場面	登場人物の気持ち
(manga panels: ㊱ お前のようなものの顔は見たくもない。 ㊲ 向こうへお行き！) * This scene focuses on a past event. Thus, the vocabulary words tend to be in the past form.	〈坊っちゃん〉 すまなかった　かなしかった こわかった　悪かった ごめんなさい 〈お母さん〉 あきれた　うれしかった なさけなかった　がっかりした うんざりした

C. 坊っちゃんが清にほめられている場面	登場人物の気持ち
(manga panels: ㊹ そういうところが、いいご気性だというんです！　㊸ 坊っちゃんがまっすぐでいいご気性だからです。　俺は世辞は嫌いだ！)	〈坊っちゃん〉 うれしい　うらやましい はずかしい　ありがたい 〈清〉 すき　かわいい　いとおしい にくらしい

D. 駅での別れの場面	登場人物の気持ち
(manga panels: ㋆① ㋆⓪)	〈坊っちゃん〉 しあわせ　かなしい さみしい　せつない　心配 もうしわけない　感情的 〈清〉 かなしい　残念　さみしい しかたがない　つらい イライラする　はずかしい なごりおしい

❻ こんな時どんな気持ちになりますか。
　できるだけたくさん言葉をリストしてみましょう。

A. テストで100点をとった時　　　B. 宿題を忘れた時
C. 先生に（または親に）怒られた時　D. 病気がなおった時
E. 恋人にふられた時　　　　　　　F. 家族や親友と別れなければならない時

表現しましょう

❶ 下の言葉を使いながら、坊っちゃんの性格について話し合ってみましょう。

無鉄砲　　まっすぐ　　ろくなもの　　えらい人　　気性

❷ 清の言葉、表情、行動・態度をまとめて、清の気持ちや性格、坊っちゃんとの関係を話し合いましょう。

清は、＿＿＿＿＿＿＿＿（だ）と思います。どうしてかというと、＿＿＿＿＿＿＿＿からです。

清という登場人物は、坊っちゃんのことを一番＿＿＿＿＿＿＿＿人だと言えるでしょう。

❸ クラスメートと好きな場面を選んで、演じてみましょう。

❹ あなたはどんな子供でしたか。坊っちゃんとあなたの子供の頃を比べて、「子供の時」という題（タイトル）で、作文を書いてみましょう。

例：「私も坊っちゃんのように無鉄砲な子供で、いつも親に心配をかけていました。今でも忘れられないのは、私が6歳の時のことです。……」

❺ あらすじをまとめて、話す練習をしましょう。

あらすじをつかむためには、「いつ、どこで、だれが、どうした」について考えます。

いつ（時）	日時、一日の時間帯（朝・昼・夜）、季節、時代、過去・現在・未来、時間の変化 The date and time, time period (morning・noon・night), seasons, historical periods, past・present・future, change in time
どこで（場所）	場所、様子・状況、風景、形・色、動き・音（オノマトペ） Place, appearance・circumstance, scenery, shape・color, movement・sounds (onomatopoeia)
だれが（登場人物）	「出来事」と「登場人物」のかかわりを考える。 Think of the relationship between events and main characters

185ページへ

どうした（出来事）	「だれ」が「どんな行動」をしたか、その「結果」はどうなったか。「出来事の変化」に注目する。 Examine who took what action and how that impacted the event. Pay attention to the change of events.

例：これから坊っちゃんの第1章のあらすじについて話します／発表します／報告します。

　第1章は、坊っちゃんの少年時代から、大学を卒業して四国へ行くまでの話が書いてあります。この話の主人公の坊っちゃんは、子供の時から無鉄砲でした。例えば……。坊っちゃんの両親はそんな坊っちゃんに愛想をつかしてしまいます。しかし、奉公人の清は坊っちゃんをとてもかわいがります。その後、両親は死に、家は売りに出されました。清は甥の家に移りましたが、清は坊っちゃんと一緒に暮らしたいと考えています。坊っちゃんは大学を卒業した後、四国で数学の先生になることになったので、清は悲しいです。最後の場面は、坊っちゃんと清が駅で別れるシーンです。

――振り向いたら

清はやっぱり立っていた。

なんだかたいへん小さく見えた。

原文に挑戦しましょう

◎最後のまとめとして、夏目漱石の原文を読んでみましょう。第1章の原文の引用文は、このテキストの(p.27)にあります。

問題集について

◎本書では、問題集は第1章しか掲載されていませんが、残りの第2章以降の問題集は、以下の「Learning Language Through Literature 英語圏版　マンガ『坊っちゃん』オンライン」で見ることができます。このサイトは学習を補助する教材と追加情報の提供をすることを目的としています。以下のURLアドレスにアクセスし、ID、パスワードを入力してログインして下さい。

URL：http://www.yumani.co.jp/Botchan-en

ID：yumani_soseki

パスワード：LLTL01

◎ This textbook contains only the Chapter 1 exercises. The rest of the exercises are located at "Learning Language Through Literature: Manga 'Botchan' Online (English edition)." This website is designed to provide supplementary learning materials and additional information. Please go to the following URL and enter the ID and password to access the website.

URL：http://www.yumani.co.jp/Botchan-en

ID：yumani_soseki

password：LLTL01

【著者　夏目漱石について】

1867年	夏目金之助、江戸（現在の新宿）に生まれる
1868年	明治時代が始まる（1912年まで）金之助は塩原家の養子になる
1874年	金之助（7歳）　小学校入学
1876年	金之助（9歳）　夏目家にもどる
1879年	金之助（12歳）　中学校（現・高校）に入学、二年後中退
1881年	金之助（14歳）　二松学舎に転校、漢文を勉強
1883年	金之助（16歳）　成立学舎に入学、英語を勉強
1884年	金之助（17歳）　大学予備門予科に入学
1888年	金之助（21歳）　第一高等中学校本科に入学、英語を勉強
1889年	漱石（22歳）　正岡子規に会い、「漱石」のペンネームをもらう
1890年	漱石（23歳）　帝国大学（現・東京大学）に入学、英語を勉強
1893年	漱石（26歳）　大学院に進む
1894〜1895年	日清戦争（First Sino-Japanese War）
1895年	漱石（28歳）　愛媛県松山中学校（現在の松山東高校）で英語を教える
1896年	漱石（29歳）　熊本県第五高等学校（現在の熊本大学）で英語を教える この年、中根鏡子と結婚
1900年	漱石（33歳）　英国留学　留学中、友人正岡子規が死ぬ
1902年	漱石（35歳）　英国留学より帰国
1903年	漱石（36歳）　第一高等学校、帝国大学で英語を教える
1904〜1905年	日露戦争（Russo-Japanese War）
1904年	漱石（37歳）　『吾輩は猫である』を発表
1906年	漱石（39歳）　『坊っちゃん』を発表
1907年	漱石（40歳）　第一高等学校、帝国大学をやめて、朝日新聞入社
1909年	漱石（42歳）　『三四郎』『それから』を発表
1910年	漱石（43歳）　『門』を発表
1912年	大正時代が始まる（1926年まで） 漱石（45歳）　『彼岸過迄』『行人』を発表
1914年	漱石（47歳）　『こころ』を発表
1915年	漱石（48歳）　『道草』を発表
1916年	漱石（49歳）　『明暗』を発表、死去

【参考文献】

広瀬正宜・庄治香久子（1995）『日本語学習使い分け辞典』講談社
出口汪　(2005)『夏目漱石が面白いほどわかる本』中経出版
夏目漱石　(2007)『坊っちゃん』 講談社青い鳥文庫
夏目漱石　(2003)『坊っちゃん』集英社文庫
牧野成一・筒井道雄（1989）『日本語基本文法辞典 [初級]』The Japan Times.
牧野成一・筒井道雄（1995）『日本語基本文法辞典 [中級篇]』The Japan Times.
東北大学附属図書館　夏目漱石ライブラリ http://www.library.tohoku.ac.jp/collect/soseki/soseki.html

語彙索引 【れ・レ】～【ん・ン】

よみ	漢字	品詞	英語	ページ
れつ	列	n	line; row	147

【ろ・ロ】

よみ	漢字	品詞	英語	ページ
ろうか		n	hallway	22
ろうふうふ	老夫婦	n	an old couple	102
ろくな		adj-pn	decent	18
ろこつに		adv	bluntly; plainly; outspokenly	122
ろんぽう	論法	n	logic; reasoning	130
ろんりてきに	論理的に	adv	logically	130

【わ・ワ】

よみ	漢字	品詞	英語	ページ
わーっ		int	Aahh; a crowd's excited roar	15
わあっ		int	wahaha; a crowd's excited roar	49
わーい		int	wow; whee-ee; a crowd's excited roar	45
[WH+か] わからない		exp	I don't know WH (question words)	107
わかれ	別れ	n	farewell	25
わかれる	別れる	v1, vi	to bid farewell (～と)	173
わけ	訳	n	reason	124
～わけ（だ）		n	conclusion from reasoning, judgment or calculation based on something read or heard	43
[V (plain form)] わけにはいかない		exp	impossible to do (although someone wants to)	58
わたしのために	私のために	exp	on my behalf	139
わな		n	trap; snare	147
わめく		v5k, vi	to shout; to cry out	144
わら		n	straw	18
わらう	笑う	v5u, vi	to laugh	50
わる		v5r, vt	to cut; to break	109
わるうなって	悪うなって	dialect	悪くなって	106
わるぐち	悪口	n	abuse; insult	147
わるもの	悪者	n	bad fellow; scoundrel	107

【ん・ン】

よみ	漢字	品詞	英語	ページ
～ん		aux	negative verb ending used in informal speech (abbr. of negative verb ending "ぬ・ない")	15
～んじゃろ		dialect	～でしょう	63

語彙索引　　【よ・ヨ】～【れ・レ】

よみ	漢字	品詞	英語	ページ
よく	欲	n	greed	64
よくあさ	翌朝	n	the next morning	68
よくじつ	翌日	n	next day	49
よけい（な）		adj-na	unnecessary	160
よこどりする	横取りする	vs	to snatch; to seize	107
よさん	予算	n	estimate; budget	125
よし		int	good; all right!; OK!	39
よしかわ	吉川	n	Yoshikawa, family name	36
よす		v5s, vt	to cease; to give up	76
よせる	寄せる	v1, vt	to come near; to gather	167
よっ		int	yah	19
よっ（＝よう）		int	hello; hey; yes	137
よっぱらい	酔っ払い	n	drunkard; someone who is drunk	144
よっぽど（＝よほど）		adv	very; quite	110
よなか	夜中	n	midnight	66
よのなか	世の中	n	the world; society	83
よびよせる	呼び寄せる	v1, vt	to invite; to have (Kiyo) come (to Shikoku)	121
よぶん	余分	adj-na, n	surplus; excess	125
よほど		adv	very; really	134
よみかき		n	reading and writing	109
よめ	嫁	n	wife; bride	106
よめにいく	嫁に行く	exp, v5k	to marry（〜に）	106
よる	寄る	v5r, vi	to visit; to drop by（〜に）	52
よろこばす	喜ばす	v5s, vt	to please; to satisfy	121
よろこぶ	喜ぶ	v5b, vi	to be delighted; to be glad; to be pleased	82
よろしくおねがいします	よろしくお願いします	exp, hon	please help me; please treat me well	39
よわみ	弱み	n	weakness	44
よわむし	弱虫	n	coward	15

【ら・ラ】				
[V (た form)] ら		conj	indicates supposition; when; if; after	26
らんとう	乱闘	n	brawling	159
らんぼう（な）	乱暴（な）	adj-na, n	violent; rough	18
らんぼうもの	乱暴者	n	roughneck; a thug	170
らんぼうをはたらく	乱暴を働く	exp, v5k	to act violently; to resort to violence	88

【り・リ】				
[Number] り	〜里	n, ctr	an old Japanese unit of distance, approx. 3.927km or 2.44 miles	29
りくつ	理屈	n	logic	169
りっぱ（な）	立派（な）	adj-na	fine; exemplary	33
りゆう	理由	n	reason	129
りょうてい	料亭	n	(Japanese-style) restaurant	136
りょうゆう	良友	n	good friend	136
[Number] りん	〜厘	n, ctr	old monetary unit (0.001 yen)	87

【る・ル】				
るす	留守	n	absence; being away from home	151

【れ・レ】				
れいの [Noun]	例の〜	adj-pn	the usual (culprit); as it always is; (the one) in question	80

語彙索引 【も・モ】〜【よ・ヨ】

よみ	漢字	品詞	英語	ページ
もんく	文句	n	complaint	171
〜もんだ・ものだ		exp	indicates one's wish when used with 〜たい and expresses some degree of shock and surprise when an unlikely event has taken place	36
もんだい	問題	n	problem; question	44

【や・ヤ】

よみ	漢字	品詞	英語	ページ
やーい		int	hey	15
やがて		adv	before long; soon; at length	76
[V (ます stem form or て form)] やがる		aux	indicates hatred, contempt, or disdain for another's action	63
やくそく	約束	n	arrangement	130
やさしいこえ	やさしい声	exp, n	soft voice	73
やさしげ（な）	優しげ（な）	adj-na	gentle; kind; sweet-looking	35
やちん	家賃	n	rent	121
やつ	奴	n, col	fellow	16
やっかい（な）		adj-na, n	trouble; burden	45
やっかいになる		exp, v5r	to be under [in] the care of somebody; to throw oneself on somebody's mercy	23
やった！		int	hooray (lit: I/we did it); yes!	51
やっつける		v1, vt	to beat; to finish off	61
やってくる		vk	to come along; to come around	151
やっと		adv	at last	29
やっぱり（＝やはり）		exp	as I thought; as expected	26
やどや	宿屋	n	(Japanese) inn	30
やどりょう・しゅくりょう	宿料	n	hotel charges	38
やまあらし	山嵐	n	nickname of the mathematics teacher	36
やましろや	山城屋	n	Yamashiroya, name of an inn (lit. mountain castle shop)	30
やめる		v1, vt	to end; to stop; to cease	50
やりこめる		v1, vt	to talk down; to corner someone in an argument	130
[V (て form)] やる		aux, col	to do something for (the sake of someone else)	35
やろう	野郎	n, vulg	rascal	96

【ゆ・ユ】

よみ	漢字	品詞	英語	ページ
ゆ	湯	n	hot spring; hot water	53
ゆうはん／ゆうめし	夕飯	n	evening meal	110
ゆうべ	夕べ	n	last night	120
ゆくさき	行く先	n	the future	18
ゆずる		v5r, vt	to turn over; to hand over	135
ゆだん	油断	n, vs	negligence; unpreparedness	83
ゆめ	夢	n	dream	66
ゆるす	許す	v5s, vt	to forgive	18

【よ・ヨ】

よみ	漢字	品詞	英語	ページ
よいいえので	よい家の出	exp	from a well-to-do family	22
〜よう（だ）		aux	seeming to be; appearing to be; appearing to be	79
ようげんじ	養源寺	n	Yôgen temple	174
ようじ	楊子	n	toothpick	25
ようじ	用事	n	errand; business (to take care of)	93
ようす	様子	n	situation; circumstances	162
〜のような [Noun]		exp	like 〜; [Noun] similar to 〜	20
〜ようなきがする	〜ような気がする	exp	to have a certain mood or feeling	112
[V (ない form)] ように		exp	in order not to (show my weakness)	44
[V (ば form)] よかった		exp	I wish I had done; I should have done	103

(49)

語彙索引 【む・ム】〜【も・モ】

よみ	漢字	品詞	英語	ページ
むすこ	息子	n	a son	125
むずむずする		onoma, vs	to itch; to feel strange	43
ムッ		onoma	annoyed; offended; same as ム〜	73
むてっぽう（な）	無鉄砲（な）	adj-na, n	reckless; rash (col)	19
むてっぽうもの	無鉄砲者	n	reckless person	33
むほう	無法	n	outrageous, unlawful act	169
むり（な）	無理（な）	adj-na, n	unreasonable; impossible	33
むろん		adv	of course; naturally	83

【め・メ】

よみ	漢字	品詞	英語	ページ
[Number] め	〜目	n	ordinal number suffix	165
め	芽	n	sprouts	18
めいえんぜつ	名演説	n	great speech; fine speech	138
めいじ	明治	n	Meiji period (1868-1912)	15
めいじいしん	明治維新	n	Meiji Restoration (1868)	22
めいひん	名品	n	fine product; masterpiece	54
めいよ	名誉	n	honor	160
めいれい	命令	n, vs	order; command; decree; directive	126
めいわくする	迷惑する	vs	to be troubled; be inconvenienced	91
めし	飯	n	(usually male) meals; food	58
めしあがる	召し上がる	v5r, vt, hon	to eat	21
めずらしい	珍しい	adj-i	unusual; rare	151
めをさます	目を覚ます	v5s, vt	to awaken	20
めんしょく	免職	n, vs	dismissal; discharge	134
めんしょくになる	免職になる	exp. v5r	to be dismissed; to be fired	162
めんどう（な）	面倒（な）	adj-na, n	bother (some) to do; tiresome	35

【も・モ】

よみ	漢字	品詞	英語	ページ
〜も		prt	as much as 〜	31
〜も		prt	about (emphasizing an upper limit); even 〜	150
[V (て form)] も		prt	even if 〜 ; even though 〜	45
[Counter] もない		exp	there is no 〜	77
[Noun1] も [Noun1] だが、[Noun2] も [Noun2] だ		exp	emphasis on the degree of an action; implies a sense of condemnation for both N1 and N2	106
もう		adv	already; now	25
もう		adv, int	used to show emotional overtone (often exasperation)	143
もういっぱい	もう一杯	exp	another bowl	48
もうすこししたら	もう少ししたら	exp	soon	122
もぐ		onoma	eating; munching sound	31
もちろん		adv	of course	119
もつ	持つ	v5t, vt	to possess; to have	24
もっていく	持っていく	exp, v5k	to take	31
もっと		adv	more; even more	148
もっとも（な）		adj-na, adv	quite right; plausible	124
もと	元	n	former; original	128
もとめる	求める	v1, vt	to seek; to pursue (pleasure)	98
もの		n	thing; a natural reaction	51
もはん	模範	n	role model; exemplar	32
もよおし	催し	n	event; festivities	151
[V (て form)] もらう		v5u, vt	to get someone to do something (to/for me or someone else)	18
〜もんか・ものか		exp	never do; how could 〜	45

語彙索引				【ま・マ】～【む・ム】
よみ	漢字	品詞	英語	ページ
まずい		adj-i	unskillful	109
マズイ・まずい		adj-i	unwise; not a good idea	59
ますます		adv	increasingly; more and more	22
～ませ		aux, pol	(used to make a polite request or demand) please	21
またか		exp	again?	152
まちがい		n	mistake	81
まちこがれる	待ちこがれる	v1, vt	to long for; to wait longingly for something or someone	104
まつ	松	n	pine tree	75
まっか（な）	真っ赤（な）	adj-na, n	bright red	136
まっすぐ（な）		adj-na, n	straightforward; honest; frank (in this particular context)	21
まったく		exp, int	good grief	18
まったく		adv	really; completely	34
マッチばこ	マッチ箱	n	matchbox	30
まっておいでたところ	待っておいでたところ	dialect	待っていらっしゃったところ	125
～まで		prt	until	44
[Noun] まで		prt	even; to the extent of ～	113
マドンナ		n	Madonna	76
マドンナさんがなもし		dialect	マドンナさんがですね	105
～まま		prt	condition; state; as is/was	125
まるで		adv	as if	79
まわる	回る	v5r, vi	to go around; to visit several places (～へ・に)	108
まんぞく（な）	満足（な）	adj-na, n	satisfied; satisfaction	173

【み・ミ】				
みえる	見える	v1, vi, hon	to come	125
みかた	味方	n, vs	friend; ally	107
みかたにする	味方にする	exp	gain [win] (a person) over to one's side (～を)	107
みかん		n	mandarin orange	149
[V (て form)] みせる		v1, vt	to show the action of ～	16
[Noun] みたい（な）		aux	- like; sort of ～	33
[Noun] みたい（に）		aux	- like; sort of ～; similar to ～	51
みだす	乱す	v5s, vt	to throw out of order; throw into disarray	147
みつける	見つける	v1, vt	to discover; to find	48
みておいでるのかもし	見ておいでるのかもし	dialect	見ていらっしゃるのですか	110
みてのとおり	見ての通り	exp	as you see; as you already know	36
みなとや	港屋	n	Minatoya, the name of a Japanese inn	171
みのがす	見逃す	v5s, vt	to overlook	96
みはり	見張り	n	keeping watch	150
みはる	見張る	v5r, vt	to watch; to look out	165
みょう（な）	妙（な）	adj-na	strange; unusual	46
みらい	未来	n	the future (usually distant)	94
[V (て form)] みると		exp	to see that ～; to find that ～	64
みをひそめる	身をひそめる	exp, v1	to hide oneself	165

【む・ム】				
ム～		onoma	grrr	49
むかい	向かい	n	across the street; the other side	165
むこう	向こう	n	over there	20
むこう	向こう	n	the other party (i.e., いか銀 and his wife)	91
むしのすかない	虫の好かない	exp	unpleasant; disagreeable	84

語彙索引　　　　　　　　　　　　　　　　　　　　　　　　　　　　　【へ・ヘ】～【ま・マ】

よみ	漢字	品詞	英　語	ページ
ヘタ（な）		adj-na, n	unskillful; poor (at fishing)	74
べつ	別	n	difference; distinction	107
べつに	別に	adv	not particularly; nothing	111
べっぴんさん		n	beautiful woman	105
へらぐちをきく	へらず口を利く	exp, v5k	to talk back	50
ペラペラペラ		onoma	fluent, non-stop talk	44
べらぼうめ		prt	refers to people "You fool" or an incident "It's absurd; it's rubbish"	45
べらんめい		n, arch	moron; idiot	167
へん（な）	変（な）	adj-na	strange; odd; weird	43
べんぜつ	弁舌	n	eloquence; speech	135

【ほ・ホ】

よみ	漢字	品詞	英　語	ページ
ほう	方	n	side; direction	24
ほう・なにがし	某	suf, pref	one; a certain	159
[V (た form)] ほうがいい	（～た）方がいい	exp	had better ～	104
ほうかご	放課後	n	after school	30
ほうこうにん	奉公人	n	maidservant	22
ホウッ		onoma	a suppressed sigh	16
ほうっておく	放っておく	exp, v5k	to leave alone; to ignore	151
ボー		onoma	echo of a large ship's air horn	172
ポカ		onoma	pow（impact of hitting with one's fist)	144
ほこり		n	dust	119
ほしい	欲しい	adj-i	want; wish for	106
ほそながい	細長い	adj-i	long and narrow	75
ポチャン		onoma	plopping; splashing sound（～と）	79
[Noun] ほど		prt	as; to the extent	93
ほど	程	n	degree; limit	67
ほとんど		adv	mostly; almost	109
ホホホホ		int	tee hee tee hee	73
ほめたたえる		v1, vt	to praise; to admire	136
ほめる		v1, vt	to praise	59
ポリポリ		onoma	sound of scratching lightly	70
ほんとう	本当	n	truth; reality	90
ほんにん	本人	n	the person oneself	64

【ま・マ】

よみ	漢字	品詞	英　語	ページ
ま（あ）		int	well	76
[V (plain form)] まい		aux	probably isn't (doesn't, won't, etc.)	70
まいる	参る	v5r, vi	to give up [in]	171
まかせる	任せる	v1, vt	to entrust (e.g., a task) to another（～を，～に）	162
まがる	曲がる	v5r, vi	to curve; to bend	75
まけおしみがつよい	負け惜しみが強い	exp	sore loser; unwilling to admit defeat	134
まごころ	真心	n	sincerity; devotion	148
まことに	誠に	adv	indeed; really	139
まさか		int	by no means; never!; you don't say!	80
まさに		adv	exactly; surely	40
マシ／まし（な）		adj-na	better; preferable	141
～まし		aux, pol	(used to make a polite request or demand) please	109
ます	増す	v5s, vi	to increase	123
まず		adv	first (of all)	32

(46)

語彙索引 【ふ・フ】～【へ・ヘ】

よみ	漢字	品詞	英語	ページ
【ふ・フ】				
プイ		onoma	movement of looking away	142
～ふう（な）	～風（な）	adj-na, n, suf	a style of ～; an appearance of ～	36
フーッ		int	blowing sound	87
ふうりゅう（な）	風流（な）	adj-na, n	elegant; refined	46
ブーンブーン		onoma	buzz; whirr; hum	67
ふかく	深く	adv	deeply; profoundly	93
ふかさ	深さ	n	depth	77
ふく		v5k, vt	to wipe; to dry	91
ふくれる		v1, vi	to swell (out)	35
ふこう（な）	不幸（な）	adj-na, n	unhappiness; misfortune	136
ふこうへい（な）	不公平（な）	adj-na, n	unfair	57
ふさがる		v5r, vi	to be occupied (e.g. accommodation)	31
ふさわしい		adj-i	suitable; appropriate	138
ぶし	武士	n	warrior; samurai	96
ふしぎ（な）	不思議（な）	adj-na, n	strange; mysterious	84
ふしぎと	不思議と	adv	strangely; curiously	22
ふしぎなことに	不思議なことに	adv	strangely; oddly enough	65
ふしょう	負傷	n, vs	injury; wound	160
ぶた	豚	n	pig	69
ぶたい	舞台	n	stage (theatre, theater)	152
ふたしか（な）	不確か（な）	adj-na	unreliable; uncertain	105
ふたりきり	二人きり	exp	just two people	74
ぶつ		v5t, vt	to hit (a person); to strike	144
ぶっしつてき（な）	物質的（な）	adj-na	material or physical (as opposed to spiritual, intangible); materialistic	98
ぶっそう（な）	物騒（な）	adj-na, n	disturbed; insecure; dangerous	115
ふとく	不徳	n	lacking virtue; immoral	93
ふとん		n	futon; bed	62
ふにんじょう（な）	不人情（な）	adj-na, n	unkindness; inhumanity; heartlessness	115
ふにんする	赴任する	vs	to arrive in [leave for] one's new post	159
ふね	船	n	ship; steamship	29
ふね	舟	n	boat	75
ふへい	不平	n	complaint	46
ふべん（な）	不便（な）	adj-na, n	inconvenient; inconvenience	137
ふやす	増やす	v5s, vt	to increase	125
ぶらぶら		onoma	leisurely; aimlessly （～と）	115
ふりむく	振り向く	v5k, vi	to turn one's face; to turn around	26
フン		int	hmph	90
ブン		onoma	swish of air; swoosh	61
ぶんがく	文学	n	literature	98
ぶんがくし	文学士	n	a man of letters; a literary man	35
ぶんがくしゃ	文学者	n	literary person	78
【へ・ヘ】				
へえ		int	oh, yes?; really?; huh?	121
[V (plain form)] べからず		exp, arch	must not; should not; do not	50
へきち	へき地	n	remote place; backwoods	137
ペコ		onoma	action of quickly bowing or lowering one's head	48
ペコリ		onoma	action of quickly bowing or lowering one's head	151
ベシャッ		onoma	splat	169

語彙索引 【は・ハ】〜【ひ・ヒ】

よみ	漢字	品詞	英語	ページ
はみがき	歯みがき	n	toothpaste	25
はめる		v1, vt	to set someone up (i.e., frame someone for a crime)	161
はやい	早い	adj-i	quick; fast	43
はやくち	早口	n	fast-talking	44
はやめに	早めに	adv	ahead of time	87
はらう	払う	v5u, vt	to pay	40
はれる		v1, vi	to swell (from mosquito bites); to become swollen	70
ばん		onoma	used when showing something amazing to someone	70
バン		onoma	bang	33
バンザイ		int, n	banzai (a celebratory cheer); something worthy of celebration	51
はんたい	反対	n, vs	opposition; disagreement（〜に）	95
はんどう	反動	n	backlash; reaction	95
はんぶん	半分	n	half	123
ばんめし	晩めし	n, col	evening meal	169

【ひ・ヒ】

よみ	漢字	品詞	英語	ページ
ピーピー		onoma	whistling sound	54
ひぇ		int	eep	171
ひきさがる	引き下がる	v5r, vi	to withdraw; to leave	130
ひきはらう	引き払う	v5u, vt	to vacate; to move out	172
ピキピキ		onoma	muscles flexing; muscle vein popping	135
ひきょう（な）	卑怯（な）	adj-na	cowardly; unfair	50
ひく		v5k, vt	to pull	101
ひさしぶりに		adv	after a long time	48
ピシャ		onoma	splashing sound	77
ピシャン		onoma	rattle; sound of quickly closing a door	31
ひじょうに	非常に	adv	very	88
びじん	美人	n	beautiful person (woman)	112
ヒソヒソ		onoma	in hushed whispering tones; conspiratorial	80
ひつよう	必要	n	necessity, need	130
ひどい		adj-i	awful; severe	143
ひどいめにあう	ひどい目にあう	exp	to have a bad time	83
ひとがいい	人がいい	exp, adj-i	generous; having a good personality	135
ひとかげ	人影	n	figure(s) or shadow(s) of a person (persons)	115
ひとがら	人柄	n	personality; character	137
ひとすじ	一筋	n	one long straight object (e.g., beam of light)	130
ひとつ	一つ	n	for one thing (often used in itemized lists)	50
ひとで	人出	n	crowd; turnout	152
ひとまえ	人前	n	the public	46
ひとまず		adv	for the present	165
ひとりひとり	一人ひとり	n	one by one; one at a time	34
ひなんする	非難する	vs	to blame; to criticize	150
ひやかす		v5s, vt	to banter; to make fun of	70
ひゅうが	日向	n	Hyūga, a place name, present-day Miyazaki Prefecture, Kyushu	123
ピューッ		onoma	toot toot	113
ピョン		onoma	hopping; skipping	60
ひらく	開く	v5k, vt	to hold	139
ひりょう	肥料	n	fertilizer	79
ひれつ（な）	卑劣（な）	adj-na	mean; cowardly	147

語彙索引 【の・ノ】〜【は・ハ】

よみ	漢字	品詞	英語	ページ
[Noun] のとちゅう	〜の途中	n	on the way to 〜 ; en route to 〜	48
〜のに		conj	even though; despite the fact that	20
のびる		v1, vi	to be postponed; to be prolonged	106
のべおか	延岡	n	Nobeoka, a place name, the northernmost city in present-day Miazaki, Kyushu	123
のべる	述べる	v1, vt	to state	94
のる	乗る	v5r, vi	to mount; to board (〜に)	119

【は・ハ】

よみ	漢字	品詞	英語	ページ
はあ		int	yes; indeed; well; huh 〜 (with some hesitation)	38
ハア		int	pant ; out of breath	61
ばあさん		n	grandmother figure; female senior citizen	107
はいえん	肺炎	n	pneumonia	174
ハイカラ（な）		adj-na, n	refers to people dressed in a western style; derives from the English word, "high-collar"	138
はいく	俳句	n	haiku poetry	98
ばか（なこと）をいう	ばか（なこと）を言う	exp	to talk nonsense	81
バカさわぎ	バカ騒ぎ	vs	to get drunk and horse around	141
ばかにする		exp, vs	to make fun of	96
[Quantity] ばかり		prt	approximately; just/only (about)	29
[V (た form)] ばかり		prt	[ta-form of a verb] just (finished, etc.)	18
[V (plain form)] ばかりでなく／ばかりか		exp	not only 〜（but also …）	96
はぎの	萩野	n	Hagino, family name of Botchan's new landlord	102
はぐ		onoma	chomp; eating, munching sounds	18
はこね	箱根	n	Hakone, a city near Mt. Fuji	24
はじ	恥	n	shame; embarrassment	67
バシ　バシ		onoma	smack, smack	61
はしけ		n	dinghy; launch; a small boat to transport people or goods from a large ship to the shore	29
[V (ます stem form)] はしない		exp	express a strong negative intention	135
〜をはじめ		exp	starting with 〜	137
はじめ	初め	n	beginning	33
はじめて	初めて	adv, n	for the first time	43
バシャバシャ		onoma	splish splash	52
ばしょ	場所	n	place; location; spot; position	97
[plain form] はず（だ）		n	expected to be; must be	120
[V (plain form)] はずがない		exp	cannot (do); it is impossible that 〜	33
はだん	破談	n	cancellation; breaking off (one's engagement)	107
パチパチ		onoma	clapping; sound of applause	137
はっ		onoma	hah; gasping sound; catching one's breath	19
ハッ		onoma	realize	31
はっきり		adv	clearly; plainly	88
ばっきん	罰金	n	fine	18
はっけよい		int	a phrase shouted by a sumo referee when both wrestlers have stopped moving; "put some spirit in it!"	17
はっしゃする	発車する	vs	to depart; to set off	110
ばっする	罰する	vs	to punish; to penalize	94
バッタ		n	grasshopper; locust (of family Acridoidea)	60
ばなし;はなし	話	n	story	119
はなしかける	話しかける	v1, vt	to accost a person; to talk (to someone) (〜に)	114
[V (て form)] はならない		exp	must not do	96
はなれる	離れる	v1, vt	to leave; to go away (place of departure を)	172
ハハハハ・アハハ		int	laughing sounds	43
ハフ		onoma	blowing sound	150

語彙索引 【に・ニ】~【の・ノ】

よみ	漢字	品詞	英語	ページ
【に・ニ】				
～に		prt	per	110
[V (ず neg. form)] に		exp	without ～ ing	16
にぎりしめる	握りしめる	v1, vt	to grasp tightly	87
にぎる	握る	v5r, vt	to grasp; to seize	112
[V (ます stem form)] にくい		aux, adj-i	hard (to do)	109
にげあし	逃げ足	n	running away; escaping on foot	156
にげかくれ	逃げ隠れ	n	fleeing and hiding	171
にげる	逃げる	v1, vi	to run away (～に、～から)	17
[Noun] にしかならん		exp	X can / will only become ～	79
[Noun] にする		exp, vs	to decide on ～	47
にせもの	偽物	n	imitation; faked antiques	133
[Noun] にだって（=にでも）		prt	even ～ ; even if ～	45
[Noun] について		exp	about ～ ; concerning ～ ; as to ～	32
にっか	日課	n	daily routine	58
につけ		n	vegetables or fish boiled in soy sauce	110
にっしんせんそう	日清戦争	n	First Sino-Japanese War (1894-1895)	144
～にて		prt	indicates location of action (formal literary form of で)	136
[V (plain form)] には [V (plain form)] が			repetition of the same verb creates the atmosphere of an uncertain outcome	24
にもつ	荷物	n	luggage; baggage	101
ニヤニヤ		onoma	smirk	53
にょうぼう	女房	n	(my) wife	40
にる	似る	v1, vi	to resemble; to be similar (～に)	40
にんげん	人間	n	human being; character (of a person)	64
にんじん	人参	n	carrots	18
にんじんばたけ	人参畑	n	carrot garden	17
【ぬ・ヌ】				
ぬくい	温い	adj-i	lukewarm; tepid	63
【ね・ネ】				
ねがう	願う	v5u, vt	to desire; to wish	138
ねこむ	寝込む	v5m, vi	to be sick in bed	24
ねどこ	寝床	n	bed	64
ねぼけぐせ	寝ぼけ癖	n	a habit of being half asleep	66
【の・ノ】				
のうか	農家	n	farmer	18
[plain form] のか		exp, fam	question with the request for further explanation	31
のがす	逃す	v5s, vt	to let escape	73
[Noun] のきみ	～の君	n	poetic second person, used to express one's longing and affection towards the person	81
のこった、のこった		int	notifies the wrestlers they are still in the ring so the fight is not over yet	17
のこる	残る	v5r, vi	to remain (～に)	165
[Noun] のころ	～の頃	n	(approximate) time; around ～	73
[Noun] のせいで		exp	because of (Noun)'s fault; to blame something on someone (or on something)	89
のぞく		v5k, vt	to peek (through a keyhole, gap, etc.)	53
のぞむ	望む	v5m, vt	to desire; to wish for	74
～のだ・～んだ		exp	the expectation is that ～ .; the reason is that ～	21
のだいこ	野だいこ	n	the clown, Yoshikawa's nickname	36
[Noun] のためになる		exp, v5r	to be of benefit for ～ ; to be useful for ～	151

語彙索引 　　　　　　　　　　　　　　　　　　　　　　　　　　　　　　　　　　　　　【と・ト】～【な・ナ】

よみ	漢字	品詞	英語	ページ
とんだ		adj-pn	unthinkable; terrible	160
とんちんかん（な）		adj-na, n	absurdity; contradiction	95

【な・ナ】

よみ	漢字	品詞	英語	ページ
～な		prt	(sentence end, mainly masc.) indicates emotion, emphasis, reflection, or a command	31
な		prt	reassures and confirms	23
[V (plain form)] な		prt	indicates a negative imperative	33
ないしょばなし	内緒話	n	secret talk	81
なかがわるい	仲が悪い	exp, adj-i	on bad terms; at loggerheads（～と）	107
なかま	仲間	n	company; fellow; colleague, associate	36
ながめる		v1, vt	to view; to gaze at	79
なきねいり	泣き寝入り	exp, n	literally, crying oneself to sleep. It means giving up in frustration; accepting meekly; or being compelled to accept a situation.	67
なぐさめる	慰める	v1, vt	to comfort; to console	114
～なくちゃ（＝なくては）		exp	if ～ not	83
～なくてはならない		exp	must do ～	32
なくなる	亡くなる	v5r, vi	to die	106
なぐる	殴る	v5r, vt	to strike; to hit	135
なげいれる	投げ入れる	v1, vt	to throw into	77
なげる	投げる	v1, vt	to throw; to cast away	155
[V (ます stem form)] なければならない		exp	have to do ～ ; should do ～	94
[V (ます stem form)] なさい		aux	do (command form)	25
なさけない	情けない	adj-i	miserable; pitiable; regrettable	114
なじみ		n	intimacy; friendship; familiarity	76
なぜ		adv	why	21
なづける	名付ける	v1, vt	to name (someone)（～を、～に）	76
なにごと	何事	n	what; something	61
なにやら	何やら	adv	something; for some reason	144
なにをいっても	何を言っても	exp	no matter what I said	114
[v (ます stem from)] なはる		aux, pol, dialect	to do	142
なびく		v5k, vi	to flutter; to be swayed by（～に）	111
なまいき（な）	生意気（な）	adj-na	sassy; smart-mouthed; smart-aleck	51
なまたまご	生卵	n	raw egg	110
なめる		v1, vt	to lick	160
なやむ		v5m, vi	to be worried; to be troubled	19
～なら		aux	if it is the case that ～ ; if it is true that ～	33
～なり		aux, arch	(meaning ～だ、～である) be (an affirmation)	50
～なる		suf, arch	who is called ～	159
なる		v5r, vi	to become（～に）	22
なる	鳴る	v5r, vi	to sound; to ring; to resound	113
なるべく		adv	as much as possible	94
なるほど		adv	I see; that's right	84
なんか／なにか	何か	exp	something	142
[Noun] なんか		prt	things like ～ ; or something like that ～ (often derogatory)	62
なんぞ		prt	and [or] the like	124
なんだか	何だか	adv	somewhat	26
なんだこりゃ（＝こりゃ／これはなんだ）			What is this?	45
なんだと	何だと	exp	What?!	159
～なんて		prt	such as ～ ; (things) like ～	45
なんで（＝どうして）	何で	adv	why?	62
なんでも	何でも	exp	whatever one likes	171

語彙索引 【と・ト】

よ み	漢 字	品 詞	英 語	ページ
どうだ		exp	How's it going?	166
とうとう		adv	finally; at last (after all that waiting)	168
どうどうと	堂々と	adv	boldly; confidently	150
とうなす	唐茄子	n	squash; pumpkin	93
とうふ	豆腐	n	tofu; bean-curd	124
どうやって		exp	how; in what way 〜	162
どうやら		adv	it seems like; somehow or other	139
どうらく	道楽	n	hobby; pastime	46
とおくはなれて	遠く離れて	exp	at a long distance	64
とおやま	遠山	n	Madonna's family name	105
とおる	通る	v5r, vi	to be heard; to be granted	57
〜とか		prt	among other things; such things as 〜	98
とき	時	n	the time	15
どきょうがある	度胸がある	exp	to have nerve; to be bold; to be daring	63
とぎれとぎれ		exp	broken; intermittent	81
とく	解く	v5k, vt	to solve	44
どく		v5k, vi	to step aside	144
どこでも		adv	anywhere	74
[V (plain form)] ところ		n	about to do an action; on the verge of 〜	40
〜どころ／ところじゃない		exp	It's not the time/condition/situation for 〜	82
ところが		conj	even so; as a matter of fact	91
ところで		conj	by the way	38
[V (plain form)] ところ（に）		n, suf	the moment; just at that time 〜	106
ドサッ		onoma	collapse; fall	31
としうえ	年上	n	older; senior	18
[Noun] として		prt	as (i.e., in the role of)	83
としをとる	年を取る	exp, v5r	to grow old; to age	115
どっー		onoma	sudden, louder laughter	49
とっておく	取っておく	exp, v5k	to set aside; to keep in reserve	89
トテチテタ		onoma	bugle sounds	33
とどく	届く	v5k, vi	to be delivered; to arrive	108
とどまる	留まる	v5r, vi	to remain	164
どどん		onoma	ba-boom	64
とにかく		adv	anyhow	91
どの [Noun] でも		exp	no matter which 〜	44
とはいうものの		exp	having said that	101
とびおりる	飛び降りる	v1, vi	to jump off of	15
とぼしい		adj-i	limited; lacking（〜が／〜に）	83
トホホ		int	boo-hoo; boo-hoo-hoo	79
とまる	泊まる	v5r, vi	to stay at（〜に）	38
とまる	留まる	v5r, vi	to stop; to remain; to stay (in the one place)（〜に）	108
とめる	泊める	v1, vt	to give shelter to; to lodge	108
とりあえず		adv	for the time being	23
とりけし	取り消し	n	cancellation	163
とりつぎにでる	取り次ぎに出る	exp, v1	to answer the door [knock, bell]	127
どりゃあ〜		int	hayaa; a loud yell; a war cry	170
とれる		v1, vi	to be interpreted (as)（〜と）	81
とん		onoma	tap; fairly quiet impact	60
トン		onoma	tap; jump	19
ドン		onoma	don!; ban!; boom	19

語彙索引 【て・テ】～【と・ト】

よみ	漢字	品詞	英語	ページ
ていせい	訂正	n, vs	correction; amendment	161
でかい		adj-i, col	huge; gargantuan	78
でかっ（＝でかい）		adj-i, col	huge	44
てがら	手がら	n	achievement; feat; meritorious deed	78
～てき（な）	～的（な）	adj-na, suf	- like; typical	96
デキがわるい	デキが悪い	exp, adj-i	(having) bad marks or results (e.g., in school)	121
できるだけ		exp	as much as possible	44
できんけれ		dialect	できないので	104
できんじゃろ		dialect	できないでしょう	63
[V（ない form）] でください		exp	please do not ～ ; without doing ～	122
でげす		aux, arch	です ; used by males from the end of the Edo to the beginning of the Meiji Period	36
～でございます（＝です）		exp, pol	to be	47
ですから		conj	therefore, …	33
デタラメ（な）		adj-na, n	nonsense	159
てつづき	手続き	n	procedure	161
てつづきする	手続きする	vs	to follow the necessary procedures	125
でて（い）く	出て（行）く	v5k, vi	(い may be dropped, particularly in plain or rough language) to go out and away	63
でてきたんぞなもし	出てきたんぞなもし	dialect	出てきたんでございますよ	106
でてくる	出て来る	vk	to come out	67
てにいれる	手に入れる	v1, vt	to obtain	134
てにのる	手にのる	exp, v5r	to be fooled by somebody's trick	163
てぬぐい	手ぬぐい	n	hand towel	25
てのひら	手のひら	n	the palm (of one's hand)	112
てほどき	手ほどき	n	learning the basics	74
てまえ	手前	n	before; towards this side	24
～でも		prt	even ～ ; even if ～	147
[Noun] でも		prt	or something	40
てやんでぇ		exp, vulg	What're you talking about?!	15
てら	寺	n	temple	174
てをあわせる	手を合わせる	exp	to beg	91
てをだす	手を出す	exp	to make a move	119
てをまわす	手を回す	exp, v5s	to use one's influence (～に)	162
てん	点	n	point	97
てんちゅう	天誅	n	heaven's (well-deserved) punishment	170
てんにんしゃ	転任者	n	a person who is transferred	122
てんにんする	転任する	vs	to be transferred	122

【と・ト】

よみ	漢字	品詞	英語	ページ
～と		conj	when	22
（おっ）と		int	uh-oh; oops; sorry	138
[Noun] という		exp	said; called thus	40
～ということ（だ）		exp	mean that ～	32
～というもの		exp	something like ～ ; something called ～	112
～といえば	～と言えば	exp	speaking of	123
～といったら		exp	speaking of ～ , talking of ～	75
どういう [Noun]		adj-pn	somehow	93
どうか		adv	please; somehow or other	95
とうきょう	東京	n	Tokyo	15
どうごおんせん	道後温泉	n	a famous hot spring	53
どうせ		adv	anyhow; in any case	76

語彙索引 【ち・チ】～【て・テ】

よみ	漢字	品詞	英語	ページ
ちゅうがえりする	宙返りする	vs	to do a somersault	20
ちゅうがっこう	中学校	n	middle school	29
[V (て form)] ちょうだい		aux, fam, fem	please do ～ for me	142
ちょうど		adv	just; right; exactly	81
ちょうどいい	丁度いい	exp, adj-i	just right (time, size, length, etc.)	39
ちょうめん	帳面	n	notebook	21
ちょくせつ	直接	adv, n	direct; firsthand	128

【つ・ツ】

よみ	漢字	品詞	英語	ページ
ついてくる	ついて来る	exp, vk	to come along with one; to accompany	39
つうじる	通じる	v1, vt	to get through; to understand（～に）	148
つかまる		v5r, vi	to be caught; to be arrested	156
つかむ		v5m, vt	to seize; to catch	135
つかれる	疲れる	v1, vi	to get tired	70
[Noun] つき	～付き	suf	furnished with ～	173
つぎ	次	n	next	32
つく	着く	v5k, vi	to arrive at（～に）	29
つくりばなし	作り話	n	made-up story	133
つけこむ		v5m, vi	to take advantage of（～に）	83
つけまわす	つけ回す	v5s, vt	to follow around	54
つごう	都合	n	circumstances	164
つづき	続き	n	continuation; sequel	51
～って		prt	indicates annoyance with someone's word or action	33
～って（＝～と）		prt, informal	indicates a quotation	159
～って（＝～という）		prt	the one you say is ～, called thus	122
～って（＝～というのは）		exp	presents a topic that is to be defined or explained	104
～って（＝～としても）		prt	assuming ～; even if ～	82
つとまる	勤まる	v5r, vi	to be fit for; to function properly	64
つまらない		adj-i	insignificant; trifling	90
つまらん（＝つまらない）		adj-i	uninteresting; boring ん＝ぬ、ない	34
つまり		adv	in short; in brief; in other words	32
つまる		v5r, vi	to be choked; to be blocked	135
[V (plain form)] つもり		n	intention to do ～	38
つよがる	強がる	v5r, vi	to bluff; to pretend to be tough	167
[V (ます stem form)] づらい		aux, adj-i	difficult (to do)	109
つり	釣り	n	fishing	73
つりざお	釣りざお	n	fishing rod	77
つりぼり	釣りぼり	n	fishing pond	73
つる		onoma	slurping noodle soup	48
つる	釣る	v5r, vt	to fish	73
つれてくる	連れて来る	exp, vk	to bring someone along（person を place に）	39

【て・テ】

よみ	漢字	品詞	英語	ページ
[Noun] で		prt	indicates means of action; cause of effect	91
～である		v5r	to be (formal, literary style)	96
であるく	出歩く	v5k, vi	to go out; to take a stroll	59
～であれ		conj	should	32
～てい	～邸	n	～'s house; residence; estate	102
ていきゅう	低給	n	low salary	130
ていしゅ	亭主	n	landlord; master; husband	91

語彙索引 【た・タ】～【ち・チ】

よみ	漢字	品詞	英語	ページ
～だって（＝～だと）		prt	a quotation	46
たっとれ	立っとれ	aux, arch	keep standing	22
たとえば	例えば	adv	for example	97
（そう）だとしたら		exp	if it's the case	162
たにん	他人	n	another person	115
たぬき	狸	n	Tanuki; badger	32
[Noun1] だの、[Noun2] だの		prt	and the like; and so forth	97
たのしみ	楽しみ	n	pleasure; amusement	98
たのしみにする	楽しみにする	exp, vs	to look forward to something	52
たのむ	頼む	v5m, vt	to request; to ask（～を、～に）	62
たのむ	頼む	v5m; arch	to ask for assistance at the entrance	121
たま	珠	n	bead	112
[V (ます stem form)] たまえ		aux, male	please do ～ (imperative form of an auxiliary verb)	35
だましうち		n	surprise attack; sneak attack	126
だます		v5s, vt	to trick; to cheat	136
たまらん（＝たまらない）		exp, adj-i	intolerable; one can't stand it	47
だまる		v5r, vi	to become silent	101
[V (て form)] たまるもんか		exp	cannot bear ～	63
ため		n	purpose; objective	134
ダメになる		exp, v5r	to be spoiled; to be ruined	147
たより	便り	n	letter; news	104
[Noun] だらけ		suf	covered all over	119
たりる	足りる	v1, vi	to be sufficient; to be enough	125
[Noun] たる		aux	(those) who are; (that) which is	32
だれにも～ない	誰にも～ない	exp	not anyone (with negative predicate)	87
だれも～ない	誰も～ない	exp	no one (with neg. verb)	52
ダン		onoma	bang; bam	19
たんけい	端渓	n	Tankei ink stone	47
だんご	団子	n	a sweet dumpling	52
たんじゅん（な）	単純（な）	adj-na, n	simple-minded	163
タンタン		onoma	tan-tan; tap tap	19
たんとう	担当	n	(in) charge (of a subject, but not necessarily supervision of the staff)	34
たんに	単に	adv	merely; only	96

【ち・チ】

よみ	漢字	品詞	英語	ページ
ち	血	n	blood	67
ちがいない	違いない	exp	to be sure; no mistaking it（～に）	78
ちかごろ	近頃	adv, n	lately	159
ちくしょうめ		int	rats; dammit	61
ちこくする	遅刻する	vs, n	lateness; tardiness	93
ちと（＝ちょっと）		adv, fam, arch	a little bit	35
ちほう	地方	n	area; countryside	138
ちゃき	茶器	n	tea utensils, used for Japanese tea ceremony	54
ちゃだい	茶代	n	a (small) tip	31
ちゃだいをはずむ	茶代をはずむ	exp, v5m	to tip handsomely	37
チャリン		onoma	jingle; sound of coin(s) falling	89
ちゃわん	茶碗	n	tea bowl	54
～ちゃん		suf, fam	an endearing way to refer to usually females of equal or lower social position	142
～ちゅう・じゅう	～中	suf	during (a certain time when one did or is doing something)	97
ちゅうい	注意	n, vs	caution; attention	97

語彙索引 【そ・ソ】～【た・タ】

よみ	漢字	品詞	英語	ページ
それで		conj	because of that	16
それに		conj	besides; moreover	45
それにしても		exp	nevertheless; at any rate; even so	37
それみろ	それ見ろ	exp	Look at that; I told you so	98
それもそうだ		exp	it may be so	135
ぞろぞろ		onoma	in groups; in succession	70
ぞんじる	存じる	v1, hum	to know	62
そんな [Noun]		adj-pn	such (about the actions of the listener, or about ideas expressed or understood by the listener); that sort of ～	33

【た・タ】

よみ	漢字	品詞	英語	ページ
ターナー		n	Joseph M. W. Turner (1775-1851)	75
たい	鯛	n	tai (species of reddish-brown Pacific sea bream)	77
～だい		prt, fam	marks a WH question (what, where, who, how long)	38
だいがく	大学	n	university; college	24
だいきん	代金	n	cost; payment	89
たいくつ（な）	退屈（な）	adj-na, n	tedium; boredom	168
だいじょうぶ	大丈夫	adv, n	all right	20
だいたい		adv	generally; for the most part	91
だいどころ	台所	n	kitchen	21
だいなし（な）	台無し（な）	adj-na, n	ruined; spoiled; spoilt	18
だいひょう	代表	n	representative	62
だいぶ		adv	considerably; greatly	70
たいへん	大変	adv	very; greatly	26
たいへん（な）	大変（な）	adj-na	difficult; hard	59
たいへんしっけいした	大変 失敬した	exp	I owe you a big apology (Lit. I was extremely rude to you).	133
たいへんなおもいをする	大変な思いをする	exp, vs	to have a terrible experience	168
たえず	絶えず	adv	constantly; always	147
だが		conj	but; however; (and) yet; nevertheless	83
たくましい		adj-i	burly; strong	36
たくみ（な）		adj-na, n	skillful; dexterous	171
たけ	竹	n	bamboo	109
～だけでなく		exp	not just ～ (but also ～)	136
～だけではなかった		exp	It was not only ～	116
[Noun] だけに		exp	being the case; (precisely) because ～ .; as might be expected (from ～)	108
たしか（な）	確か（な）	adj-na	reliable	102
たしかに	確かに	adv	surely; certainly	78
たすける	助ける	v1, vt	to rescue	171
たずねておいでたぞなもし	訪ねておいでたぞなもし	dialect	訪ねていらっしゃいましたが	151
たずねる	訪ねる	v1, vt	to visit	121
ただ		conj	but; however	109
ただいま	ただ今	adv	presently; just now	95
たたきつける		v1, vt	to smash; to smoosh; to slap something onto a surface	61
ただし		conj	but; however	50
ダダダ		onoma	dash; running sound	65
ただの [Noun]		adj-pn	only; mere; ordinary	33
[Noun] たち		suf	plural suffix (esp. for people & animals; formerly honorific)	48
たつ		v5t, vi	to pass; pass by [away]	115
ダッ		onoma	charge; sound of footsteps	116
[Noun] だって		prt	also; even ～	163
だって		prt, col	but; however	124

語彙索引 【せ・セ】～【そ・ソ】

よみ	漢字	品詞	英語	ページ
せいせき	成績	n	results; record; grades	121
せいだい（な）	盛大（な）	adj-na, n	grand; magnificent	139
せいと	生徒	n	pupil	32
せきにん	責任	n	liability (for the incident); duty; responsibility	94
せじ	世辞	n	flattery	21
せっかく		adv	with trouble; at great pains; long-awaited	142
ぜっけい	絶景	n	picturesque scenery	75
ぜったいに	絶対に	adv	absolutely	33
せつめいする	説明する	vs	to explain	63
ぜひ		adv	by all means	74
せまい	狭い	adj-i	narrow; confined	31
[Noun] せめ・ぜめ	～責め	n	persecution; hounding; pestering	47
せわする	世話する	vs	to look after; to help	122
せわになる	世話になる	exp, v5r	to receive favor; to be much obliged to someone; to be indebted to someone	40
せわのやける	世話のやける	exp	to be annoying; to be troublesome	153
せわをやく	世話をやく	exp, v5k	to take care of; to meddle	64
[Number] せん	～銭	n, ctr	hundredth of a yen	52
せんじつ	先日	n	the other day	89
せんどう	船頭	n	boatman	75
せんどうする	先導する	vs	to lead (the way)	159
ぜんにん	善人	n	good person; virtuous person	103
ぜんにんしゃ	前任者	n	predecessor	121
せんりょうする	占領する	vs, vt	to occupy	103

【そ・ソ】

よみ	漢字	品詞	英語	ページ
～ぞ		prt, male	(sentence end) emphasizes what the speaker is saying	16
そいつ		pn, col	that (person)	76
[V (plain form)] そう（だ）		aux	people say that; I hear that	22
[stem form] そう（だ）		aux	appearing that; seeming that	70
そういうところ		exp	such; that sort of; aforementioned quality or trait	21
そういえば	そう言えば	exp	which reminds me; come to think of it	101
ぞうきゅう	増給	n	salary increase	119
そうじゃ		dialect	そうだ	63
そうすれば		exp	if so; in that situation	103
そうだんする	相談する	vs	to consult（～について、～と・に）	161
そうちょう	総長	n	(college) president	120
そうどう	騒動	n	incident; uprising; revolt	51
[V (ます stem form)] そうにない		exp	showing no signs of (verb); extremely unlikely to	64
そうべつかい	送別会	n	farewell party	134
そそのかす		v5s, vt	to instigate; to coax	81
そつぎょうする	卒業する	vs	to graduate	23
そっくり（な）		adj-na	just like ～; the spitting image of ～	75
～ぞなもし		prt, dialect, pol	indicates polite certainty, emphasis, or contempt (similar to よ, but it is a polite expression); states one's opinion politely (～と申し上げます); and makes a request politely (Similar to なもし see 3章コマ10).	49
そのうえ	その上	conj	in addition; on top of (that)	139
そのうち		adv	eventually; sooner or later	101
そのとおり	その通り	exp	just like that; quite so	46
そら		exp	look!; look out!	77
それいらい	それ以来	exp	since then; from that time	107
それっきり		adv	(stronger version of それきり) since then	173

語彙索引 　　　　　　　　　　　　　　　　　　　　　　　　　　　　　【し・シ】～【せ・セ】

よみ	漢字	品詞	英語	ページ
しんけい	神経	n	nerve; sensitivity	167
しんし	紳士	n	gentleman	93
しんじる	信じる	v1, vt	to believe; to believe in; to place trust in	128
しんぱい（な）	心配（な）	adj-na, n, vs	worried; nervous	18
しんぱいする	心配する	vs	to worry	37
しんばしえき	新橋駅	n	Shinbashi station located in Tokyo. Shimbashi is the original terminus of Japan's first stretch of railway, the Tōkaidō Main Line, and is one of Japan's oldest stations.	173
じんぶつ	人物	n	character; person	93
しんぶんはいたつ	新聞配達	n	(newspaper) carrier	147
しんまい	新米	n	newcomer; beginner; literally, new rice crops	96
しんようする	信用する	vs	to trust	120
しんようにかかわる	信用にかかわる	exp, v5r	to reflect (badly) on one's trustworthiness; to affect people's confidence in one; to damage one's standing/credit	129

【す・ス】

よみ	漢字	品詞	英語	ページ
すいしょう	水晶	n	crystal	112
ずいぶん		adv	very; considerably	46
すうがく	数学	n	mathematics	34
すうじつご	数日後	adv, n	several days later	73
スー		onoma	door sliding smoothly and quietly	47
[V (ます stem form)] すぎ		n	too (much)	49
すききらい	好き嫌い	n	likes and dislikes; taste	130
すきじゃけれ	好きじゃけれ	dialect	好きだから	63
スキヤキ		n	thin slices of beef, cooked with various vegetables in a table-top cast-iron pan, written as すきやき and すき焼	149
すぎる	過ぎる	v1, vt	to pass by	166
すぐ		adv	immediately	142
スクッ		onoma	standing up quickly	113
すぐに		adv	soon	24
スコン		onoma	clunk	142
ズサッ		onoma	sound of something heavy falling	154
すじあい	筋合い	n	reason; logic	90
ずじょう	頭上	n	overhead; high in sky	130
すず	鈴	n	Suzu, given name	142
すずり		n	ink stone	47
ずっ		onoma	slurp	18
ズッ		onoma	sip	124
すっかり		adv	completely	97
ずっと		adv	far and away	24
すてる	捨てる	v1, vt	to break up with (someone)	111
ズデン		onoma	thud; falling motion; faint	54
～すべき		exp	should do ～ (abbr. of する + べき); ought to ～	96
すまない		exp	inexcusable; sorry	109
すもう	相撲	n	sumo wrestling; a Japanese style of wrestling	17
ズラリ		adv, onoma	parallel, aligned（～と）	34

【せ・セ】

よみ	漢字	品詞	英語	ページ
～ぜ		prt, male	(sentence end) indicates assertion	45
せいぎ	正義	n	justice	171
せいじつ（な）	誠実（な）	adj-na, n	sincere	137
せいしょ		n, vs	clean copy	109
せいしん	精神	n	spirit	32
せいしんてき（な）	精神的（な）	adj-na	mental; emotional	98

語彙索引 【し・シ】

よみ	漢字	品詞	英語	ページ
しぬ	死ぬ	v5n, vi	to die	23
しばらく		adv	little while	23
しはんがっこう	師範学校	n	normal school; teacher training school	152
しはんせい	師範生	n	students at teacher training school (normal school)	159
じひょう	辞表	n	letter of resignation	163
じびょう	持病	n	chronic disease	111
じぶん	自分	pn	oneself	21
しまいに		adv	at the end	119
[Noun] じみる		suf, v1	to have a touch of; to look like	127
しめた		exp	I've got it; all right	78
じもと	地元	n	home area; home town; local	102
ジャーッ		onoma	sound of flowing water	19
～じゃけれ、ここじゃろうて		dialect	～なので、ここにいらっしゃるだろうと思って	151
～じゃけれど		dialect	～ですが	105
しゃせいする	写生する	vs	sketching; drawing from nature	84
[Noun] じゃなさそう（だ）		exp	does not seem; unlikely; improbable	40
じゃまもの	邪魔者	n	someone who is a nuisance or a burden	167
～じゃろうが		dialect	to question or state something	50
～じゃろうがなもし		dialect	～でしょう	105
じゅうだい（な）	重大（な）	adj-na	serious; important	123
じゅうぶん（な）	十分（な）	adj-na, n	enough	37
しゅくじょ	淑女	n	lady	138
しゅくしょうかい	祝勝会	n	victory celebration	147
しゅくちょく	宿直	n	night duty; night watch	57
しゅくちょくしつ	宿直室	n	night duty room	58
しゅっけつする	出血する	vs	to bleed	156
しゅっせする	出世する	vs	to achieve success in the world after leaving home	22
しゅっぱつ	出発	n, vs	departure	25
しゅにん	主任	n	person in charge; senior staff	36
しゅやく	主役	n	leading part	143
じゅんさ	巡査	n	police; policeman	155
じゅんぼく（な）	純朴（な）	adj-na, n	rustic simplicity; honest	137
しょうかい	紹介	n	referral	173
しょうがっこう	小学校	n	elementary school	15
しょうきゅうする	昇給する	vs	to get a salary raise	122
しょうこ	証拠	n	evidence; proof	135
しょうじ	障子	n	shoji (paper sliding door)	167
しょうじき（な）	正直（な）	adj-na	honest; straight-forward	83
しょうしょう	少々	n, adv	small quantity	93
じょうだん	冗談	n	jest; joke	50
しょうちする	承知する	vs	to accept; to agree	57
じょうとう（な）	上等（な）	adj-na, n	superior; first-class	97
しょうねん	少年	n	boys	94
しょくいん	職員	n	staff member; personnel	93
しょぶん	処分	n, vs	punishment	93
しらせ	知らせ	n	notice	166
しらんぞな	知らんぞな	dialect	知らないです	69
しりまへん	知りまへん	dialect	知りません	142
しりもちをつく		exp, v5k	to fall on one's backside	60
じれい	辞令	n	notice of appointment (for his new job)	32

(33)

語彙索引 【さ・サ】 ~ 【し・シ】

よみ	漢字	品詞	英語	ページ
さきほど	先ほど	adv, n	some time ago	38
さく	策	n	plan; strategy	167
さくりゃく	策略	n	scheme; tactic	126
ざくろぐち	ざくろ口	n	the small, low entrance to the bathing pool	53
ざしき	座敷	n	tatami room	37
さすが		adv	(with affirmative sentence) as one would expect	77
さすがの [Noun] も		exp	even ~	103
さぞ		adv	I am sure; no doubt	70
さそいだす	誘い出す	v5s, vt	to lure（～を、～に）	162
さそう	誘う	v5u, vt	to invite	161
サッ		onoma	swoosh; a quick motion of erasing the blackboard	49
ザッ		onoma	sound made when knocking or swiping things (e.g., coins) off a table with one's hand	133
さっき		adv	some time ago	31
さっそく		adv	immediately; without delay	101
さっぱりする		vs	to feel refreshed	53
さつまいも		n	sweet potato	110
さびしい		adj-i	lonely; lonesome	74
さら	皿	n	plate; dish; platter	52
さる	去る	v5r, vi	to leave; to go away (place of departure を)	136
ザワ		onoma	unsettled atmosphere of chatter; people murmuring and fidgeting	43
さんかくけい・さんかっけい	三角形	n	triangle	43
さんこう	参考	n	reference; consultation	94
さんせい	賛成	n, vs	approval; agreement	95
ざんねん（な）	残念（な）	adj-na, n	deplorable; it is a shame	23
さんぽ	散歩	n	walk; stroll	48

【し・シ】

よみ	漢字	品詞	英語	ページ
～し		conj	(at the end of a phrase) identifies one of several reasons	31
し～ん		onoma	silence	65
しいる		v1, vt	to force; to compel; to coerce	129
しかし		conj	however; but	49
しかたない	仕方ない	exp, adj-i	it cannot be helped; there is nothing to do but	136
[V (plain form)] しかない		exp	to have no choice, but (to do something)	31
しかる		v5r, vt	to scold (a person with the intention of correcting wrong behavior)	114
しき	式	n	ceremony	148
しきてん	式典	n	ceremony	147
しこく	四国	n	Shikoku, the smallest of the four main islands of Japan	24
じこしょうかい	自己紹介	n	self-introduction	34
じじょう	事情	n	circumstances; conditions; situation; reasons	69
じしょくする	辞職する	vs	to resign from (work or position)	123
しずかに	静かに	exp	be quiet	147
しずまりかえる	静まりかえる	exp, v5r	to fall silent	65
したがき	下がき	n, vs	rough copy; draft	109
しっけい（な）	失敬（な）	adj-na, n	rudeness; acting impolitely	38
じっと		adv	fixedly (e.g., to stare); patiently	168
じつに	実に	adv	indeed; truly	161
じつは	実は	adv	as a matter of fact; actually	122
しつれい（な）	失礼（な）	adj-na, n	impolite; rude	143
しつれいながら	失礼ながら	exp	Perhaps I shouldn't say so [this], but...	83
しでん	市電	n	municipal railway; city streetcar	173

語彙索引 【こ・コ】〜【さ・サ】

よみ	漢字	品詞	英語	ページ
こぞう	小僧	n	youngster	153
ごぞんじがなもし	ご存知がなもし	dialect	ご存知でしょうか	105
こたえる		v1, vi	to take its toll; to have an effect on	98
こだんな	小旦那	n	young master	76
こづかい	小遣い	n	allowance	21
こづかいさん	小使いさん	n	janitor	16
こっとうや	骨董屋	n	antique store	39
[Noun] こと		n	a matter of 〜	169
コト		onoma	clink	148
[V (た form)] ことがある		exp	someone has experienced doing something	73
ことに		adv	especially; particularly	137
[V (plain form)] ことにする		exp, vs	to decide to do 〜	30
[V (plain form)] ことになる		exp, v5r	it has been decided (so) that 〜 ; it has been arranged (so) that 〜	23
ことば	言葉	n	language; word	40
ことわる	断る	v5r, vt	to decline; to turn down	74
このたび	この度	n	this occasion; at this time	139
このつぎ	この次	n	next time; another time	45
このまえ	この前	n	the other day	114
このやろーっ（＝このやろう）		exp	this rascal	61
こばむ	拒む	v5m, vt	to refuse; to decline	129
こびなた	小日向	n	a place in Tokyo	174
ゴホッ		int	cough; deep coughing	24
ごまかす		v5s, vt	to deceive; to falsify	135
こまる	困る	v5r, vi	to be troubled; to be worried（〜に）	88
ごめん		int, n	your pardon; permission	102
ごもっとも		exp	(you are) quite right	164
こらー!		int	hey!	17
こりゃ		exp	(from これは) hey there; I say; see here	60
ゴルキー		n	a kind of fish, similar to wrasse (ベラ in Japanese)	78
これくらい・これぐらい		n, adv	this much; this amount	70
これほど		adv	this much	168
ゴロリ		onoma	rolling around	148
こわい	恐い	adj-i	scary; frightening	83
こんちくしょう		exp	dammit	159
こんど	今度	n	this time	119
こんな [Noun]		adj-pn	such (referring to something/someone; or to ideas expressed by the speaker); like this	22
こんなことになる		exp	turn out be like this	161
こんや	今夜	n	this evening; tonight	57
こんやくしゃ	婚約者	n	fiancé; fiancée	107

【さ・サ】

よみ	漢字	品詞	英語	ページ
〜さ		prt, male	(sentence end) indicates assertion	135
さいご	最後	n	end; conclusion	138
さいしょ	最初	n, adv	beginning	130
さいしょに	最初に	adv	foremost; at first	32
さいなん	災難	n	disaster	160
さいわい	幸い	adv, n	fortunately	122
さがく	差額	n	the difference in amount; the balance	130
さき	先	n	way past that point; the other side	24
さきに	先に	adv	before; earlier than	143

語彙索引 【け・ケ】～【こ・コ】

よみ	漢字	品詞	英語	ページ
けしかける		v1, vt	to instigate (a fight)	159
けしからん		exp	outrageous; inexcusable	91
けしき	景色	n	scenery	75
げしゅく	下宿	n	boarding; boarding house	38
げしゅくにん	下宿人	n	lodger	39
げしゅくやのにょうぼう	下宿屋の女房	n	innkeeper's wife	91
けずる		v5r, vt	to reduce; to curtail	129
げた	下駄	n	geta (Japanese footwear); wooden clogs	127
げっきゅう	月給	n	monthly salary	40
けっきょく	結局	adv, n	in the end	163
けっこう（な）	結構（な）	adj-na	sufficient; fine	47
けつれつ	決裂	n, vs	breakdown; rupture	87
けはい	気配	n	indication; sign; hint	165
～けれ		prt, dialect	indicates a reason	44
けんか		n	quarrel; fight	152
けんかする		vs	to fight	18
げんかん	玄関	n	entranceway	121
げんばをおさえる	現場をおさえる	exp, v1	to catch in the act (of)	150
けんぶつする	見物する	vs	to sightsee	50
けんり	権利	n	right; privilege	57

【こ・コ】

よみ	漢字	品詞	英語	ページ
ご [Noun]		pref	honorable	20
コイ		n	koi, carp	73
こいつ		pn, col	this guy	18
こいつあ（＝こいつ）		pn, col	usually refers to a person, but here to the fact that Hagino noticed a lot about Botchan	104
[Noun] こう	～公	suf	familiar or derogatory suffix (after a name, etc.)	127
こうして		conj	thus	64
こうしゃ	校舎	n	school building	16
こうしょう（な）	高尚（な）	adj-na, n	noble; refined	96
ごうじょうっぱり（な）	強情っぱり（な）	adj-na, n	obstinate; stubborn	134
こうしんする	行進する	vs	to march; to parade	147
こうすい	香水	n	perfume	112
こうちょうしつ	校長室	n	principal's office	32
こうなれば		exp	If this is how it is	67
こうやって		conj	thus; in this way	148
こえ	声	n	voice	35
こえをかける	声をかける	exp, v1	to greet; to call out to someone	73
こおりみず	氷水	n, arch	shaved ice (usually served with sweet flavored syrup)	40
こが	古賀	n	Koga, family name	35
ごきげんよう		exp	please take care of yourself	25
こぐ		v5g, vt	to row	75
ごくろうさまです	ご苦労様です	exp	thank you very much for your ～; I appreciate your efforts	57
ここら		pn	around here	105
こころ	心	n	heart	115
こころにもない	心にもない	exp	(something) one does not really mean; insincere	137
こしらえる		v1, vt	to make	104
こしをぬかす	腰を抜かす	exp, v5s	to dislocate one's lower back; to be paralyzed with fright	16
こじん	個人	n	individual	136
～こそ		prt	for sure (to emphasize a preceding word)	156

語彙索引　　　　　　　　　　　　　　　　　　　　　　　　　　　　【き・キ】～【け・ケ】

よみ	漢字	品詞	英語	ページ
きょうしゃ	強者	n	strong man; man of power	57
きょうとう	教頭	n	vice principal	35
きょうり	郷里	n	birthplace; hometown	128
きょねん	去年	n	last year	106
ぎり	義理	n	sense of duty; social obligation	164
きれる	切れる	v1, vi	to be disconnected	109
ギロ		onoma	stare	92
きをつける	気をつける	exp	to be careful; to pay attention（～に）	83
きんじょ	近所	n	neighborhood	18
きんつば	金つば	n	a type of traditional Japanese confection, or wagashi	21

【く・ク】

よみ	漢字	品詞	英語	ページ
[V (ます stem form)] ぐあい		n	condition; manner	75
ぐいっ		onoma	to yank (down)	68
くう	食う	v5u, vt, male, vulg	to eat	48
くさる		v5r	to rot	170
くしゃ		onoma	sound of crumpling a piece of paper	159
クスクス		onoma	giggling	80
クスッ		onoma	a little laugh	80
くせ	癖	n	a habit (often a bad habit); peculiarity	60
くたびれる		v1, vi	to get tired; to wear out（～に）	111
くちぐせ	口癖	n	favorite saying	22
くちをきく	口をきく	exp, v5k	to speak; to utter	120
グツ		onoma	boiling sound	149
くになる	苦になる	exp, v5r	to be bothered (by something); to suffer	119
くみ	組	n	class; homeroom; there are several kumi for each grade	50
くやしい		adj-i	regrettable; awful	73
[Noun] くらい・[Noun] ぐらい		prt	just; only; the extent that; approximately	16
くらう	食らう	v5u, vt, vulg	to eat	169
くらしむき	暮らし向き	n	one's (living) circumstances; standards of living	106
くらす	暮らす	v5s, vi	to live	24
ぐり		onoma	grinding sound	154
[V (て form)] くる		aux	to do ～ and come back	25
[V (て form)] くる		aux	to come to ～	106
ぐるぐる		onoma	turning round and round; going around in circles	101
くるま	車	n	meant jinrikisha; rickshaw in the Meiji Period	30
くるまや	車屋	n	rickshaw man	101
くれる	暮れる	v1, vi	to get dark	58
[V (て form)] くれる		v1, vt	to do something for me	21
くわしく	詳しく	adv	in detail; fully	148
くんし	君子	n	man of virtue	93

【け・ケ】

よみ	漢字	品詞	英語	ページ
けいけん	経験	n, vs	experience	83
げいしゃ	芸者	n	geisha; a professional female entertainer who is hired to create a lively atmosphere at social gatherings by singing, dancing, and conversing.	76
げいにん	芸人	n	player; performer; actor	36
けいようする	形容する	vs	to describe	112
けいれき	経歴	n	career	164
げいをおぼえる	芸を覚える	exp, v1	to master an art/a technique/a performance (through personal experience)	103
けさ	今朝	n	this morning;	125

語彙索引 【か・カ】～【き・キ】

よみ	漢字	品詞	英語	ページ
かんげいする	歓迎する	vs	to welcome	83
かんじ	感じ	n	feeling	43
かんしゃく		n	temper; irritability	109
かんしゃする	感謝する	vs	thanks; gratitude	139
かんじん（な）	肝心（な）	adj-na	crucial; essential	135
かんしんする	感心する	vs	to admire	120
かんだい（な）	寛大（な）	adj-na	lenient; tolerant	94
がんばる		v5r, vi	to persist; to insist on; to try one's best	82
かんばん	看板	n	sign; signboard	48
かんべんする	勘弁する	vs	to pardon; to forgive	133

【き・キ】

よみ	漢字	品詞	英語	ページ
きがつく	気がつく	exp, v5k	to notice（～に）	161
ききとる	聞きとる	v5r, vt	to catch (a person's words)	43
きこえる	聞こえる	v1, vi	(can) hear	128
きさま	貴様	pn, vulg	you	170
きし	岸	n	shore	29
きじ	記事	n	article; news article	162
きしゃ	汽車	n	steam engine train	30
きしゅくせい	寄宿生	n	boarding student	62
きしょう	気性	n	disposition; temperament	21
きずがつく	傷がつく	exp, v5k	to damage; to harm（～に）	164
きたえる		v1, vt	to train; to discipline	96
きっと		adv	most likely (e.g. 90 percent)	18
きっぱり		adv	clearly; decisively	59
きてき	汽笛	n	whistle of a steam-operated train	113
きになる	気になる	exp, v5r	to be bothered by; to feel uneasy; to be on one's mind; to care about	90
きのあった	気の合った	exp	congenial	84
きのう／さくじつはしっけい	昨日は失敬	exp	Thanks for yesterday	87
きのどく（な）	気の毒（な）	adj-na, n	pitiful; unfortunate	107
きのはやい	気の早い	exp, adj-i	quick-tempered; hasty	38
きびしく		adv	severely; strictly	94
きぼう	希望	n	hope; wish	33
きぼうする	希望する	vs	to hope; to wish	97
きまる	決まる	v5r, vi	to be decided	126
きみ	君	pn	you; buddy; pal	35
きみの（orが）わるい	気味の（orが）悪い	exp, adv	in a creepy manner; weirdly	73
きみらのことば	君らの言葉	n	your language.	44
きめる	決める	v1, vt	to decide	38
きもちがいい	気持ちがいい	exp, adj-i	to feel good; feel comfortable	60
きゅうしゅう	九州	n	Kyushu, southernmost of the four main islands of Japan	23
きゅうに	急に	adv	suddenly	140
ぎゅうにく	牛肉	n	beef	149
ぎゅうにゅうや	牛乳屋	n	dairy; milkman	103
きゅうりょう	給料	n	salary	70
きよ	清	n	Kiyo, a woman's given name	18
きょういく	教育	n	education	32
きょういくしゃ	教育者	n	educator	32
きょういんひかえじょ	教員控所	n	teacher's room; teacher's lounge	34
きょうし	教師	n	teacher	24

語彙索引 【か・カ】

よ み	漢 字	品 詞	英 語	ページ
かぜをひく	風邪を引く	exp, v5k	to catch a cold	24
[Noun] がた	〜方	suf, hon	honorific pluralizing suffix (used only for people)	96
ガタ		onoma	rattle	95
かたち	形	n	shape	75
かたをもつ	肩を持つ	exp, v5t	to side with; to support	96
カチッ		onoma	click; the sound of cracking eggs	110
カチャ		onoma	the sound of a knob turning	45
ガチャッ・カチャッ		onoma	the sound of a knob turning	50
カチン		onoma	argh; used when the particular word someone says triggers your anger	51
カッ		onoma	motion of opening eyes wide in rage or alarm	82
カッ		onoma	clack	126
ガッ		onoma	impact of hitting something	66
ガッ		onoma	thump; impact of geta stepping hard on the ground	153
ガッシュ		onoma	hiss	26
かって（な）	勝手（な）	adj-na, n	one's own convenience; one's way	49
かってに	勝手に	adv	of its own accord; involuntarily	67
かど	角	n	corner	20
かどや	角屋	n	Kadoya, name of a Japanese inn (where Red Shirt and the geisha meet)	150
〜かな、もし・〜なもし		prt, dialect, pol	makes a request polite	44
かならず	必ず	adv	surely	165
かなり		adv	considerably	46
かのうせい	可能性	n	possibility	122
かべ	壁	n	wall; barrier	119
かまう		v5u	to mind; to be concerned about	143
かまど		n	kitchen range; cooking stove; hearth	20
かまわない		v5a	no problem; it doesn't matter	129
がまん		n, vs	patience; endurance	23
〜かもしれない		exp	perhaps; maybe	25
かもな		exp	That may be the case	162
かや	蚊帳	n	mosquito netting	61
ガヤ		onoma	clamorous racket; chatter; crowd of people talking	43
かゆい		adj-i	itchy	70
かよう	通う	v5u, vi	to commute (〜に)	52
カラ		onoma	rattle; light sound of opening a sliding door	54
からかう		v5u, vt	to ridicule; to make fun of	67
ガラガラ		onoma	rattling	19
からだ	体	n	body; health	35
ガラン		onoma	loud (metallic) sound	19
かりる	借りる	v1, vt	to rent	151
[Adj-stem] がる		suf, v5r	to feel; used to describe a third person's apparent emotion or feeling	130
かわいがる		v5r, vt	to love; to dote on someone	22
かわいそう（な）		adj-na	pitiful	165
[Noun] のかわりに	〜の代わりに	exp	in place of 〜; replacement	126
かわりに	代わりに	adv	instead of	97
かわる	代わる	v5r, vi	to take the place of	151
かん	完	n	The End	174
かんがえ	考え	n	thinking; ideas; intention	134
かんがえなおす	考え直す	v5s, vt	to reconsider	164
かんけい	関係	n	relation; connection	149
かんげい	歓迎	n	welcome; reception	138

語彙索引 【お・オ】～【か・カ】

よみ	漢字	品詞	英語	ページ
おぶう		v5u, vt	to carry (child) on one's back	16
おべっかづかい	おべっか使い	n	flatterer; someone who sucks up to another	77
おぼえ	覚え	n	memory; experience	88
おまえ		pn, fam, male	you	20
おまえら	お前ら	n, col	you scoundrel	51
おめにかかる	お目にかかる	exp, v5r, hum	to meet (someone of higher status)	120
おもい	思い	n	a thought. Here it is used to refer to an experience such as くやしい思い (awful, bitter experience).	73
おもえる	思える	vl, vi	to seem, to appear likely	115
おもわぬ [Noun]	思わぬ～	adj-pn	unexpected; unforeseen	83
おや		int	oh!; oh?; my!	58
おや	親	n	parent(s)	64
おやじ	親父	n	one's father	23
おゆき・おいき	お行き	exp	go	20
およぐ	泳ぐ	v5g, vi	to swim	53
および		conj	and; as well as	95
[V (て form)] おる		aux, pol	indicates continuing action or state (i.e. to be ..ing)	24
おれ	俺	n, male	I; me (tough, rough, or arrogant-sounding first-person pronoun)	19
おろす		v5s, vt	to drop	76
おわび		n	apology	93
おわる	終わる	v5r, vi	to finish; to end	45
おんこう（な）	温厚（な）	adj-na	gentle; mild-mannered; easy-going	92
おんせん	温泉	n	hot spring bath (house); onsen	52

【か・カ】

よみ	漢字	品詞	英語	ページ
～か		prt	indicates a question, choice, doubt, or a rhetorical question (a forceful statement with no expected response)	16
～か、～か		prt	either ～ or not	92
[V (volitional, plain form)] が [V (neg, stem form)] まいが		exp	whether V or not	90
[Noun1] が [Noun1] なら、[Noun2] も [Noun2] (だ)		exp	both of them are equally horrible (something negative)	94
カア		onoma	used when a person gets really upset	52
～かい		prt, fam	marks a yes-no question	37
[Number] かい	～階	ctr	counter for floors of a building	16
がい	害	n	harm; evil influence	163
がいしゅつする	外出する	vs	to go out	97
かいらく	快楽	n	pleasure	98
かう	飼う	v5u, vt	to keep; to raise (pets)	62
かえす	返す	v5s, vt	to return (something)	33
かえって		adv	on the contrary; instead	95
かえりに	帰りに	exp	on one's way home	52
かおいろがわるい	顔色が悪い	exp, adj-i	looking pale; looking unwell	35
かおつき	顔つき	n	look; face	36
かおをする	顔をする	exp, vs	to have an expression on the face like ～	127
ががく	画学	n	the study of drawing	36
かかる		v5r, vi	to hang	130
がくもん	学問	n	study; learning	96
かけじく	掛軸	n	hanging scroll	46
かける		v1, vt	to take (time, money); to expend (money, time, etc.)	109
かざん	峯山	n	Kazan, the name of a famous Japanese artist	46
かしつ	過失	n	error; accident; negligence	93
かす	貸す	v5s, vt	to rent out; to lend (～を，～に)	102
かせいする	加勢する	vs, n	assistance; reinforcements	151

語彙索引 【お・オ】

よみ	漢字	品詞	英語	ページ
おいでなんだぞなもし		dialect	おいでにならなかったんですか	104
おいでになる		v5r, hon	to come; to go; to be（～に）	104
～おいでるぞなもし		dialect	～いらっしゃいます	104
おおいに	大いに	adv	very; much; greatly	136
おおきな	大きな	adj-pn	big	43
おおごえ	大声	n	loud voice	44
おおさわぎ	大騒ぎ	n, vs	clamor; uproar; tumult	82
おおさわぎする	大騒ぎする	vs	to clamor; to make a big fuss	50
おおぞら	大空	n	heavens; sky	79
おおもの	大物	n	important person; big-shot; big game (animal, fish)	78
おかあさま	お母様	n	(your) mother	20
おかしい		adj-i	ridiculous; strange; funny	45
おかしなことに		exp	oddly enough; the odd thing is that ～	79
おかまいなく		exp	please don't fuss over me; don't go out of your way	111
おかわり		n, vs	another helping	18
おき	沖	n	open sea	75
おきづり	沖釣	n	offshore fishing	77
おきのどく	お気の毒	exp, adj-na	my sympathies; that's too bad	161
おきのどくじゃなもし	お気の毒じゃなもし	dialect	お気の毒でございませんか	124
おきゃん		n, arch	girl with "attitude"; lively minx	111
おく		v5k, exp, arch	to put; to place; to keep（～を、～に）	103
[V（て form）] おく		aux	to do something in advance	37
[V（て form）] おくれんか		dialect	to make a request; similar to ～てくれませんか	44
～おくれんかなもし		dialect	～いただけませんでしょうか	125
おこしいれ	お輿入れ	n, vs	marriage (into a family); wedding; bridal possessions	106
おこす	起こす	v5s, vt	to cause	81
おことわり	お断り	n, pol	declining; refusal	126
おこまりじゃけれ	お困りじゃけれ	dialect	困っていらっしゃるので	125
おごり		n	a treat	40
おこる	怒る	v5r, vi	to get angry	50
おごる		v5r, vt	to treat (someone); to pay for someone	133
おこんばんは	お今晩は	exp, arch, dialect	a polite way to say good evening Here, geisha use the greeting when entering the room. It is not a commonly used expression.	139
おさえる	抑える	v1, vt	to hold back one's anger; to restrain	167
おしい	惜しい	adj-i	regrettable; disappointing;	84
おしこめる	押し込める	v1, vt	to confine（～に）	31
おしはかる		v5r, vt	to guess	81
おしまい		n	end	109
おしむ	惜しむ	v5m, vt	to regret (e.g. a loss); to feel sorry (for)	141
おじゃまします		exp	to excuse me for disturbing (interrupting) you	111
おじょうさん	お嬢さん	n	(term of respect for) someone else's daughter; daughter of a high-class whelthy family	105
おたく	お宅	n, hon	your house	151
おたのみて	お頼みて	dialect	お頼みになって	125
おちぶれる	落ちぶれる	v1	to be ruined; to fall low	22
おっしゃるとおり	おっしゃる通り	exp, hon	as (someone) says	33
おっぱらう・おいはらう	追っ払う・追い払う	v5u, vi	to chase away; to drive away	167
おどかす		v5s, vt	to startle; to surprise	33
おとしいれる		v1, vt	to hatch a plan and deceive someone	138
おどろく	驚く	v5k, vi	to be surprised; to be astonished（～に）	103
おなご	女子	n, arch, dialect	woman	104
おなじ（な）	同じ（な）	adj-na	same; identical	58

(25)

語彙索引 【い・イ】～【お・オ】

よみ	漢字	品詞	英語	ページ
いわ	岩	n	rock	76
いんそつする	引率する	vs	to lead; to supervise (students)	147
いんぼう	陰謀	n	plot intrigue; conspiracy	73

【う・ウ】

よみ	漢字	品詞	英語	ページ
ウィッチ		n	witch	40
うおおお		int	a very powerful scream	66
うけとる	受け取る	v5r, vt	to receive; to get ; to accept	90
うけもち	受け持ち	n	the class assigned to (Botchan)	38
うける	受ける	v1, vt	to receive; to accept	74
うごく	動く	v5k, vi	to move	67
うしなう	失う	v5u, vt	to lose; to part with	136
うそ	嘘	n	lie	136
うそつき		n	a liar	120
うたう	唄う	v5u, vt	to sing traditional Japanese songs such as nagauta (long epic song) and kouta (a Japanese ballad) accompanied on the shamisen (three-stringed Japanese guitar)	142
うち		n	my; our (referring to one's family, school, company, etc.)	48
[Noun] のうちに		exp	within ～	129
[V (ない form)] うちに		exp	within ～ ; while ～	164
うつ	打つ	v5t, vt	to hit	20
うつす	移す	v5s, vt	to move or change the object of one's interest or focus （～を、～に）	115
うつる	移る	v5r, vi	to move (to another place) （～に）	38
うつる	映る	v5r, vi	to be reflected; to be projected	167
うまい		adj-i, fam	delicious	48
うまい		adj-i	skillful	109
うめる	埋める	v1, vt	to bury (e.g. in the graveyard)	174
うら	裏	n	out of sight; behind the scenes	119
うらおもて	裏表	n	both sides; double-dealing; literally "back" and "front"	84
うらなり		n	Koga's nickname; weak-looking fellow; pale-faced man; a vegetable (Japanese squash) grown near the top end of the vine	35
うりつける	売りつける	v1, vt	to palm off; to force a sale	133
うれしい		adj-i	happy; glad	36
うんぬん、かんぬん		exp	and so on; and so forth; blah, blah, blah	32

【え・エ】

よみ	漢字	品詞	英語	ページ
えいきょうをおよぼす	影響を及ぼす	exp, v5s	to have an effect on	32
えいよう	栄養	n	nutrition; nourishment	110
ええぞなもし		dialect	いい / よろしいでございます（よ）	104
えき	駅	n	train station	25
えどっこ	江戸っ子	n	true Tokyoite	36
えふで	絵筆	n	paintbrush	160
エヘン		int	ahem; attention-drawing cough	138
えらい		adj-i	great; distinguished	22
えんぜつ	演説	n, vs	speech; address	135
えんにち	縁日	n	temple festival	73
えんまん（な）	円満（な）	adj-na, n	perfect; harmonious; peaceful	138
えんりょ	遠慮	n, vs	diffidence; thoughtfulness	143

【お・オ】

よみ	漢字	品詞	英語	ページ
お［V(ます stem form)］する		exp, hum	creates a humble form of a verb	69
おい	甥	n	nephew	23
おいだす	追い出す	v5s, vt	to expel	163

(24)

語彙索引 【い・イ】

よみ	漢字	品詞	英語	ページ
いうとおり	言うとおり	exp	as (you) say	129
いうとるぞなもし	言うとるぞなもし	dialect	言っていらっしゃいます（よ）	105
いかが（ですか）		adv	how; how about	46
いかぎん	いか銀	n	Ikagin, name of both the antique shop and the proprietor	39
いかり		n	anchor	76
いくら [V(て form)] も		exp	No matter how much one does 〜	15
いけん	意見	n	opinion; view; comment	94
いけんする	意見する	vs	to comment; give one's opinion（〜に）	107
いざとなったら		exp	if one has to; when occasion demands	162
〜いじょう	〜以上	adv	once 〜 ; since 〜 ; seeing that 〜 (commonly 'and more')	94
いじょう	以上	adv	this is all; the end	138
〜いじょうに	〜以上に	adv	beyond 〜 ; more than 〜	64
いせいのいい	威勢のいい	exp	vigorous; full-blooded	167
いたいめにあわす	痛い目にあわす	exp	to make a person sweat for it	135
いたずら		n	prank	63
いたたたた	痛タタタ	int	ouch-ouch-ouch	66
いたって		adv	very much; extremely	121
いちどう	一同	n	all present; all concerned	96
いちにちめ	一日目	n	the first day	45
いちにちもはやく	一日も早く	exp	lose no time (in) doing	138
いちねんじゅう	一年中	adv	all year around	35
いちばんのり	一番のり	n	the first person to do (e.g., catch a fish)	78
いっしょうけんめいに	一生懸命に	adv	very hard; with utmost effort; with all one's might	79
いっしょに	一緒に	adv	together (with)	24
いったい	一体	adv	the heck (e.g., "what the heck?"); 〜 in the world (e.g., "why in the world?"); 〜 on earth (e.g., "who on earth?")	124
いつでも		adv	any time; whenever	47
いつのまにか	いつの間にか	exp	before one knows or realizes it (something has happened)	75
いっぱい		adv, n	a lot; much	31
いつまで		exp	how long 〜 ; till when 〜	38
いつものとおり	いつもの通り	adv	as always	54
いつものように		exp	as always	53
いてっ、いててて		adj-i	painful; a contracted form of いたい	20
いと	糸	n	fishing line; string	77
いなか	田舎	n	rural area; countryside	45
イナゴ		n	locust (of family Catantopidae); rice grasshopper (of genus Oxya)	62
いばる		v5r, vi	to brag; to boast about	15
いまどき	今時	adv, n	recently; nowadays	104
いまに	今に	adv	before long; even now	101
いや（な）	嫌（な）	adj-na, n	disagreeable; unpleasant	90
いやなものはいや		exp	dislike	130
いよいよ		adv	at last; finally	144
いらんものはいらんっ		exp	When I say I don't want it, I mean I don't want it!	47
いりぐち	入口	n	entrance	52
いる		v5r, vi	to need	70
いれちがい	入れちがい	n	passing each other	103
いれる	入れる	v1, vt	to put in（〜を、〜に）	62
いれんがな	入れんがな	dialect	入れません	63
いろいろ（な）	色々（な）	adj-na	various	37
いろのくろい	色の黒い	adj-i	dark-skinned	32
いろまち	色町	n	red-light district	52

語彙索引 【あ・ア】～【い・イ】

よみ	漢字	品詞	英語	ページ
【あ・ア】				
あいいれない	相いれない	exp, adj-i	impossible to reconcile; incompatible	163
あいさつ	挨拶	n	greeting	30
あいつ		pn, col	that guy; that person	127
あいてにする	相手にする	exp, vs	to deal with	147
あいにく		adv	unfortunately; sorry, but ...	31
あかシャツ	赤シャツ	n	Red Shirt, the vice principal's nickname	35
あがる	上がる	v5r, vi	to enter (from outdoors)	127
あきれる		v1, vi	to be amazed; to be shocked; to be disgusted（～に）	103
あく	空く	v5k, vi	to be empty; to be vacant	31
あくそう	悪僧	n	dissolute priest	36
あくるひ	あくる日	n	the next day	87
あげる	上げる	v1, vt	to raise	126
あさごはん	朝ごはん	n	breakfast	70
あじ	味	n	charm; style; flavor	73
あしのうら	足の裏	n	sole of the foot	43
あせをかく	汗をかく	exp, v5k	to perspire; to sweat	87
あそぶ	遊ぶ	v5b, vi	to play; to enjoy oneself	35
あたえる	与える	v1, vt	to give (esp. to someone of lower status)	96
あたためる		v1, vt	to warm; to heat	112
あだなをつける	あだ名をつける	exp, v1	to give someone a nickname	35
あたまにうかぶ	頭に浮かぶ	exp, v5b	to come to mind; to pop into one's head	64
あたり		n	neighborhood; vicinity	101
あたりまえ（な）	当たり前（な）	adj-na, n	normal; natural; reasonable	88
あっち		pn	that place (somewhere physically distant from both speaker and listener, or somewhere not visible but known by both speaker and listener)	120
あては（or が、も）ない		exp	aimless; no definite object (e.g., place) in view	101
あと		adv	remaining; further	149
あとから		adv	afterward	133
あばら		n	ribs	20
あばれる		v1, vi	to act violently; to act up	94
あまのがわ	天の川	n	Milky Way	130
あまる	余る	v5r, vi	to be in excess	94
あやしい		adj-i	suspicious; dubious	122
あやまる	謝る	v5r, vt. vi	to apologize	67
あらよっと		int	up we go; off we go; here I go.	19
ありがたい		adj-i	grateful; thankful	64
ある [Noun]		adj-pn	a certain (place or person)	15
あるひ	ある日	n	one day	17
あれ、まあ		exp	oh my; my goodness; expression of surprise	173
あわれ（な）		adj-na	pitiable; pitiful; pathetic; miserable	50
あんしんする	安心する	vs	to feel relieved; to stop worrying	125
あんた		pn, fam	you (familiar form of あなた)	142
【い・イ】				
[V（て form）]（も）いいです		exp	indicates permission; you may (also) do ～	36
[V（ば form）]いい		exp	you had better ～ ; you have only to ～	44
[V（ば form）]いい		exp	usually is used for advice, but here conveys more a nuance of letting something take its own course	67
いいがかり	言いがかり	n	false accusation	91
いいなずけ	許嫁	n	fiancé; fiancée	115
いいわすれる	言い忘れる	exp, v1	to forget to say; to forget to mention	97

(22)

Part-of-Speech (POS) Codes

adj-i	adjective
adj-na	adjectival nouns or quasi-adjectives
adj-pn	pre-noun adjectival
adv	adverb
aux	auxiliary
conj	conjunction
ctr	counter
exp	expressions (phrases, clauses, idiomatic, etc.)
int	interjection
n	noun
pn	pronoun
prt	particle
pref	prefix
suf	suffix
v1	ichidan verb (〜 iru and 〜 eru ending verbs)
v5	godan verb (〜 u ending verbs)
v5u, v5k, etc.	godan verb with `u', `ku', etc. endings
vs	noun or participle which takes the aux. verb suru
vk	kuru verb-special class
vi	intransitive verb
vt	transitive verb

Miscellaneous Codes

abbr	abbreviation
arch	archaism
col	colloquialism
fam	familiar
fem	female term or language
hon	honorific or respectful (*sonkeigo*) language
hum	humble (*kenjōgo*) language
male	male term or language
onoma	onomatopoeic or mimetic word
pol	polite (*teineigo*) language
sl	slang
vulg	vulgar expression or word

Notes:
- Words listed in the word boxes may have multiple parts-of-speech (for example, adverbs may be used as nouns also). The parts of speech and examples listed therein are those relevant to their usage in the text and are not intended to be an exhaustive list.
- For the English definitions, I mainly used Prof. Jim Breen's EDICT/JMdict dictionary at http://www.edrdg.org/cgi-bin/wwwjdic/wwwjdic. With his kind permission, I have adopted some of the Parts-of-Speech (POS) Codes & Miscellaneous Codes at http://www.edrdg.org/wwwjdic/wwwjdicinf.html#code_tag. I, however, am solely responsible for the usage of these codes in the text.

現代の日本において『坊っちゃん』を中学生を読者対象にして書かれた作品として想定する傾向は、この物語をマンガとして取り組もうとする日本語学習者の状況と皮肉にも類似していると言えます。以前マンガ小説（グラフィック小説）は当たり前のように子どもの文学だと言われましたが、もちろん今はほとんどそのようには思われていません。しかし、この有名な文学作品をマンガとして再創造することは、より単純化をしたのではないかと思われる方もいるかもしれませんが、これは誤解だといえます。

　マンガは日本語での読書をより楽しいものにします。さらに、読者が何を「得られる」か、読者に読解能力を求めます。それは、文法や語彙がどのように登場人物たちの対立する意図や行為についてのニュアンスを表現しているかを読み取ることであり、少しも単純なことではありません。また、マンガは、視覚的コンテクスト（場面や顔の表情など）を通し、全体的な理解を促す手助けをしてくれます。

　『坊っちゃん』は、自分自身を近代的な人間だと称する者たちの姿勢や偽善を非難する学園喜劇なのです。一部の読者は、この時代の現実性が欠如したものだと嘲笑しながら、国家的寓話の一種として見なすかもしれません。私は日露戦争（1904〜1905）の日本の勝利において起こった勝利主義へのある種の矯正手段としての文学と見なしたいのです。漱石は巧みな手法を用い、学校や他の団体の文化を形づくる些細な短所、見当違いの期待、気まずいやりとり、不慮の成り行きなどに対する愛着を描いています。漱石は文学が与える影響にたいして興味関心を持っていました。それと同じように、このテキストを学ぶ学習者がその言語やマンガの中で何を楽しみ、そしてどのように予想と違った展開になるかについて考える、そんな取り組み方を促したいと思います。

あまり教養のない読者のためのふりがなが一切抜ありませんでした。福田は、作品にふりがなを加え、より平易な漢字に置き換え、さらに漢字を平仮名に書き換え、そして学者ぶった箇所やわかりにくい箇所を削除することで、戦後の若い読者にとって読みやすく、そして親しみやすくなるように作品を改訂しました。1958年の改訂版がその後も増刷され続け、1960年代半ば以降は児童小説として最も読まれました。また、中学校の教科書編纂者もその認識もないまま、改訂版から引用、作成しました。『坊っちゃん』は親しみやすい冒険ものとして、また、中学校という設定が青少年に最適なため、広い層の読者に最も親しみのある作品として普及していきました。しかし、漱石の他の作品が徹底的に研究される一方、『坊っちゃん』はそういった真剣な文学批評の題材としては扱われていない傾向があると言えます。[7]

学園喜劇

近代の学園生活を懐かしむような漱石の陽気な学園喜劇は、平安時代の宮廷小説の繊細なユーモアとは異なっています。明治政府が掲げたより高貴な道徳教育の目標とかけ離れていた『坊っちゃん』は、近代的な新しい学校という設定で、江戸時代の大衆小説に見られるユーモアと趣意を合わせたものです。江戸っ子が理解できない四国の方言に直面しながら、いくつもの勘違いを引き起こす姿がユーモラスに描かれています。この作品は、田舎から都市へ越してきた世代の読者に支持されました。そういった読者は、地方と都市の間における役割の逆転に、すぐさま喜劇的な価値観を見い出したからです。読者らは、常に忠実な奉公人で、"主人がすることはすべて正しく映る"といった清によって具体化される、明治時代以前の時代遅れの主従関係も理解したでしょう。中学校という設定と生徒とのどんちゃん騒ぎにもかかわらず、人間関係（教員の中の一人が芸者と関係を持っていること）や、おそらくもっと重要である坊っちゃんの権威に対する反抗（校長や教頭を「狸」、「赤シャツ」と呼ぶ態度など）から、読者は『坊っちゃん』の内容の一部は成人向けであると理解するでしょう。

坊っちゃんは教員で構成されるエリート集団を滑稽なあだ名で紹介します。ずるい校長の「狸」、彼の共謀者で異常に高い声で話す教頭の「赤シャツ」、そしてごますりの「野だいこ」などです。坊っちゃんはそれとは反対の、青白い顔をした英語教師「うらなり」や数学教師の「山嵐」側につきました。皮肉なことに、近代の日本を成功に導くと予測される教科英語や数学の担当の教員は、学校の権力関係で失敗する結末となります。あれこれと問題があったにもかかわらず、最終的にはすべて坊っちゃんにとっては納得の行く結末となります。『坊っちゃん』は、江戸時代の勧善懲悪に見る、善が悪をやっつけるという関係より、権力を握っている人の裏をかくには俊敏に反応して動く能力が必要だという現代の話です。

え、東京一帯でも「坊っちゃん」という言葉は甘やかされた気楽さと未熟さを意味していると言えます。[5] この「坊っちゃん」というあだ名は、奉公人の清によって愛情のこもった敬意をもって使われていますが、中学校での同僚からは、幾分かからかったような悪意をこめて使われています。[6]

喜劇的な比喩

　漱石の『坊っちゃん』は、二つの喜劇的な比喩的用法を表しています。一つ目は、近代的で知識人である江戸っ子（江戸の子／東京人）が、遥かに洗練されている地方の陰謀者に遭うという設定です。坊っちゃんという登場人物は、筋金入りの世間知らずで、強情で頑固、無頓着なほど正直で、どんな批判的自意識もないといった人物で、首都東京で育った社会的背景や学歴から想定される主人公とはまったく正反対の人物です。物語では直接的に松山という町の名前を言及しませんが、多くの地理的描写や坊っちゃんの住む町と温泉まで行く汽車の話からも、簡単に松山だと特定できます。漱石は松山を田舎と言っていますが、読者は東京とは対照的な場所とだけ理解すれば良いでしょう。二つ目の主要な比喩は、明治時代のエリートとしての坊っちゃんの立場です。意識的に国づくりを目指した明治の有力者たちの真剣な試みとは対照的に、坊っちゃんには野心がありません。彼は、ただ他により良い選択肢もなかったので何の期待もないまま、中学の教員職を受け入れます。坊っちゃんは、日本の近代における模範像とはまったく違って衝動的でむしろ未熟、ある種永続する思春期にいる、安易で無力な人物です。1890年に発表された教育勅語の倫理上の徳を描写した修身の教科書に登場する模範的な人物の美談とはまったくかけ離れている存在です。しかし、驚いたことに、倫理上の徳がなくても、坊っちゃんは人間として道徳的に正しい選択をしているのです。それは、うらなりが僻地にある学校へ転任させられた際、坊っちゃんは自分の増給話を断ったり、山嵐が辞職させられた時も、なぜ同じ喧嘩に加わった自分も首にしないのかと言った上、よく考えもせずに辞表を出したりなど、坊っちゃんは長期的な影響を考えずに行動し、その結果自分の不利益になることがしばしばありますが、これらの行動は道徳的には正しいのです。つまり、坊っちゃんは明治政府が求めていた高徳の人物のアンチテーゼとして機能し、それに成功したといっても過言ではないかもしれません。

改訂

　日本で一般的に読まれている『坊っちゃん』は、1958年に福田清人が大幅に改訂したものです。初版の『坊っちゃん』は、文芸雑誌『ホトトギス』での連作としてもともとは大人向けに出版されたものだったので、多くの漢字を含んでおり、若い読者や

と思っていた人物が、実際には実の母親であったことを知ったのは後のことでした。漱石は、二松学舎では中国古典文学の基礎を徹底的に勉強しながら、後に東京帝国大学（今の東京大学）で英文学を学ぶといった、新旧両方の教育制度からの教育を受けました。今、日本語を学習している皆さんにはおそらく理解するのが難しいかもしれませんが、当時の教育システムの最高峯にたつ大学から学士号を取得したことによって、漱石は明治のエリート集団の仲間入りをしたのです。漱石は、大学院生として研究を続けながら、非常勤として東京高等師範学校で教鞭をとりました。それゆえ、漱石が1895年に四国の松山で中学校の教員としての職を受け入れたのは珍しいことだったと言えます。漱石はそこで一年間教えた後、熊本の第五高等学校でのよりよい職へと移りました。当時第五高等学校は、国家によって設立運営された五つの学校のうちの一つで、そこの生徒は帝国大学へ進むことができました。また、熊本で漱石は中根鏡子と結婚しました。漱石の松山という田舎へ行くといったとっぴな行為が、しばしば『坊っちゃん』の話の土台となったと言われています。漱石は日本政府より1901年から1903年の間、英国で英文学を学ぶ奨学金を得ましたが、この奨学金を受けたことで、漱石は生活苦を体験することとなりました。奨学金は彼が生活するのに十分な額でなかったことを、後に『文学論』の序章で「余は英国紳士の間にあって狼群に伍する一匹のむく犬の如く、あはれなる生活を営みたり」と記しています。さらに、漱石は自分の殻に閉じこもり、彼を訪ねた数人の日本人は彼の精神状態を案じたと書いています。1903年に日本へ帰国した後、漱石は第一高等学校と東京帝国大学での講師職を任命されました。漱石は生活のため明治大学でも教鞭をとりました。この頃の講義が、のちの漱石の文学理論の基礎となりました。

「坊っちゃん」というあだ名

　漱石が選んだ「坊っちゃん」という言葉は、主人公の社会的地位や主人公がどのように見られていたかという両方の意味を含んでいます。小説家の谷崎潤一郎（1886～1965）は、自分の子ども時代の思い出のエッセイの中で、「坊っちゃん」という言葉が1890年代にいかに使われていたかを書いています。「坊っちゃん」は貴族的な邸宅が立地する高台の山の手（江戸時代、武家屋敷のあった清閑な地区）で使われたものであり、下町（人口密度の高い江戸の都心にあたる平地）では、裕福であったとしても、使用される言葉ではなかったと記しています。それゆ

> 「坊」という音、そしてそのバリエーションは、現代の日本語においても聞くことができます。元来、この漢字はお坊さんやお坊さんの住まいを表していますが、幼い男の子や裕福な家庭で育った世間知らずの若い男を指し示すようになり、また親しみの意を込めて名前の後に付けられるようになりました。また、「坊」という音は、「赤ん坊」（赤ちゃん）、「朝寝坊」（朝早く起きられない）、「三日坊主」（三日であきらめる人／何かをやり始めて続かない人／ダイエットや新年にすべきことを決めてもすぐやめる人）など、ある特定の癖をもった人を描写する際によく聞くことがあります。

あまり受け入れられなかったようです。漱石は『三四郎』(1908)のなかで彼自身の経験を風刺しています。『三四郎』の中で三四郎という23歳の学生は、英文学の日本人の教授に、前の外国人の教授の方が好きであったことを告げました。事実、漱石は東京大学でラフカディオ・ハーン(1850～1904)の後任の英文学講師として赴任しました。[4] 漱石が他者と違っていたところ特異性は、東京帝国大学の名誉ある講師職から1907年に突然辞職し、その年の四月に朝日新聞社に入社したことからもわかります。これは当時の同輩に言わせれば、驚くべきことでした。漱石は朝日新聞社に勤務しながら、数々の小説をそこで出版し、多くの批判や賞賛を受けました。皮肉なことに、漱石が一般大衆向けに書き始めた時には、彼の作品はより暗さを帯びており、読者の読解力が必要とされていました。

『坊っちゃん』

漱石の作品の中で『坊っちゃん』を特徴づけるのは難しいことです。漱石は主に小説家として著名ですが、多様な文学や芸術形態の作品 —— 十数以上の小説、短編集、スケッチ、エッセイ、日記、文学批評、漢詩、俳句そして絵画など —— を出版しました。現代でも漱石は、最も広く読まれ、研究される文壇の大家であり続けています。大衆文化における漱石の存在は、1980年初期に日本の紙幣を新しくデザインし、近代の歴史的人物も加えられることになった際、1984年から2004年まで最も広く社会に流通する紙幣であった1000円札に彼の肖像が採用されたことからも明らかでしょう。また、かつては『坊っちゃん』は、日本の中学校の教科書によく引用されていました。『坊っちゃん』は漱石の中で、必ずしも最も面白く、成功し、また洗練された作品ではないかもしれませんが、軽快なタッチで描かれた一人の青年の混沌たる近代化との遭遇は批判的な評価を受けながらも、広く読者に親しまれ、愛されています。

> 毛利八十太郎、ウメジ・ササキ、アラン・ターニー、J・コーエン、そしてマット・トレイバンドの5人の『坊っちゃん』の英訳のうち、2つのものがオンラインで読むことができます。
> (注：毛利は「プロジェクト・グッテンベルグ」http://www.gutenberg.org/cache/epub/8868/pg8868.html)。『坊っちゃん』は、1923年に初めてフランス語に翻訳され、すぐにドイツ語版が出版されました。それ以来、中国語、ヘブライ語、インドネシア語、韓国語、マレー語、ロシア語、スペイン語、シンハラ語、トルコ語、そしてベトナム語の読者のために翻訳がなされています。

教育

漱石は、夏目金之助として、現在の東京都新宿区にあたる場所で慶応3年(1867年、明治元年の一年前)に生まれましたが、漱石の生みの親である老夫婦は、彼を養子に出しました。漱石が9歳のときに養父母が離婚したため生家に戻りましたが、祖母だ

き方、つまり過去も未来も考えず、現在の快楽がすべてだとする生き方を捉えています。『助六』(1713)は、復讐、立ち居振る舞い、台詞のきっかけを受けそこなった滑稽なへま、そしてドタバタ喜劇のテーマを含めた演目でしたが、それを見るために人々は集まりました。

> 井原西鶴は、金持ちになるためにはどうしたらよいかという商人の話、また、町人の男と女の恋愛ものについて描きました。十返舎一九の『東海道中膝栗毛』の中に現れる、江戸から京都までの東海道の町を旅する際に次々と冒険に遭遇するのんきな二人の旅行談は、ドタバタ喜劇やおどけた行いに満ちた江戸喜劇がどのようなものであったのかを知るのに、最適な一例です。

ユーモアは言われたことと予期された応答の言い回しを巧妙に変えていく中に表れました。また、近代初期の喜劇に関連した「俳諧の連歌」の読みあいでは、多くの歌人が日常生活の話題を話し言葉で詠み、（ユーモアを）競い合いました。これは、人々を驚かせるような連歌の「並列」を達成するための古くて技巧化されすぎた古典的伝統とは対照的でした。凝り性で人気の寄席芸人がつくるごろ合わせは、平安時代の清少納言の言葉遊びや機知に対抗させたもので、味わい深くなったものです。

特異性：漱石は明治時代の作家とどう違うか？

漱石の特異性には多くの局面があります（夏目は姓で、漱石は彼自身が選んだペンネームであり、この名で知られることとなります）。最もよく知られた喜劇作品を出版した時、漱石は教育制度の頂点である東京帝国大学の英文学講師でした。この時期の漱石の講義は、際立ってオリジナルで洗練された、抽象的な文学へのアプローチを示していました。これは、読書の経験を特徴づける心理学的、かつ、社会学的モデルを大いに生かしたものです。漱石の『文学論』(1907年出版)は2009年に翻訳されたため、英語を母国語とする読者でも、これが英文学の典型的な概説からどれほど逸脱したものであったのかが理解できます。漱石は、彼自身が「コスモポリタン」と呼ぶ普遍的な研究方法を求めました。漱石の文学論は自然科学の普遍性を基にしたもので、物理的な世界の認識から始まり、我々がどのようにして意味を汲み取るのかまで、近代文明で文学がどのように機能したのかを体系的に理論づけようとしたものです。漱石は、読書体験の瞬間の流れを特徴づける方法として、意識の波線グラフや方程式を構築するため、当時の科学を応用したのです。[3] 類似した原理を前提とし、熱力学のシステムとして文学を特徴づけることで彼の広範囲に及ぶモデルを結論づけました。漱石のモデルは、当時支流であった文学分析モデルと相反するものでした。それは、芸術感覚を特権化し、具体的で差別的な「感覚」の正当化を擁護する西洋中心（特に英国）の文学概念に挑戦したものでした。漱石にとって、文学の価値も相対的で歴史的であるため、流動的で変化していくものだったのです。

漱石の文学理論は一連の大学の講義で紹介されていましたが、彼の記述によると、

めとする宮廷文女性作家の古文を読み、さらに、宮廷文化における美学を理解しなければならなかったからです。かなり前になりますが、コロンビア大学で日本語の古文を学んでいた時、紫式部の『源氏物語』の和歌の一節に当惑しました。そこでは、気品ある主人公の源氏は、彼の恋人の一人を「末摘花」、つまり紅花と描写しました。紅花は赤みがかった染料を作り出す黄色い花なのですが、教授に日本語で「はな」の別の意味を考えるよう言われるまで、私は若い姫の長くて赤い鼻を描写するための掛詞だとは気づかなかったのです。私は抽象的な概念について考えすぎたあまり、作品に使われた実際の言葉そのものを十分に考えてはいなかったのです。

> 『坊っちゃん』での一般的な謎掛けと言葉遊びは、古典的な伝統に根付いています。定子皇后に仕える女官 (986-1000) の清少納言により編纂された『枕草子』には、宮廷生活のスケッチに加えて、「美しいもの」「心ひかれるもの」「醜いもの」、現代の読者には多少面白いとか単なる意地悪ではと思われるような様々なリストが示されています。ある一節では卑しい身分の親を恥じて海に投げ捨て、其の後親のお盆の供養を熱心にした宮廷に仕えている男のことを述べ、清少納言は、この出来事を戒める歌を「いとおかし」と感じました。どうして「いとおかし」と感じたのでしょうか。それは「盆」は、親を「ぼん」と海に投げ捨てた時に発した水の音の同音語だったからです。おわかりになりましたか。
> 萩谷宅著者 (1983) 清少納言『枕草紙解環 五』東京：同朋舎、278。

現在、私たちは日本文学のユーモアにおける文化の複雑さを奥深く探求した近年の研究のおかげで、文学をより楽しむことができます。[2] アダム・カーンによる18世紀後期の江戸時代の風刺マンガの分析は、大衆文化の消費者、つまり読者がどれほど文化的に洗練されていなければならないかについて指摘しています。しかし、その一方、日本では複数の喜劇伝統の系譜があるにもかかわらず、どれもが大衆の多くに受入れられてきました。貴族の言葉で演じられる質素で厳格な能楽には、それと相対するおおっぴらな間狂言があります。狂言は話し言葉で演じられ、必ず役割や権力の逆転を描写しており、観るものを楽しませてくれます。

> 説話文学や、その後数世紀に続く、その土地固有の一般的な物語の口承文学は、もっと滑稽な場面を見せてくれます。12世紀初頭に編纂された、インド、中国、そして平安時代の日本の物語集である『今昔物語集』は、淡々とした様子で架空の出来事を紹介しています。例えば、「東の方に行く者、蕪を婁ぎて子を産む話」、「加賀の国の、蛇と蜈（むかで）と争う島に行きたる人、蛇を助けて島に住む話」などですが、興味をそそる題名は、現代の漫画においても、適当なものかも知れません。
> 森正人、校注 (1996) 新日本古典文学大系37『今昔物語集 五』東京：岩波書店、6, 44.

江戸時代（1603～1868）の日本文学には、多種多様な喜劇もの、やや下品な韻文、滑稽な歌舞伎芝居などがあります。この時期の機知は浮き世という言葉に捉えることができます。浮き世というのは、特に町人の間に見られた刹那的な生

> 永きにわたって好まれる狂言劇『附子（ぶす）』は、二人の弟子がどのようにして師匠の僧侶を出し抜くかという話です。さらに、御伽草子の短編の絵入り物語（12世紀後期～17世紀初期）は、仮名を使い話し言葉で書かれています。『物ぐさ太郎』は、平凡な農民がとんちの利いた言葉やユーモアで、身分の高い人たちを出し抜くといった物語で、そのてんで狂言を引いているようなユーモアも見られます。

エッセイ

ジョーン・E・エリクソン

　現代の日本語学習者は、夏目漱石の『坊っちゃん』をどのように読むべきでしょうか？著者である夏目漱石は、語学教師は言うまでもなく、読者が何かを「得る」ことを期待しているのでしょうか？

　夏目漱石（1867〜1916）は最も有名で愛されてきた近代日本小説家の一人であり、漱石の作品は明治時代の日本がどのように西洋社会と関わってきたかを象徴する文学として読まれてきました。明治時代の小説は、特に言文一致運動（文語体で書かれていたものを話し言葉としての口語に一致させようとした運動）に見られるように、それまでの文学的伝統からは、明らかに異なった特徴をもっています。この時期現代文学を作り出そうとした日本人作家らは、写実主義や自然主義といった西洋の文学ジャンルに新しい発想を得、自我という概念を深く見つめ始めました。それゆえ、明治時代の文学は、江戸時代後期のしばしばユーモラスな戯作文学とは大きく異なり、その作風は深刻な相を帯びていると言えるでしょう。

　夏目漱石の翻訳者として有名なエドウィン・マクレランは、漱石の小説を「ドラマ性の高い現代の知性を持ち合わせた作品」と特徴づけました。[1] しかし、実際に一般的大衆の注目を集めたのは『吾輩は猫である』（1905）や『坊っちゃん』（1906）などの初期の喜劇小説でした。漱石が他の作品で探求した斬新な形式や文体群は、簡単に分類したり要約できるものではないでしょう。さて、このエッセイでは、『坊っちゃん』のユーモアや他の特徴が、なぜ他の日本人作家らと一線を画しているのかを読者の皆さんに紹介したいと思います。

ユーモア

　言語や文化、そして時代が異なれば、ユーモアを理解するのはしばしば困難になります。私たちは古い時代の冗談をいつも理解できたり、面白いと思ったりする訳ではありません。冗談の本当の意味を「捉えよう」と努力しているが、文法や漢字の複雑さのため、理解するので精一杯だと言う日本語学習者もいるのではないでしょうか。私もそんな日本語学習者の皆さんに共感します。実は、私もユーモアを理解するのに大変な思いをしてきたからです。日本文学研究者となるためには『源氏物語』をはじ

1 Edwin McClellan, *Kokoro* (Lanham, MD: Regnery Publication, 1996), xi.
2 Joel R. Cohn, *Studies in the Comic Spirit in Modern Japanese Fiction* (Cambridge, Harvard University Asia Center, Harvard University Press, 1998); Howard Hibbett, *The Chrysanthemum and the Fish: Japanese Humor Since the Age of the Shoguns*. (Tokyo: Kodansha International, 2002); and especially, Adam L. Kern, *Manga from the Floating World: Comicbook Culture and the Kibyôshi of Edo Japan* (Cambridge: Harvard University Asia Center, Harvard University Press, 2006).
3 Joseph A. Murphy in "Natsume Soseki and the Ten-Year Project," Introduction to *Natsume Soseki's Theory of Literature and other critical writings*. Edited by Michael K Bourdaghs, Atsuko Ueda and Joseph A Murphy. (New York: Columbia University Press, 2009), 12.
4 The popular Hearn (1850-1904) is today most well known for his work as a journalist and as a recorder of old Japanese folktales and ghost stories *(kaidan)* for an English audience. He took the name Koizumi Yakumo when he became a Japanese citizen.
5 Tanizaki Junichiro *Childhood Years, A Memoir*. Paul McCarthy, trans. (London: William Collins Sons & Co, 1988), 42.
6 J. Cohn's fine introduction to his 2005 translation of *Botchan* provides a fuller discussion of the term and the text.
7 As Angela Yiu notes, "there are thousands of essays, journal articles and monographs published on Soseki each year." Her critical appreciation of a wide range of his works is an insightful example of contemporary criticism in English, though she does not discuss Botchan. *Order and Chaos in the Works of Natsume Soseki* (Honolulu: University of Hawai'i Press, 1998), 7.

well received by urban readers who themselves had, within a generation or so, come from rural areas to the city; they would immediately have seen the comic value in the reversal of roles between the country and the city. They would also have understood the outmoded master-retainer relationship of the pre-Meiji Period as embodied by Kiyo, the ever-loyal servant in whose eyes her young master can do no wrong. Despite the middle school setting and student hijinks, they would have seen some of the content of Botchan as being adult in terms of both human relations (e.g., the geisha as possible mistress to one of the teachers) and, possibly more importantly, resistance to authority [e.g., Botchan's reactions to the principal, "Tanuki" (Badger) and vice principal, "Red Shirt"].

Botchan exposes the elite group of teachers at the middle school by giving them absurd nicknames. On one side we have the shifty Principal "Tanuki," his accomplice, Vice Principal "Red Shirt" who has an unusually high voice, and the brown-noser "Nodaiko" (The Clown). Botchan joins the opposing ranks of the pale-faced English teacher and "Yama-Arashi" (Porcupine) the mathematics teacher; ironically, those who teach subjects that one would expect to lead to success in modern Japan end up failing to succeed in school politics. Everything works out in the end for Botchan, despite his bouncing from one problem to another. It is less a case of virtue overcoming vice, seen in the Edo Period concept of kanzen chôaku (encouraging virtue and chastising vice), and more a modern tale of being vigilant in order to outwit those in charge.

The tendency in contemporary Japan to conflate *Botchan*'s setting with its intended audience, in other words to assume that it was written for the middle school crowd, presents an ironic parallel for students of Japanese who approach the story as a manga. Graphic novels long ago shed their automatic equation as kid's stuff, however much that association lingers in some circles. Yet reimaging this well-known literary work as a manga means another redaction, with possibly even greater simplification. However, this is misleading. Manga can make reading in Japanese fun. This manga can also challenge the reader to see what they can "get" : to work through how the grammar and vocabulary convey shades of meaning about the conflicted intensions and actions of the characters. It is anything but simple. Manga also provides a visual context (e. g., a setting, facial expressions) that helps with overall comprehension.

Botchan presents a campus comedy of manners that indicts the hypocrisy and posturing of those presenting themselves as modern. There might be an inclination among some readers to take this as a kind of national allegory, ridiculing the lack of authenticity of the era. I would be inclined to see the work as an antidote to the triumphalism of national narratives in the wake of Japan's victory in the Russo-Japanese War of 1904-05. Soseki employs a deft touch to portray his affection for foibles, those misplaced expectations, awkward interactions and unintended consequences that shape the cultures of schools and other institutions. Following Soseki's own interest in the affect of literature, I would encourage students of this text to identify what, in the language and the manga, they enjoy, and how it cuts against the grain of their expectations.

Meiji elite. In contrast to the serious endeavors of Meiji movers and shakers, who self-consciously sought nation-building, Botchan lacks ambition; he accepts the middle school teaching position for lack of anything better to do and with no expectations. Botchan is impetuous and rather immature, a kind of perpetual adolescent, unobservant and clueless, far from the exemplary models of Japan's modernity. It should be noted that at this time short biographies of exemplary gentlemen populated middle school textbooks to illustrate the moral virtues set forth in the 1890 Imperial Rescript on Education. It can hardly be overstated that Botchan serves as the antithesis of those exemplary gentlemen, and yet he succeeds in presenting a model of morality in making the right choices, though without particular finesse or grace. He fails to weigh the long-term repercussions of his actions, often to his own detriment, as when he refuses a raise when "Uranari" is transferred to another more remote school or when he asks why he has not been fired at the same time as "Yama-Arashi" (Porcupine) since they had both been wrongly accused and then rashly tenders his resignation.

Revisions

The Botchan text commonly read in Japan underwent a significant revision in the 1958 edition edited by Fukuda Kiyoto. The initial editions of *Botchan*, originally published for an adult audience in serialized installments in the literary journal *Hototogisu*, included many kanji without any furigana that would aid the younger or less well educated readers with pronunciation and meaning. Fukuda revised the text to make it easier and more accessible for a younger, postwar audience, adding furigana, substituting simpler kanji or shifting kanji to hiragana, and deleting some of the more pedantic or obscure sections. The 1958 edition has been the one that publishers continue to reprint, most commonly in children's literature series since the mid 1960s, and from which middle-school textbook compilers draw excerpts, without acknowledging the redactions. Botchan has come to be viewed as an accessible adventure, as a kind of juvenilia suitable for its middle school setting, which has cemented its familiarity with the widest possible range of readers. But it has also tended to fall off the radar as a subject of serious literary criticism, while his other works continue to receive exhaustive scrutiny.[7]

A Campus Comedy

Soseki's light-hearted school comedy, reminiscent of the modern campus novel, differs from the subtle humor of courtly Heian Period literature. Far from being in keeping with the high moralistic educational goals of the Meiji government, *Botchan* combines a humor and tenor more readily found in the popular literature of the Edo Period with the new setting of a modern school. A Tokyoite confronting a near unintelligible Shikoku dialect provides much of the humor, creating layers of possible misunderstanding. The novel was experience a very difficult time in his life. Soseki would later observe in the introduction to his *Theory of Literature* that the award was barely enough for him to survive. "Among English gentlemen I lived in misery, like a poor dog that had strayed among a pack of wolves." By his own account, he shut himself off, and his few Japanese visitors worried about his sanity. Upon his return to Japan in 1903, he was appointed a lecturer at the First Higher School and the Imperial University in Tokyo. He also taught at Meiji University to help support his growing family. During this time, Soseki prepared lectures on English literature that were to be the basis of his theoretical writings.

The Sobriquet "Botchan"

Soseki's choice of the term Botchan, the young master, conveyed both something of the main character's social status and the multiple ways he was viewed. The word "Botchan" comes from a background of privilege. In his childhood memoir, the novelist Tanizaki Jun'ichirô (1886-1965) describes the use of "Botchan" in the 1890s as typical of the more "aristocratic uplands of Yamanote" [the hilly, sparsely-settled districts of Tokyo that had housed former daimyo estates during Edo] and not a term used even by well-to-do families of Shitamachi [the densely-settled flat lands of Edo's urban core] so that even within Tokyo circles it signified a particular kind of cosseted ease and inexperience.[5] The term is applied to the protagonist of Soseki's novel with affectionate respect by the elderly family retainer, Kiyo, but some of his colleagues at the middle school come to use the term with thinly-veiled mocking disparagement.[6]

> The sound 坊 "Bô" and its variants can still be heard in contemporary Japanese. Originally designating a monk (obôsan お坊さん), or a monk's dwelling, the sound has also come to be used to designate a young boy, (bôya 坊や) or an inexperienced young man from a well-to-do family (Bon Bon 坊々), or placed after a young boy's name to show familiarity. As we see in this novel, Kiyo refers to her young master affectionately as "Botchan"; however, some of the teachers at the middle school mock him with the same term. More commonly you will hear the sound "bô" to describe someone who has a particular attribute: akanbô 赤ん坊 (baby), asanebô 朝寝坊 (someone who sleeps in), or mikkabôzu 三日坊主 (literally someone who gives up after three days; someone who starts a project but does not stick to it, such as a diet or a New Year's resolution).

Comic Tropes

Soseki's *Botchan* presents two comic tropes. The first is of the city sophisticate-the Edokko (child of Edo/Tokyo)-who encounters provincial connivers far more worldly than he. The character Botchan exhibits an earnest naiveté; he is rather headstrong and stubborn, disarmingly direct and without any critical self-awareness, the antithesis of what his social background or educational achievements in the capital would suggest. Soseki would refer to the city of Matsuyama-never named directly in the tale, but easily identified from many geographic references as well as by the train between the town where Botchan lives and the hot springs onsen-as *inaka* (countryside), but readers should only take that as a contrast with Tokyo. The second principal trope is that of Botchan's standing as a member of the

Botchan

Botchan's place in Soseki's body of work is difficult to characterize. Soseki published in a wide variety of literary and artistic forms—more than a dozen novels, short stories, sketches, essays, diaries, literary criticism, Chinese verse (*kanshi*), haiku, and paintings—although it is as a novelist that he is principally remembered. He remains a giant in the modern canon, among the most widely read and studied. His standing in popular culture is perhaps best illustrated by his place on the ¥1000 bill from 1984–2004; when Japanese currency was refashioned in the early 1980s to include faces of modern historical figures, Soseki's image was selected for the most widely circulated note. *Botchan* used to be commonly excerpted in Japanese middle school textbooks. *Botchan* may not be considered Soseki's funniest, most successful or most sophisticated work, but it remains accessible and endearing to a wide audience, revealing a critical appraisal, with a light touch, of a young man's encounter with the untidy edges of modernity.

> Of the five English translations of Botchan—by Yasotaro Morri (1918), Umeji Sasaki (1968), Alan Turney (1972), J. Cohen (2006), and Matt Treyvand (2009)—two are available in electronic form (Morri in Project Gutenberg and Treyvand in a Kindle edition http://www.gutenberg.org/cache/epub/8868/pg8868.html). The book was first translated into French in 1923, quickly followed by the German version. Since then, readers of Chinese, Hebrew, Indonesian, Korean, Malay, Russian, Spanish, Singhalese, Turkish, and Vietnamese have had access to this novel.

An Education

Soseki was born Natsume Kinnosuke in what is now Shinjuku Ward in Tokyo in the year before the beginning of Meiji to an older couple who gave him up for adoption; he returned to his natal home after his adoptive parents divorced when he was nine, but it was not until later that he found out that the person he thought was his grandmother was actually his mother. In his education, Soseki benefitted from a combination of the old and the new forms of education, gaining a solid grounding in Chinese classics at the Nisho Gakusha, followed by study of English literature at Tokyo Imperial University (now Tokyo University). It may be hard for undergraduates today to appreciate how Soseki's B. A. (1893) from that pinnacle of the education system put him within the rarified circles of the Meiji elite. He continued his studies as a graduate student and taught part-time at Tokyo Higher Normal School, so it was strikingly unusual for him to accept in 1895 a position as a middle school teacher in Matsuyama on the island of Shikoku. He taught there one year before moving on to a far more prestigious position at the Fifth Higher School in Kumamoto, one of five nationally designated and financed institutions that tracked students to the single Imperial University. In Kumamoto he married Nakane Kyoko. Soseki's provincial escapade in Matsuyama is often described as providing the basis and setting for his tale *Botchan*.

The Japanese government awarded Soseki a scholarship to study English literature in England between 1901 and 1903. However, in accepting this honor, Soseki was to said versus what was expected. In comic linked poetry, or *haikai no renga*, of the early modern period, multiple poets competed to compose poetic links expressed in colloquial language and addressing everyday topics that contrasted with the older codified classical conventions to achieve startling juxtapositions. Puns of the popular *yose* storyteller monologists matched the wit and wordplay of the Heian diarist Sei Shonagon and were piled on thick and deep.

Exceptionalism:
What sets Natsume Soseki apart from other Meiji writers?

Soseki's exceptionalism was multifaceted. [Natsume was his family name; Soseki was his chosen pen name and is the name by which he is known in Japan.] When he published his best-known comic works, he was a Professor of English Literature at Tokyo Imperial University, the apex of higher education in Japan. Soseki's lectures in this period presented his strikingly original sophisticated and abstract approach to literature, an approach that drew largely on psychological and sociological models to characterize the experience of reading. English readers can see from his recently translated (2009) *Theory of Literature* (1907), how much of a departure this was from the typical contemporary survey of English literature. Soseki sought a universal approach, which he would term "cosmopolitan," modeling itself on the universality of physical science. He sought to systematically theorize how literature worked in a modern civilization, beginning with the perception of the physical world and ending with how one derives meaning. Soseki utilized the scientific thought of his day to construct "wave diagrams and quations for consciousness"[3] as a way of characterizing the moment-to-moment stream of the experience of reading. He concluded his far-ranging model by characterizing literature as a thermodynamic system, subject to similar laws. Soseki's theory of literature was constructed in direct opposition to the dominant modes of literary analysis of his day. In particular, he was challenging an Anglo-centric notion that privileged the aesthetic sensibilities of particular (principally English) literatures and championed specific discriminating judgments of "taste." For Soseki, the value of any literature was relative and historical, and so it was fluid and subject to change.

His theory of literature was presented in a series of lectures that, by his own account, were not well received. Soseki would satirize his own experience in *Sanshiro* (1908) where the twenty-three-year-old student named Sanshiro tells his Japanese professor of English Literature that he liked the former foreign professor better. In reality, Soseki had followed Lafcadio Hearn (1850-1904) in this position at Tokyo University.[4] Soseki's exceptionalism was exemplified in his abrupt and, for his peers, startling resignation from his prestigious professorship to work at a newspaper, the *Asahi Shinbun*, in April 1907. There he would publish the bulk of his novels to much critical and popular acclaim. Ironically, when he began to write for the popular press, his work tended to take a darker tone and demand far more from the reader.

to describe the long red nose of the young princess. I was thinking too much about abstract concepts and not enough about the actual language of the text.

We now have the benefit of recent scholarship that plumbs the complex cultural practices in the humor of Japanese literary traditions.[2] Adam Kern's careful discernment of late 18th century comic book satire offers an informative model of just how sophisticated the consumers of popular culture could be expected to be. Yet much in the multiple lineages of Japanese comic tradition was rather broad humor. Paired with those spare and austere medieval noh dramas, presented in the language of the aristocracy were those "in your face" kyogen interludes set in the vernacular, invariably depicting reversals of roles and power and inevitable just desserts.

Japanese literature in the Edo Period (1603–1868) presents a much wider range of comic narratives, ribald poetry and farcical kabuki dramas. The esprit of the period can be captured in the word *ukiyo* (floating world) that describes the manner in which townspeople especially seemed to live for the moment without serious regard for the consequences. People flocked to the kabuki theatre to watch such plays as *Sukeroku* (1713), which included revenge, comic miscues of manners and language, and slapstick. Humor commonly appeared in a clever turn of phrase in what was

---

Puns and word-play, common in Botchan, have deep roots in the classical tradition. Sei Shonagon's observations in *The Pillow Book* (*Makura no soshi*), compiled when she was lady-in-waiting for Empress Sadako (from 986-1000), offered a variety of lists-things said to be beautiful, charming or ugly-that contemporary readers find mildly amusing or simply catty, in addition to vignettes of court life. In one puzzling passage, she mentions a case of a courtier who was so embarrassed by his lowly parents that he threw them into the sea and then became a faithful observer of Bon (the Buddhist festival of the dead that pays homage to ancestors). Sei Shonagon found an admonishing poem about the event "delightful." Hint: "bon" is a homonym for "splash".
Sei Shonagon, *Makura no sōshi kitan*, 5. Hagitani Taku, ed. (Tokyo: Dōhōsha, 1983) ,278. In translation, this passage appears in Ivan Morris' 1967 edition (Vol. 1, p. 249) from Columbia University Press, but it is not included in his condensed Penguin edition.

The oral traditions of tale literature (setsuwa bungaku) and popular vernacular narratives in subsequent centuries provide more farcical scenes. *The Collection of Tales of Time Now Past* (*Konjaku monogatari shū*, compiled in the early 12th century), a collection of tales from India, China, and Heian Japan, presents fanciful events in a matter-of-fact tone. These intriguing titles might not be out of place in a contemporary manga: How an East-Bound Traveler Fathered a Child by a Turnip" or "How Men of Kaga Province Who Went to an Island Where a Snake Was Warring with a Centipede, Aided the Snake, and Settled in the Island".
Mori Masato, ed., Shin Nihon Koten Bungaku taikei 37 Konjaku monogatari shū 5 (Tokyo: Iwanami shoten, 1996), 6, 44.
 Shin Nihon Koten Bungaku taikei 37 Konjaku monogatari shū

The perennial favorite kyogen play *Busu (Poison)* presents a story of two servants who cleverly outwit their master. In addition, short narratives of the *otogizoshi* tradition (late 12th century-early 17th century) provided stories written in vernacular Japanese for those who could read kana. The tale *Lazy Taro (Monogusa Taro)* presents an ordinary peasant man with an endless ability to engage in verbal wit and humor, who ends up outwitting those above him socially, very much in the kyogen tradition.

Ihara Saikaku (1642-93) painted vignettes of merchants in how-to-get-rich stories, or of townspeople, both men and women, who loved love. The travelogue of two devil-may-care fellows in Jippensha Ikku (1765-1831)'s *Shank's Mare (Tokaidochu Hizakurige)* who encounter one adventure after another as they travel from town to town along the Tokaido from Edo to Kyoto is an excellent example of Edo comedy replete with slapstick and buffoonery.

Botchan

Joan E. Ericson

How should contemporary students of Japanese language read Natsume Soseki's *Botchan*? What does the author, to say nothing of your language teachers, expect you to "get"?

Natsume Soseki (1867-1916) was among the most renowned, beloved writers of modern Japanese fiction, and his works are often taken as emblematic of the Meiji (1868-1912) era's engagement with the West. Meiji fiction was marked by a significant rupture from previous literary traditions, notably in the *genbun itchi* movement (the unification of written and spoken language). Japanese writers of this period who sought to create a modern literature found new ideas in Western literary genres such as realism and naturalism; as these literary approaches were introduced in Japan, they came to focus on a search for the individual. Often there was a self-consciously serious tenor and intent in these Meiji works that differed greatly from the often humorous popular literature of the late Edo Period.

Edwin McClellan, distinguished translator of Natsume Soseki's writings, characterized his novels as combining "modern intellectuality with dramatic effectiveness."[1] Yet it was Soseki's early comic novels—*Wagahai wa neko de aru* (I am a cat, 1905), and *Botchan* (The young master, 1906)—that brought him to the attention of the public. The wide array of innovative forms and styles that he explored in his writings eludes any simple categorization or summary. This brief introduction seeks to alert the reader to *Botchan*'s humor, and other qualities that set the work and its author apart from other Japanese authors.

Humor

Appreciating humor is often difficult across languages, cultures and time. We do not always get the jokes or think that they are funny. Students of Japanese language may be justified in feeling burdened in trying to master complexities of grammar and kanji while attempting to "get" what is really being said. They have my sympathies. I've been there. In my education, *The Tale of Genji* (*Genji monogatari*, ca. 1008), together with other Heian (794-1185) writings by court women, was taught as an exemplar of the court aesthetic that served as a touchstone for subsequent literary sensibilities and, in my classes, we struggled to demonstrate competency in the classical language while also grasping that aesthetic. Years ago, when I was studying classical Japanese at Columbia University, I confronted a passage from Murasaki Shikibu's *The Tale of Genji* that baffled me. In a poem, the elegant protagonist Genji was describing one of his loves as "*suetsumuhana*" or safflower, a yellow flower that produces a reddish dye. Only after my professor told us to think of the different meanings of "*hana*" in Japanese did I understand that the author was using a pun

本の出版にあたり、いろいろな方々にアドバイスをいただき、エリクソン、増山より、特に下記の方々に感謝を申し上げたいと思います（敬称略）。

○ 文法の注釈・説明：下條光明（オノマトペ執筆）／安部さやか
○ セリフ・練習問題：関口千亜紀／マッケール菅野尚子／杉山朗子／加藤陽子
○ エッセイ：Steven J. Ericson ／ Michael Kleinkopf ／ Jim Matson ／ Laurel Rasplica Rodd
○ 語彙翻訳：Mary Knighton ／ Phillip Shea

【監修】
ジョーン・E・エリクソン

コロラド・カレッジ日本文学・日本語教授。日本語プログラムディレクター。日本語・日本文学学会元会長。日本の女性文学と児童文学について著書、翻訳がある（林芙美子『放浪記』英訳など）。ハワイ大学で日本文学修士課程修了。ドナルド・キーン氏とポール・アンデラー氏指導のもと、コロンビア大学日本文学博士課程修了。

Joan E. Ericson is NEH Professor of the Humanities, and Professor of Japanese at Colorado College. A former president of the Association of Teachers of Japanese, her research interests include Japanese women's literature (*Be a Woman: Hayashi Fumiko and Modern Japanese Women's Literature*, University of Hawai'i Press, 1997) and children's literature from the Meiji through early Showa eras. She received her Ph.D. in Japanese Literature at Columbia University.

【著】
増山和恵 （ますやま かずえ）

カリフォルニア州立大学サクラメント校外国語学部准教授。日本語プログラムディレクター。アセスメント、オンライン教育、国際教育について数々の論文を執筆。全米日本語教師会 Teacher of the Year（2006）、カレッジボード・アドバンスト・プレースメント（AP）テスト試験作成委員（2007-2011）。ニューヨーク州立大学バッファロー校教育学大学院（外国語・第二言語教育）博士課程修了。

Kazue Masuyama is currently Associate Professor of Japanese and Director of the Japanese Language Program at California State University, Sacramento. She has published widely on Japanese assessment, online education, and international education. She was a recipient of the Teacher of the Year from the National Council of Japanese Language Teachers (2006) and served on the Development Committee for the AP Japanese Language and Culture Test (2007-2011). She obtained her Ph.D. (Foreign and Second Language Education) at the State University of New York, Buffalo.

【マンガ】
月館蛍人 （つきだて けいと）

徳島県出身。京都精華大学美術学部卒業。『モーニング』（講談社刊）で、「第30回ちばてつや賞一般部門大賞」受賞後デビュー。その後『ビッグコミックオリジナル』『ビックコミックスペリオール』（小学館刊）で、『アート探偵ＤＡＲＵＭＡ』『山田さんがころんだ』など、シリーズ連載を展開。現在は複数のペンネームで、クロスオーバーなジャンルのマンガを月産100ページのペースでこなす。

From Tokushima Prefecture, Tsukidate Keito graduated from the Art Department of Kyoto Seika University. She debuted with the prize winning *Mooningu* (Morning) (Kodansha) which earned her First Prize in the General Category of the 30th Chiba Tetsuya Award. Since then, she has published such titles as *Biggu komikku orijinaru* (Big Comic Original) and *Biggu komikku superiooru* (Big Comic Superior) (Shogakukan), as well as serialized *Aato tantei DARUMA* (Art Detective DARUMA) and *Yamada-san ga koronda* (Yamada-san Fell Down). Currently she writes under several pen names and keeps up a pace of one hundred pages of cross-over manga per month.

英語圏版　マンガ『坊っちゃん』
2011年9月25日　初版1刷発行

原　作	夏目漱石
監　修	ジョーン・E・エリクソン
著	増山和恵
マンガ	月館蛍人
発行者	荒井秀夫
発行所	株式会社ゆまに書房
	東京都千代田区内神田2-7-6
	郵便番号　101-0047
	電話　03-5296-0491（代表）
印刷・製本	株式会社シナノ
デザイン	佐藤千恵

©2011 Yumani Shobo Printed in Japan
ISBN978-4-8433-3526-0 C1081

落丁・乱丁本はお取替えします。